Doing Justice to Young Peo

Doing Justice to Young People
Youth crime and social justice

Roger Smith

WILLAN
PUBLISHING

Published by

Willan Publishing
2 Park Square
Milton Park
Abingdon
Oxon
OX14 4RN

Published simultaneously in the USA and Canada by

Willan Publishing
270 Madison Ave
New York
NY 10016

First published 2011

ISBN   978-1-84392-839-3 paperback
       978-1-84392-840-9 hardback

British Library Cataloguing-in-Publication Data

A catalogue record for this book is available from the British Library

Project managed by Deer Park Productions, Tavistock, Devon
Typeset by GCS, Leighton Buzzard, Bedfordshire
Printed and bound by T.J. International, Padstow, Cornwall

Contents

Introduction: a recurrent problem?

Back to Square One

Youth justice in England and Wales has taken a wrong turn. The early to mid 1990s witnessed a seismic shift in the ways in which young people were dealt with by the criminal process, as evidenced by the subsequent rises in criminalisation and incarceration which have by now been very well documented. It has also been suggested that this was not a feature simply of changing moods and practices in one jurisdiction, but had an international dimension (Muncie and Goldson 2006). It seems to be a distinctive feature of late modernity that our recurrent fears about the threat posed by our young people have been intensified and refocused in recent years and, as a result, there has been a parallel increase in the determination of the 'normal' institutions of society to find sure and certain means of quantifying and controlling the 'problem'. This preoccupation with the 'risk' posed by young people who do not conform with conventional norms has, by now, been well documented and extensively criticised, but it has nonetheless resulted in a range of highly programmatic and controlling forms of intervention which seek to anticipate and/ or prevent further manifestations of unacceptable behaviour.

There seems to be a persistent and largely insatiable appetite in some quarters for the demonisation of young people, or large elements of the youth population and their unruly qualities. This is not new, of course, and dates back at least to Shakespeare's time, but it is also hugely problematic in that it creates an intensely politicised arena in which the behaviour of the young comes under scrutiny, and in which an infraction of whatever kind (and sometimes, this encompasses just 'being there') establishes a *prima facie* case for the exertion of some form of social control over them.

This ravening mood has been assuaged to some extent by contemporary measures to introduce a degree of scientific certainty into the identification, assessment and management of potential sources of trouble and disorder – whether these are young people themselves, or 'risky situations' (street corners perhaps, or sometimes school premises and their environs). Science has thus intervened to rationalise and give substance to what seem to be rather more irrational and unfocused fears of those who are different in certain ways. These processes of 'othering' then result in young people being constructed in a quite superficial fashion, relating to one dimension of their social being, and indifferent to their own distinctive and situated experiences, aspirations, needs and expectations.

Indeed the essential problem with such approaches is that they do not engage with, or even admit as relevant, the realities of the lives of children and young people; as a result, they are unable to enter any kind of meaningful relationship with those they purport to 'know' through the application of 'validated' risk assessment tools and standardised inquiries into those aspects of their lives that are deemed pertinent. Interventions are geared towards 'responsibilisation' and imposing change, surveillance and control from without, rather than addressing internal patterns of thought and young people's own constructions of self, others and the social world; hence, the contemporary popularity of behavioural models of practice which concentrate on changing what young people do rather than who they are. These narrowly conceived and routinised forms of practice are, of course, incapable of 'doing justice to young people', and in many cases, they are demonstrably the source of additional harm, in addition to their role in reinforcing the forms of behaviour they claim to be 'tackling'.

The purpose of this book is to assert the importance of locating the concept of 'youth justice' itself within a broader landscape, in order to demonstrate that we cannot isolate concerns with criminality and anti-social behaviour from the 'bigger picture', either in seeking explanations for such behaviour, or in proposing and implementing solutions to it. It will therefore be necessary to acknowledge and take account of the changing shape and context of young people's lives, if we are to achieve anything like a plausible and realistic account of their involvement in 'crime' and their relationship with the processes of criminal justice. As a result it will also be necessary to develop an understanding of how young people's experiences are shaped by structural influences – and the social construction of adolescence and the 'transitions' associated with it – in order to reflect on the specific processes which problematise them, and then go on to 'target' them for interventions when things go wrong.

Importantly, it will be necessary to give due attention to the perspectives of young people themselves, and the accounts they offer of their own changing lives. We must assume that they can play an active role in making sense of the world around them, and the messages that are conveyed to them by the formal (and informal) institutions of society such as schools and the media. They cannot be expected simply to follow the paths mapped out for them which represent a normal process of development and maturation. Clearly, social inequalities and other forms of 'difference' are significant here – but in addition, we need to allow for the fact that young people are social actors, and will play a part in making sense of the messages they receive and respond accordingly. They will, inevitably, construct their own 'rules of the game', incorporating distinctive moral principles and guidelines for action, which may or may not comply with what is formally expected of them by the established institutions of society.

In light of these reflections, the normative mechanisms which are in place to account for young people's progress and status will need to be treated as problematic in themselves. It will certainly be important to unpick the role they play in rationalising and giving practical and moral authority to the processes in place for categorising and then intervening with young people who are identified as problematic in some way. The consequences – in terms of the influence of 'systems' on young people – must be recognised and problematised in their own right if we are to avoid a purely one-sided account that focuses on their behaviour and attributes in isolation. Indeed, as we shall see, the justice system itself will be identified as a subject of major concern, purely because it contributes so extensively to constructing certain young people as 'failures' who are in need of strong measures of coercion and control. Models of risk assessment and risk management, in particular, can be seen as highly culpable in this respect, in that they offer a spurious legitimacy to processes which are arbitrary, selective and discriminatory. The damage caused to young people, collectively and individually, by recent and contemporary youth justice practices, has been well documented of course, being the subject of intense criticism at all levels, including strong international messages of concern. Therefore the need to rethink and reconstruct the approach taken, especially in England and Wales, has been clearly established.

In place of the oppressions that young people face in the name of 'justice' it is vital to take a positive view of what can be achieved. This should be grounded in a recognition of the need to view the young 'holistically' and inclusively, incorporating their views and ideas into interventions with them. By suggesting that there are practical and achievable alternatives to contemporary practices, I also wish to argue that we should avoid any tendencies to be nihilistic, on the one hand, or merely idealistic, on the other. It will be helpful here to consider those existing and acknowledged forms of practice with young people which offer the potential to transform and signpost any structures and methods of working with young people which do represent and deliver the principles of social, and not just criminal, justice.

The structure of the book

The book has essentially been organised into three parts. It reflects firstly on the broader constructions and experiences of 'youth', within which the process is played out, whereby certain young people and certain groupings become problematised and singled out as objects of social concern; before going on to consider critically the relationships between young people and criminalisation in more detail. Finally it considers the practical implications of this in terms of the ways in which contemporary practices 'get it wrong' and the alternatives that are available and achievable both now and in the future.

Chapter 1

This chapter provides an overview of current understandings of youth, considering ideas about adolescent development and transitions in particular. These will enable us to gain a broad picture of the ways in which young people are conventionally thought about, against which we will be able to consider what we know about the lived experience of youth transitions and various 'turning points'.

In this way, we will be able to contrast idealised assumptions about 'normal' processes of growing up with disparate evidence of the kinds of concrete realities that young people experience. Key factors which shape their lives will also be considered here, such as inequality, discrimination, diversity and disruption and the associated implications for opportunity and choice.

This review will also help us to gain an understanding of divergence in the moral standpoints of some young people from conventional norms. A growing sense of injustice, for example, may help to underpin the justifications they develop for their own choices of lifestyle and potentially anti-social or harmful behaviour.

Chapter 2

This chapter goes on to evaluate some of the theoretical models developed to explain divergent patterns of identity, belief and behaviour among young people, and the resultant tensions in their relationships with dominant interests and prevailing norms. It first asks the question of how young people can interpret and make sense of their experiences and influences, drawing on the interpretive accounts of key theorists in particular, such as Merton and Matza, whose ideas seem to capture the dynamic tension between structural influences and individual choice.

A critical exploration of these ideas also provides the basis for a contemporary evaluation of the social processes and outcomes for young people in the present era, drawing on modernist and postmodernist ideas in particular.

Chapter 3

At this point, it will be helpful to consider some of the mechanisms by which influences and material realities can shape the emergence of young people's identities and cultures. The place of key elements such as family, peers, community and media will be considered in order to give substance to the theoretical account developed in the previous chapter.

We will also consider here how effective are the various kinds of explanatory framework developed to account for divergent and 'problematic' outcomes, such as the empiricist perspective of 'developmental criminology'. The deficit model of youth criminality with which this sort of depiction is associated will be juxtaposed with others which emphasise young people's creativity, resilience and independent capacity to establish alternative 'conformities'. This may be helpfully elaborated with reference to ecological accounts of youth behaviour, including those of the 'Chicago school', and recent work by Yates (2006). Issues of 'race' and discrimination are clearly of relevance here, too.

Chapter 4

The second part of the book shifts the focus away from young people themselves and towards the processes by which they (or some of them) are criminalised and are then 'dealt with' by the formal justice system. Why do we demonise young people? Why are we afraid of them and of specific groups within the wider population? This will lead us to consider firstly the importance of 'discourse' and the way in which various assumptions and stereotypes are generated and maintained that predispose us towards others in a certain way. The impact of dominant discourses can be identified at two levels – that of the process of 'othering' (Garland 2001) which generates a sense of difference, of 'us' and 'them' and of threat, and the active processes by which certain characteristics, ascribed behaviour, or circumstances become defined as legitimate grounds for 'targeted' interventions, risk management and special treatment, all of which combines to set certain young people apart, figuratively and literally (YISPs, for example, can be seen as an illustration of these tendencies).

These one-sided characterisations of young people, which locate the 'problem' within them, are, of course, additionally problematic to the extent that they confer legitimacy on the very intervention processes which compound and intensify social exclusion, while deflecting the possibility of questioning these processes and what lies behind them.

Chapter 5

This chapter considers in more detail the lived consequences (Smith *et al.* 2001; Hine 2004) of the generalised assumptions described previously as they act upon young people and shape their lives in various ways. It focuses on the processes by which young people become excluded and find their choices restricted through the interweaving of different strands of experience in the family, neighbourhood and school. Young people gain a sense of their 'place' from an early age and this is confirmed for them by their treatment by others.

Concrete examples of this kind of process of negative reinforcement will be introduced, such as the impact of school exclusions, being 'in care', anti-social behaviour policies, specialised intervention programmes, and the formal processes which recruit 'young offenders' to the justice system.

Chapter 6

This chapter illustrates the patterns elaborated previously by reference to the justice process itself and the patterns of intervention it reveals. Trends and developments in criminal justice will be discussed here, focusing on the acknowledged recent intensification of interventions across the spectrum of 'problem' behaviour.

This chapter also provides a concrete answer to the question of 'who is being punished?' and how the justice system itself operates in a partial and discriminatory fashion, fuelled by the kind of ideological messages discussed previously. The insights of 'labelling theory' will be utilised here to underpin our understanding of the ways in which ideological and structural influences operate systematically to 'criminalise' and segregate certain sectors of the population. Once characterised in this way, it is clear that these out groups are then liable to forms of punitive individualised intervention which take no account of social difference or systemic processes of discrimination. It will also be important to go on here to discuss some of manifestations of systemic injustice of this kind, including institutional racism and the persistent mistreatment of vulnerable young people 'inside' (Goldson 2002).

Chapter 7

This chapter builds on the evidence offered previously to show how current practices within youth justice are getting things wrong. It focuses both on the failures of the system to achieve the goals it sets for itself – in terms of inefficiencies and waste, ineffectiveness, unintended consequences, and popular disquiet – and on the wider consequences in terms of a failure to meet needs, harmful outcomes for young people, breaches of human rights, and a compounding of social divisions.

In particular, the aim here will be to show how contemporary practices fail in their own terms, through the mistreatment of young people within the system, a failure to 'reform' them, and the fractured and disrupted lives which are the consequences of a misconceived approach to dealing with the 'problem of crime'.

Wider social problems, such as drug dependency, family disruption, poverty and 'poor parenting', can be shown to be as much a consequence of criminal justice interventions as a trigger for them.

The chapter concludes that the contemporary youth justice system is simply not 'fit for purpose'.

Chapter 8

By contrast, this chapter considers attempts to modify the negative impact of the youth justice system and to develop effective reforms 'from within'. We focus here on examples of good practice, their achievements and constraints. Localised examples of innovation and creative interventions are considered, with a view to assessing the kinds of benefits they have been able to deliver, while also considering the question of what it is that seems to prevent them being sustained or incorporated into the mainstream. The problem of 'quick fixes' and short-term measures is discussed further in order to decide whether this is an endemic characteristic of youth justice innovations, or if sustainability is achievable.

Recent years have seen the introduction of many ostensibly innovative measures to deal with the problems associated with youth crime, and these are evaluated for their potential to offer (or signpost) progressive improvements in interventions as well as their likely shortcomings.

The further complications of reform initiatives are also discussed here, such as the question of 'compromise' and the extent to which programme goals (such as alternatives to custody) are achievable. Or must we accept that within a reformist frame of reference 'nothing works'?

Chapter 9

At this point, we cast the net rather wider for examples of progressive innovations in youth justice which pursue more radical or systemic change, based on alternative principles, such as problem solving, making good, reconciliation and participation.

The chapter introduces a range of specific interventions nationally and internationally which offer potential in these respects, such as 'conferencing', community justice, diversion, participative justice, and other restorative practices. These are assessed critically to identify both their potential to reshape youth justice and the (perhaps inevitable) obstacles they encounter.

Chapter 10

The concluding chapter develops the lessons from earlier discussions, while also incorporating a wider perspective on the 'welfare rights' of young people. It furthers the argument that youth justice reforms need to be complemented by a reshaping of the broader relationship between society and its young people. Principles of participation, legitimation and inclusion depend not just on improved practices but also on transforming social relationships and positively valuing young people in general.

It is thus shown that there is a necessary relationship between generalised principles of rights, respect and a valuing of young people, and the kind of positive approaches to resolving the issues of 'problem behaviour' that are sketched out here. In conclusion, it is argued that a fair and effective youth justice system is necessarily dependent on and operates in the context of a realisation of the wider principles of social justice.

Chapter 1

The production of youth

Working models: the idea of (normal) development

Youth and young people are much debated and highly contested elements of the social world. As a consequence, it is unsurprising that a considerable number of alternative models for describing and accounting for aspects of adolescence have emerged. However, the sheer diversity of such models also indicates that the key questions which they seek to resolve still remain unanswered, at least with any degree of certainty. The aim here will be merely to enumerate some of the most influential and significant manifestations of our attempts to account for and characterise youth and all its various aspects. In doing so, the intention is not to delve too deeply into the theoretical and ideological underpinnings of these ideas at this point, but just to articulate some of the ideas and analytical frameworks which contribute to our contemporary understandings of the subject. This will provide the basis for a more substantial discussion and critical analysis subsequently, specifically of the ways in which young people are problematised and 'othered' (Garland 2001).

Firstly, though, we will use relatively conventional frames through which we can begin to enumerate the range of understandings conveyed to us as well as their aims and objectives. Patterns of development, ideas of 'normality', and the concepts of transitions, identity, culture and maturity all feature here as common themes in the explanatory repertoire available. Youth is a time of change, progression and aspiration, it seems, during which young people will encounter a series of predictable challenges to their sense of self, personal goals, self-esteem and status. These cannot be avoided and must be negotiated according to the capacities and resources available to them, which are also the subject of classificatory inquiry and analysis.

At the same time, the terrain of youth is also subject to the claims of alternative disciplines from among the social and biological sciences, which have themselves generated distinctive frames for describing and explaining the changing lives and circumstances of young people. These may also be seen to vary according to their position on one or more of a number of explanatory axes: for instance, determinism–freedom; nature–nurture; individual–collective; identity–culture; natural–social, structural–personal and continuity–change. As we shall see subsequently, this array of possibilities allied to the politicised and contested nature of the subject matter almost inevitably generates a high degree of contestation, controversy and complexity, especially concerning the manner and means by which we set boundaries and influence and control the behaviour of the young, usually with the aim of securing social conformity of one kind or another. At this point, however, the aim is simply to elaborate some of these agendas and explanatory frameworks without leaping to conclusions. There will be plenty of time for that later on.

So – what is 'normal'?

Right from the start, it is important to acknowledge that the idea of 'normality' is both a crucial and a hotly contested issue in relation to young people, their upbringing and their behaviour. Normality is construed both as a neutral descriptive and analytical term – according to which characteristics and actions can be assessed and evaluated – and at the same time a normative term – which ascribes levels of desirability and approval or disapproval to the attributes and behaviour of the young. The term itself thus carries a very substantial power and authority to define and categorise, and thereupon to legitimise subsequent forms of intervention. Hendrick (2003) suggests that the concern with what is normal, and by extension what is abnormal, has its origin in 'several late 19th-centruy and early 20th-century anxieties' (p. 13), particularly associated with the emergence of 'modern', industrialised societies and associated 'social problems' such as family disruption, poverty and disorder. One way in which the notional opposition between normality and abnormality becomes important is via the establishment of an exclusive relationship between the two; straddling this divide was (and still is, perhaps) seen as an impossibility. Young people must therefore fall into one or other category and be treated accordingly.

Early attempts to systematise and legitimise our understandings of child development are associated with the Child Study Movement and the work of Stanley Hall (Hendrick 2003; France 2008). Longstanding assumptions about the nature of adolescence are grounded in this body of work, such as the concept of 'storm and stress' (Arnett 1999). Although it has been suggested that early proponents of such ideas were aware of the capacity for both individual and social variations within such generalised portrayals of young people's development, they certainly appear to have laid the basis for much subsequent analysis. One example takes it as axiomatic that adolescence:

> is a transition period where behavior is characterized by instability, unpredictability and change – a time when actions and emotions are often more extreme, more intense and more unpredictable, and are elicited with less provocation than ever before. (Judd 1967: 466)

Thus, during a period of time bracketed by puberty and physical and emotional maturity, we can expect young people's behaviour and attributes to be endemically erratic and problematic. In other words, disorder of one kind or another is 'normal'. More recently, the idea that 'change' is a consistent feature of adolescence has been further supported by developments in neuroscience which seem to suggest significant differences between children, young people and adults in their patterns of brain activity (Sebastian et al. 2008). These, in turn, are linked with developing concepts of the 'self', which may have implications for behaviour and social integration (p. 465).

However, to suggest that a certain period in the lifecycle is characterised by change is not to suggest that this is also associated with stress and disruption, and counter arguments have been evident for some time:

> it seems that there are many ways of coping with the developmental demands of adolescence ... only some of these coping styles will be related to later psychopathology, and the competent child will most likely be the competent adolescent. (Weiner 1977: 88)

Similarly, empirical studies have indicated a rather more nuanced view of the 'concept of adolescent turmoil' (Rutter *et al.* 1976). Feelings of 'misery and self-depreciation' have been found to be quite common (p. 55), but their significance may well have been 'over-estimated' and over-generalised. Other signs of stress and disruption (such as conflict with parents) are much less common than some models would suggest it seems. Indeed, an alternative explanation for differing perspectives on upheavals in adolescence is offered in the form of contextual accounts which suggest that these may be historically specific, with the 'idea of adolescence as a turbulent, rebellious period' being found to have increased in popularity during the decades of the 1960s and 1970s which themselves witnessed 'considerable social and attitudinal change' (Smith *et al.* 2003: 292).

On the other hand, within this explanatory frame it is equally possible to assert that change is a constant feature of young people's lives, but that this may still be experienced in ways which are both normal and pathological. Thus, there are 'many paths which eventuate in effective coping in adulthood', but at the same time 'adolescents' problems are not necessarily fleeting ones' (Weiner 1977: 90). Even if 'storm and stress' is a relatively common feature of the adolescent life stage, it is 'not something written indelibly into the human life course' (Arnett 1999: 324). Indeed, there are notable cultural and individual differences in the ways in which these aspects of young people's lives are viewed and experienced. Equally, disruption and change should not be viewed merely as negative and destructive influences, since they also provide the opportunity for learning and growth: 'The paradox of adolescence is that it can be at once a time of storm and stress and a time of exuberant growth' (p. 324).

Other research, too, has suggested that change is experienced differentially by young people. Adolescence is a period associated with certain types of 'events', both positive and negative, which are negotiated by most, if not all, in this phase of their lives. However, the relationship between 'external global events and internal states', while intensified, is not manifested consistently across the population. It is 'only a minority of adolescents' whose experience of change is translated into 'stress and duress' (Larson and Ham 1993: 138). These findings are supported by wider reviews of the available evidence, which suggest that adolescence is, typically, a period of 'transition', but one with which most young people 'cope reasonably well' (Coleman and Hendry 1999: 225). For some, though, the combination of events impacting on them may lead to a range of negative consequences. Importantly, however, the distinction is made between a historical view which sees youth as inherently problematic, and an approach which is much more concerned with identifying recognisable 'risks and stressors' (p. 208), partly in order to establish a basis for effective intervention with and for young people themselves.

It is possible, nonetheless, that the concern with common events, transitions and trajectories which has underpinned the study of adolescence has also tended to underestimate certain other key mediators of 'normality', including such features as gender, sexuality, ethnicity, class and disability. To what extent might events experienced by the population in general be mediated by significant differences between them? Is it helpful to think more in terms of 'difference' and less in terms of commonality, then?

> Within the sociology of youth there is an increased interest in the diversity of the experience of youth, the centrality of identity and the subtle interplay of individual agency, circumstance and social structure ... The relationship between timing, opportunity and identity lies at the heart of these contemporary concerns. (Thompson *et al.* 2002: 336)

A recognition of diversity and complexity has led to the formulation of theoretical accounts of adolescence which attempt to integrate the 'continuity' of human development with the 'context of human development' (Coleman and Hendry 1999: 12). This suggests, in turn, that we are unlikely to be able to achieve any consensual view of what is 'normal' in adolescence, because 'the person and the context are inseparable' (p. 13). In addition, it is suggested here, we should recognise the role a young person has in making choices and constructing his/her 'own world' and developmental pathway.

Thus, in academic and analytical terms, it seems that contemporary thinking is less inclined to deal in the logic of 'normality' or 'optimal' functioning (Weiner 1977: 90), and more in terms of contexts, individual biographies and 'critical moments' (Thompson *et al.* 2002: 339). This does not mean that we are left without any basis on which to evaluate and compare the experiences and actions of young people – however this is a process which requires a multi-faceted approach to inquiry and understanding key features of their lives. The search for normality, on the other hand, must be seen much more as a project of 'normative' construction which has important political and ideological uses in the fields of social welfare and social control (Hendrick 2003: 14).

Expectations and influences: the normative project

Having established that the concept of 'normality' is highly problematic, and increasingly suspect, we must now turn to the supplementary question of the ways in which 'normal' or conventional expectations of young people are determined. Over time, there have been a number of influential attempts to enumerate these processes, often organised around the principle of maintaining the social relations of production. Willis's (1977) exploration of 'How working class kids get working class jobs' is one such example. Despite subsequent criticisms, this account remains significant to the extent that it explores the relationship between power, structures, expectations and experience in young people's lives. Rather than set out a simple functionalist view of social structures and the reproduction of existing social relations, Willis developed a framework to account for the mediating influence of culture and daily experiences in young people's lives. According to his account, young people are not simply trained or programmed to take up pre-assigned roles in the future workforce, but actively engage with the structures and symbols represented in concrete forms of social organisation such as school. It is through a process of 'disaffection' with school and what it conventionally offers that an alternative culture and future takes shape. In this sense, the reproduction of class relations becomes a subjective and subjectively-owned process:

> It is only in the uncovering of this subjective assent that we will understand their [young people's] behaviour in a way which properly presents their own full powers, and appreciates the contradictory, half real notion of freedom at stake for them (and others) in a liberal social democracy. (Willis 1977: 103)

In this way, for example, 'the lads' that he encountered expressed a sense of superiority about manual as opposed to non-manual labour.

Of course, as he observed, there remains a paradoxical edge to this account, to the extent that school's expressed aim was not simply to entrench dominant class interests but to create opportunities for self-realisation and social mobility. And yet, the evidence seemed to suggest that 'social reproduction of the class society' was precisely what was achieved, indicating in turn that 'some of the real functions of institutions work counter to their stated aims' (p. 177).

This portrayal finds parallels in the concept of the 'hidden curriculum' (Kehily 2007: 171), which represents the covert and unintended processes of teaching and learning taking place in schools. There are two aspects to this process: the implicit messages conveyed by teachers and other staff and the processes of discovery and informal learning going on between school students. In an interesting counterpoint to Willis's account, we are provided with sixth-former accounts that construct themselves as 'superior' to former peers who 'think they look cool' but have left school and become 'wasters' (Kehily and Pattman 2006: 41).

What these different portrayals seem to share is their representation of processes of 'normalisation', whereby institutional practices and specific cultural contexts and exchanges combine to create a sense of what is expected of young people and what is in effect natural for them. In the sphere of education, these elements have been referred to as 'frames of reference' whereby the choices and actions of young people are given shape and texture by the 'different forms of local ... culture, the recent socio-economic history of the place, the internal systems of the school and, we would add, the consequences of educational policies' (MacDonald and Marsh 2005: 54). Thus, there is evidence of a significant degree of continuity between the experiences and understandings of young people from similar (working-class) communities over a significant period of time and substantial geographical distance. Certain 'identities' are clearly and actively rejected by young people, such as that of class 'swot' (p. 55), and these processes are associated with the establishment of 'oppositional pupil cultures' which have a powerful influence over the formation of forms of social identity. Thus young people who 'wanted to work harder at school' were dissuaded from doing so in light of 'the low-level disruption of learning caused by the implicit imperative to 'mess about' and the 'informal sanctions' to which they would be exposed if they appeared too enthusiastic about doing schoolwork (p. 55).

There is a sense in which this kind of active process of cultural adaptation and identify formation reflects Bourdieu's concept of 'habitus'. It is a matter of making realistic choices about oneself and one's social relationships within the context of what is possible and acceptable:

> The habitus is this kind of practical sense for what is to be done in a given situation – what is called in sport a 'feel' for the game, which is inscribed in the present state of play. To take an example from education, the 'feel' for the game becomes increasingly necessary as the educational tracks ... become diversified and confused ... (Bourdieu 1998: 25)

In other words, there is a persistent level of tension between the variable demands and expectations embedded in the formal education system and the experiences and relationships of young people passing through it. In some formulations of this dynamic, this may be referred to as 'role confusion' (Briggs 2002: 13) which generates uncertainty and tension in young people's search for a specific and stable 'identity'. This can only be negotiated effectively as they develop a 'feel' for where they stand in relation to each other, to wider social systems and institutions, to cultural influences and the expectations of their communities. These tensions and conflicting pressures are by no means exclusive to adolescence, but there is a tendency to think of this as a specific time of life when they become particularly acute. Change has to be negotiated with a view to mapping out relatively fixed directions of travel. As Griffin (2004: 16) puts it, youth is *both* a time of 'inevitable turmoil' *and* 'a time when the path to "normal life" must be found and followed'.

Implicit in this formulation is the idea of movement from a state of relative uncertainty and multiple possibilities towards an increasingly fixed position, comprising a limited range of characteristics and functions. These changes are represented both in terms of the emergence of stable self-identities and in terms of collective social and cultural formations. This process of 'normalisation' is both an individual and collective project undertaken by young people themselves, and at the same time it is echoed and reinforced by social processes and messages from outside of the kind evident in the educational process (MacDonald and Marsh 2005). If we take this essentially iterative approach to understanding, it enables us to begin to account for the relationship between the choices young people make about themselves and the expectations which others have of them and sometimes impose upon them. Thus, for example, observable characteristics such as (some) disabilities, gender and ethnicity may lead us to anticipate certain outcomes for specific groups, but these are clearly mediated by a range of experiences and processes of interpretation and choice-making which then generate the possibility of a range of responses that at some level are effectively 'owned' by those concerned. This characterisation has implications not only for the young people themselves, but also for the manner in which we seek to gain a greater understanding of their own normative and cultural processes. Thus, for example:

> For us, too little room is given in orthodox criminological studies
> to understanding both the active role of young people and the

particular historical, cultural and socio-economic conditions of neighbourhoods in the making of criminal careers. An ethnographic approach can help us understand criminal careers close-up; as they unfold in time and place, from the point of view of participants who simultaneously face, and make, limited choices in respect of this and the other careers that make up youth transitions. (MacDonald and Marsh 2005: 172)

'It's just a phase ...'

Choices and adaptations, then, are acknowledged features of youth, suggesting that 'transitions' and change are endemic. Within this context of flux and a constant reworking of the self, there may also be an increased need for fixed points and certainty. Knowing who you are probably matters more when nothing else seems certain.

Of course, it is important to acknowledge that the nature of the transitions young people experience is variable – and, similarly, these too are mediated by external expectations. In other words, we expect a degree of turbulence in the teenage years and this expectation may itself be a contributory factor in giving substance to this very outcome.

As we have already seen, there is a wide variety of actual and potential factors impacting on young people's lives whose effects are rendered yet more unpredictable to the extent that they interact. While the concept of 'transition' provides an overarching theme, this cannot be seen as one-dimensional or uniform. For instance, we can distinguish relatively straightforwardly between types of transition which may be physiological, formal/legal, cultural social or personal. Some of these points of change may be relatively clear cut, such as the onset of puberty (Alsaker 1995). However, as adolescence itself has become more clearly recognised as a distinct life stage, and as it has tended to cover an increasingly extended period, so the nature and timing of various transitions have also become less consistent. Different types of transition will occur at different times for different groups of the population. It has become something of a truism, for example, that young people from middle-class backgrounds are able to rely on the family home as a base for much longer than those who are materially disadvantaged (Coleman and Hendry 1999: 9).

Certainly it is important that we attempt to clarify the range of possibilities in relation to the stages of adolescence. While it might be seen as a 'universal experience' (Coleman and Hendry, 1999: 10), more nuanced explanatory models have emerged which refer to a 'constellation of events', the 'precursors and outcomes' of specific life changes, and the importance of considering the 'timing and sequence of events that occur within a transition period' (Graber and Brooks-Gunn 1996: 768). Thus, for example, what happens in the period before adolescence cannot be ignored if we are to make sense of changes during that period, however it is defined. Young people's gender roles and gendered relationships may well have been substantially developed by this point in their lives, given what we know about the prevalence and influence of stereotypes in this context. So it is 'noted that individual differences in the experience or negotiation of a transition are associated with a variety of conditions, including development before the transition, the timing of transition for an individual, the individual's experience of the transition and the context in which the transition occurs' (p. 768). Even predictable physiological occurrences such as puberty may be associated with discrepancies because of the 'asynchrony' between the stage of biological maturity and the extended pre-adult stage which is a characteristic of many contemporary societies: 'this discrepancy between physical and social characteristics may give rise to some socialization conflicts', it is argued (Alsaker 1995: 441). Subsequent research appears to demonstrate a clear link between puberty and a range of psychosocial 'disorders' as well (Ge et al. 2006). Therefore this is a relatively well-defined 'transition' which appears to generate certain problematic consequences, in terms of 'socialization', in particular. But, this is perhaps to understate the normative dimension of this kind of explanation:

> The most obvious – but easy to forget – prerequisite of a successful socialization process is that the norms and rules to be conveyed are clear. Problems may therefore appear if there are very different norms in different groups in the same society, if important agents convey different norms, or if the rules for the regulation of certain types of behaviour have vanished. (Alsaker 1995: 429)

For other transitions which are much more obviously socially determined at the outset – changing schools, leaving home, moving into work, for example – the relationship between normative expectation and personal experience becomes even more complex. There is yet another range of transitional events as well which are associated with this life stage, but which are less explicitly defined and more open to personal and interpersonal negotiation, such as becoming sexually active (and asserting one's sexual orientation), peer relationships superseding family ties, explicitly identifying with certain cultural forms of expression and becoming independent. Most of these changes are particularly associated with adolescence while also meeting the definitional criterion for transitions, which is that they 'require reorganization at either the structural or functional level' (Graber and Brooks-Gunn 1998: 768). That is to say, they necessitate a substantial reorientation of one's sense of self and/ or behaviour. Recognising the sheer scale and complexity of these changes at a variety of different levels has led to attempts to refine the idea of transition and to acknowledge the significance of 'turning points' (Coleman and Hendry 1999: 10) where particular challenges or stresses might arise. Thus, there are both critical events – which might include puberty – and 'cumulative or simultaneous events' – which may overload the individual concerned. Alternatively, tensions might be manifested through the absence of a 'goodness of fit' between the context and personal characteristics or needs, such as the well-documented issue of multiple placement moves for young people in the care system, whose lives have already been affected by instability and insecurity (Taylor 2006: 103).

Although there have been criticisms of the idea of 'transitions', and the rather unitary and predictable notions of progress associated with it (Wyn and Woodman 2006), there is no doubt that 'youth' (as a concept, as a structural form and as a mode of experience) has a distinct material reality, which means that ideas about 'transitions' and 'turning points' are helpful conceptual tools to enable us to make sense of this particular life stage. This does not mean that the changes we can identify in their lives are exclusive to young people, or that they are uniform and predictable. Indeed, based on our earlier considerations, normative or prescriptive accounts of adolescence are part of the problem and have to be considered critically. Nonetheless:

> Discovering *empirically* that the transitions that some young people make are messy and complicated, and that the steps taken sometimes lead sideways or backwards, does not require that we jettison the *concept* of transition. (MacDonald and Marsh 2005: 35; original emphasis)

In one sense, it does not matter whether youth and adolescence are conceived in terms of 'natural' (biological) or 'constructed' (social) phenomena; what is more significant is that irrespective of this, they are terms which have material substance and act in the ways described previously to impact on young people's lives. These impacts and their interplay are distinctive and have a particular social meaning, notably in the ways in which young people are problematised. Youth may be a specific feature of contemporary societies, and indeed it is clearly differentiated within these (MacDonald and Marsh 2005: 36), but it is this which creates the impetus towards a critical evaluation and analysis of variable experiences and outcomes for the young. We are also reminded here that these are changing elements of modern (late modern/postmodern?) societies and that it is arguable that young people are being increasingly exposed to 'new risks' and 'stresses and strains' (Furlong and Cartmel 1997: 9), partly reflected in changing levels of engagement in formal political processes (Roberts 2007). Their reference points, however, are peculiar to them. In comparison to their parents, their material experience of youth is distinctive. Thus: 'Today's young people ... simply accept current conditions as *normal* [my emphasis], and are confident that they can manage and shape their own lives under these conditions' (p. 268). Transitions, then, have come to have a dual meaning, in that they represent the changing *social* conditions of youth, as much as they do the determinate, if differentiated, life stage which is experienced by those passing through it.

Difference and diversity: changing youth

In light of this, it is important also to consider the extent to which transitions and 'normalisation' are processes which are mediated by difference and variations in young people's lives. While some aspects of their experience and lifestyle may be contingent and negotiable others are clearly more determinate – and thus less amenable to manipulation. Nor, in many cases, can these facets of existence be ignored or subsumed under other forms of adjustment or engagement. Thus, clearly, characteristics such as gender, ethnicity and disability are to varying degrees viewed as 'constants' which necessarily give a distinctive shape to young people's pathways through adolescence.

This, in turn, leads us to consider a number of further conceptual challenges. For instance, the notion of a 'normal' adolescence itself becomes subject to modification – normality itself is bounded, both by inherent characteristics and by the choices young people make in relation to these characteristics. By extension, too, transitions and the extent to which they follow expected trajectories will also be seen as variable and distinct according to the categories into which young people fall.

Gender is one such obvious divide and it has long been assumed that this is highly predictive of the shape and direction of young people's development and maturation. While this is clearly the case in a physiological sense, the available evidence also offers strong indications that it is true in terms of their personal and social lives. Indeed, it has been argued that gender differences are 'intensified' during adolescence for a number of reasons:

> This 'gender intensification hypothesis' posits that behavioral, attitudinal, and psychological differences between adolescent boys and girls increase with age and are the result of increased socialization pressures to conform to traditional masculine and feminine sex roles. (Galambos *et al.* 1990: 1905)

These differences may in turn be manifested in behavioural outcomes such as the level of self-reported offending (see Fitzgerald 2003, for example). Clear and persistent gaps appear between the propensities of males and females to carry out (or to claim they have carried out) a variety of 'delinquent behaviours'. On the other hand, these variations are not consistent across all types of criminal activity (Fitzgerald 2003: 11; Walklate 2004) and there may be some degree of variation over time.

Similarly, of course, ethnicity has been identified as one factor with considerable significance in relation to young people's transitions, particularly in the context of criminal justice processes. Once again, this is a factor which is viewed as relatively 'solid', the effects of which are clearly discernible in terms of both behaviour (Sampson *et al.* 2005) and experience (Smith 2007).

However, significant variations have also been recorded, for instance in the levels of violence between ethnic groupings; and of 'all the factors' associated with this 'neighbourhood context was the most important source of the gap' (Sampson *et al.* 2005: 231). These observations also find echoes in quite different types of research which seek to account systematically for processes of division and fracture in society that are concerned with situated patterns of behaviour and conflict (Wacquant 2003). Empirical findings such as these are important not just for their policy implications but also because of what they mean for the ways in which we conceptualise adolescence and the processes by which experience and behaviour are 'normalised', both subjectively within communities and from the outside. Clearly, too, these observations act as an important reminder of the risks involved in making normative judgements about the choices that young people make and their moral status. This is not to suggest that all forms of behaviour are equally acceptable and there is no observable basis on which moral choices are made:

> One person's order is disorder for another, one group's 'normal' behaviour creates intolerable conditions for others. (Young 1999: 139)

What it does mean, though, is that the contexts and the bases on which notions of normality are constructed are likely to be variable and situationally specific. Ideas of complexity and uncertainty in the moral order are, of course, associated with what are identified as parallel developments in the social world, with the emergence of the 'postmodern condition', the 'fragmentation of modernity and social class' (Hopkins Burke 2008: 75), and the increasingly pluralist societies associated with these developments (Young 1999) 'where the old moral certainties seemed increasingly less appropriate' (Hopkins Burke 2008: 75).

In this sense also the processes of adolescence seem to have moved on from the class-based model underpinning Willis's (1977) analysis. In parallel with these social changes, analytical strategies have also become more interested in wider questions of diversity and change (Griffin 1993: 211). Diversity, though, is also associated with increasing uncertainty, and the loss of a generic sense of identity. Thus, a somewhat later analysis shows a greater degree of ambivalence:

> While we have rejected suggestions that traditional social divisions are becoming less powerful determinants of life chances, we do accept ... that one of the central characteristics of late modernity is a weakening of collective social identities. (Furlong and Cartmel 1997: 113)

In this respect, there appears to have been an increasing emergence of 'individuated transitions' which are 'contingent' and 'buffeted by unanticipated critical moments' (MacDonald and Marsh 2005: 196). However, it is impossible to decouple these trends entirely from the parallel and interconnected developments which have seen entire communities and complete cohorts of young people marginalised and 'excluded', whether in 'Britain's poorest areas' (p. 217), or in the almost exclusively black and disenfranchised neighbourhoods in some American cities (Wacquant 2003).

As these and other forms of exclusion, separation and diversity become more substantial elements of the contemporary social world, so it becomes increasingly difficult to think in terms of uniform definitions of normality, or institutions (such as schools) and structures (such as the justice system) which are experienced or understood in the same ways across very significant divides. Indeed Garland (2001: 40), draws attention to those ideological processes and policy changes which seek to implement strategies of 'normalisation' in order to give moral authority to specific legal practices. Apparently neutral and scientific forms of problem specification, assessment and intervention are unlikely to be able to do justice to very different kinds of experience and understanding. This reminds us once again that it is vital to retain a sense of 'context' (Coleman and Hendry 1999) when seeking to make sense of young people's lives and experiences. Importantly, the value of understanding context is not just framed in terms of explaining the vulnerabilities or threats associated with certain groups of young people, but also in terms of their capabilities and strengths:

> We are particularly interested in approaches which give due recognition both to the adolescent's resources and potential for resilience, as well as to the possible circumstances in which an individual may become vulnerable. (Coleman and Hendry 1999: 11)

Set against the deficit or deviant models of adolescence implicit in some analyses, this perspective seeks a more balanced view, acknowledging young people's circumstances and their capacity to make sense of and construct their own identities, culture, meanings and moral templates in context, and against a backdrop of difference, and sometimes disadvantage and discrimination. Choices are made which fit the circumstances – they may be constrained and they may not reflect deeper aspirations. For some, they are about creating something, however limited, out of nothing (MacDonald and Marsh 2005: 191). If this kind of choice would also lead to challenge and resistance, this should not be seen as being inherently problematic or invalid. But it should not be romanticised either, 'since this often ignores the perspective of the young people concerned' (Griffin 1993: 210).

Explaining youth: development, discourse or rational choice?

We have thus reached a point where the importance of establishing a cogent and coherent explanatory framework for youth and adolescence is clear. Notions of 'normality' and desirable outcomes have tended to dominate our conventional understandings of a 'good' childhood and adolescence. However, these have also tend to embed in such conceptual models a rather limited frame of reference which is inclined to judge all young people against a series of aspirational benchmarks. These have been shown by what has preceded to be both value laden and one-dimensional. They do not account for or offer validity to the experiences and pathways of very great numbers of young people – whether our distinctions are made on 'obvious' grounds such as gender or ethnicity, or whether these are less clear cut, depending on contexts, constraints, and variable access to socially desirable resources. As a result, it has become increasingly clear that we need to develop explanatory models which can take account of (and not prejudge) many and diverse trajectories and 'transitions', albeit that these are all captured under the umbrella term of 'adolescent'.

For such explanatory frameworks we can turn to a number of sources, including multi-faceted developmental models – those which highlight the processes of youth, captured in the form of ecological 'discourses', and those which focus on resources and 'structured' choices. Bronfenbrenner (1979: 11), for instance, set out 'to provide a unified but highly differentiated conceptual scheme for describing and interrelating structures and processes in both the immediate and more remote environment' as they shape human development. Thus, he suggested that psychologically-based accounts of development were too narrowly focused and relied on highly specific and 'artificial' experimental studies which had very little wider meaning. In effect:

> much of developmental psychology, as it now exists, *is the science of the strange behaviour of children in strange situations with strange adults for the briefest possible period of time.* (Bronfenbrenner 1979: 19; original emphasis)

By contrast, any effective understanding of human development must be based on a study of the interactive processes between an 'active, growing human being' and the 'immediate (and wider) settings' in which that person lives.

In order to construct a suitable explanatory framework, Bronfenbrenner postulated a series of interlocking and interactive 'systems' where each one could be articulated in its own terms, but the meaning and impact could only be appreciated in light of its interactions with others: a 'microsystem', such as operates in the home; a 'mesosystem', where two or more settings come into contact (e.g., school and peer groups); an 'exosystem', where events or activities are undertaken which help to constitute the lived environment (e.g., local crime reduction partnerships); and a 'macrosystem', which constitutes or overdetermines the cultural and ideological forms that, in turn, permeate aspects of daily life (e.g., religious beliefs).

If we are to make sense of the kind of transitions experienced in childhood and beyond, we must be prepared to seek out the connections and interactions between these multiple systems, because 'transitions are a joint function of biological changes and altered environmental circumstances' (Bronfenbrenner 1979: 27). This analytical model (or variants of it) has been applied in a number of areas of interest, including 'adolescent bullying' (Barboza *et al.* 2009) and youth offending (Smith and McVie 2003). These approaches appear to be very effective in drawing together a range of differential associations which model possible interactive relationships, although some proponents of this approach are also cautious about its explanatory power: 'There is something in this pattern [of findings] to support nearly every criminological theory' (Smith and McVie 2003: 191), is the comment of the authors of the *Edinburgh Study of Youth Transitions and Crime*, for example.

Apart from their apparent eclecticism and indivisibility, such accounts of youth transitions and development are also limited by the extent to which they take account of the contextualised choices made by young people themselves. However much 'systems' and settings are important in shaping their experiences, it is also important to leave room in our explanations for their capacity to interpret and act upon these in distinctive and specific ways. So, for instance:

> intersecting influences of family, popular culture, schooling and society for young people often involve negotiating multiple contradictory choices. (Ryan 2008: 71)

This type of account shares a number of characteristics of ecological perspectives, but also highlights the responsive and creative capacities of young people. Thus, the two approaches share the view that young people's lives are shaped by multiple, multi-level, complex and sometimes contradictory influences. Where they part company is in the extent to which they allow for 'varied perspectives and priorities' among those concerned. So, as Brown (1987: 22) points out, this is an important consideration if we are to explain why some 'working-class pupils' go on to succeed academically, in the face of cultural influences and structural demands.

These accounts can also help us recognise that contradiction is not simply an external condition of young people's lives, but may also be revealed through their own personal accounts and activities. Ryan's (2008: 86) account of educational processes illustrates the duality of a form of schooling which both rewards students for 'colluding' with the 'school system' and encourages them 'to critique notions of power and think in ways that can enact change for a more just and equitable society'. As might be expected, this proves 'to be difficult terrain' for young people to negotiate.

As a result, we can observe the very real tensions and ambiguities in young people's relationships with the world in general (Eckersley 1997) and with specific activities such as drug use (Aldridge *et al.* 1998). They are aware of the 'downsides' of drug-taking, but they are also sensitive to their cultural meanings and their role in creating 'the brilliant night out' (Aldridge *et al.* 1998: 168). Equally, 'street kids' may be legitimately described as 'savvy, self-reliant, resourceful, [and] adapted to their world' (Eckersley 1997: 248), while also having to experience and manage extreme emotional stresses and negotiate intense physical danger. As a result young people will both incorporate and reflect this kind of ambiguity in their day-to-day strategies for sense-making, identity-claiming and negotiating significant transitions. This kind of account also helps us to make another important distinction – between aspirations and beliefs, on the one hand, and attitudes and adaptations, on the other. What young people believe in and value may, in fact, also be at odds with their views about what is necessary to survive and thrive in a hostile world:

> Surveys suggest they appear to be adopting attitudes and values they believe are demanded by the world they live in, and the future they expect – mistrust, cynicism, self-reliance, detachment, materialism, impatience, etc – not those needed to achieve the world they want. (Eckersley 1997: 248)

Systemic accounts, which helpfully introduce a range and depth of potential influences in the lives of the young, must therefore be tempered by those which acknowledge the interactive nature of their engagement with the social world, and the ways in which their own choices and actions reflect this process, both individual and situated, and collective and generalised. Of course these choices and the 'deposits' they give rise to – in the form of accomplished actions, new identities, social structures and events – will in due course become part of the context which informs the next turn of the wheel, and so on. Descriptive and analytical accounts must themselves be responsive and adaptable.

At the same time, however, they must remain sensitive to persistent features of the youth debate, such as the prevalence of stereotypes ('angels' and 'devils'), and well-established divisions, along the lines of age, physical status, class, gender and ethnicity. These are continuing material influences which may be less susceptible to change and thus need to be accounted for in terms of underlying, but not entirely fixed, trends and social forces.

Youth: construction, production and reproduction

Briefly, then, this has been an attempt to develop a number of analytical themes and strategies which will inform a more detailed understanding of the worlds of young people and the pathways they follow within them.

The language of 'normality', 'development' and 'transitions' forms the backdrop for an attempt to generate a more nuanced and multi-faceted explanatory framework. While these themes are relatively fixed core elements of contemporary (westernised) attempts to explain and account for the changes and outcomes of the lifestage known as adolescence, they must also be critically evaluated and problematised – especially if we are to begin to make sense of pathways which do not follow the normative routes mapped out for them. Even where this is the case, we must be aware of the issues of social reproduction, which may perpetuate inequality, oppression and harmful outcomes for certain groups and interests. In this way, even supposedly 'normal' trajectories can be seen to encompass complex meanings and contestable consequences.

Implicitly also, the argument pursued here has raised questions about those accounts of youth which are hermetically sealed against alternative disciplines. Neither personal life stories nor demographic surveys can provide complete or comprehensive accounts, as Bronfenbrenner (1979) and others (e.g., Sampson and Laub 2005) have demonstrated.

As we move on to consider the relationship between young people and acceptable and unacceptable behaviour, it will become clear that much contemporary analysis is framed in those terms. What is not so clear, as indicated above, is whether and how such accounts do justice to the emerging interest in 'agency' which is informing many other areas of study in relation to children and young people (Smith 2009). As we progress, the aim will be to ensure that this perspective is also integrated into both our understanding of the 'problems' of youth and crime and the subsequent attempts to sketch out effective ways of addressing these. This is a project whose aims are shared with others, although this does not mean that their destinations will coincide, of course:

> From our perspective, the implied next step is to reconcile the idea of choice or agency with a structural notion of turning points. We refer to this as 'situated choice'. (Sampson and Laub 2005: 43)

For reasons which will hopefully become clear as we progress, I would be more inclined to describe young people's decisions and outcomes as the products of 'constrained choice'. This is largely because the relationship between individual and structure is, in the end, an unequal one. It would be unwise to revert to a purely relativist account which accorded individual decisions the same weight as overarching social systems and forces, whether these are located in the state, the media or other major institutions. It is, of course, these forces too which take the primary role(s) in determining in advance just what behaviour (and what manifestations of it) are to be deemed 'anti-social' or criminal, and we must not overlook this dimension in any account of young people, crime and justice.

Chapter 2

The road to deviance: adaptation, drift or lifestyle choice?

Choosing pathways?

We have previously identified a number of analytical concerns in relation to the progression of young people through adolescence. In particular, it has become clear that their pathways and transitions are not pre-determined in any fundamental fashion, although certain characteristics such as gender and ethnicity may be significant. Following on from this observation, we have also considered a number of strategies and frameworks which may help in the task of making sense of the experience of youth. These have been characterised in various ways, but the most convincing of them appear to suggest that we must adopt a multi-faceted and multi-level analytical perspective, which links individual and personal attributes and experiences with wider structural and systemic factors. These interactive processes are significant in two distinct ways: they help to shape the lives, experiences and actions of young people themselves and they also determine the view taken of them from the 'outside' by other people and social institutions and agencies. The aim of what follows is to treat these two aspects of young people's lives as analytically separate in the first instance, in order to then consider their relationship and what this means for models of crime, youth justice, and, ultimately social justice.

To begin with we will consider the processes by which young people make sense of their own lives and opportunities and the choices they make about their own behaviour, which may or may not conform to conventional norms. The central frame for this discussion is work by

Merton (1957) and his analysis of the ways in which young people make sense of their social circumstances and how these processes are related to their lifestyle choices. This theoretical project offers an effective focal point for our consideration of the mechanisms which are at play in determining the pathways that young people will opt for, both individually and collectively. These can be further illustrated using work by Matza (1969) on the implicit and contingent factors which inform young people's adoption of particular cultural norms and identities. In turn, more recent discussions of culture, 'habitus' and social capital (Portes 1998) can also shed light on the ways in which divergent life courses emerge and are adopted by young people, in order to establish their own position and standing in relation to the communities that matter to them.

In conclusion, I will give some space to contemporary analyses which would seem to suggest that processes of fragmentation and atomisation have rendered this kind of choice increasingly contingent, situated and temporally specific. According to this kind of argument, a commitment to certain kinds of activity, norms and infractions can only be seen as provisional and superficial, resulting in a highly restricted and unstable form of self-identity (Giddens 1991). In consequence, it could be suggested that there has been a progressive erosion of moral certainties and agreed behavioural standards; these have been reduced to a matter of individual preference and 'living for the moment', it is believed, with the associated loss of any sense of social cohesion or common purpose. This analysis certainly coincides with populist visions of moral meltdown and behavioural chaos, although we should also retain a critical view of this kind of apocalyptic vision, given its well-documented historical persistence (Pearson 1983).

Making sense of their own lives: what is adolescence for?

Much of the analysis of young people's lives already available to us attempts to pre-empt their understanding and expectations. It was not until relatively recently that explanatory accounts sought to recognise the importance of their own perspectives on the nature and outcomes of adolescence (see Barry 2006, for example). However, it may be helpful to consider some of the evidence that is available in this respect before moving on to also consider established and emerging theories *about* young people from outside (much in the same manner as the present text). Vaughan (2003), for example, suggests that it is becoming increasingly expected of young people that they will have views about the nature of the pathways they will follow and the transitions they will make. In other words, contemporary discourses of self-determination and consumerism have prompted a much greater emphasis on self-awareness and a purposive orientation towards future outcomes. This is a product of our times:

> Active involvement of the individual is a characteristic of modern Western society generally. But it is *explicitly* embedded in transition policy. (Vaughan 2003: 3; original emphasis)

As she acknowledges, this expectation of a form of reflexive awareness and forward planning does not necessarily result in a conscious and careful process of preparing for the rest of one's adult life. Indeed, given that there are more possibilities than before, 'there is greater potential for young people to make "bad choices" ' (p. 4). What is clear however is that they are expected to acknowledge and then progressively accept responsibility for the choices they make in recognition of their transitional status. Vaughan also suggests (p. 4) that the idea of 'becoming' is itself a peculiarly modern phenomenon. Futures and careers were fixed in previous generations, so there was no need to consider alternatives or to make judgements about one's own direction of travel.

In subsequent work, Vaughan and a colleague gave more substance to this suggestion, arguing that young people are involved in a self-conscious process which could be represented as a 'dual "production" of identity and career' (Vaughan and Roberts 2007: 91). In other words, their views about themselves become progressively aligned with what they see as 'possibilities' and directions of travel in their lives. This particular study of young people and their early career choices led to the construction of four distinct groupings, described here as 'Hopeful Reactors', 'Passion Honers', 'Confident Explorers', and 'Anxious Seekers' (p. 96). These categories represent both a pattern of concrete choices about the type of work or training to undertake, and a more reflective view of what sort of person you are. This has been characterised in a rather negative sense elsewhere as a matter of 'knowing your limits' (Archer and Yamashita 2003: 58) and thereby determining 'what you're good at' and what might be, comparatively, 'risky' choices. Fear of rejection may thus impose significant invisible constraints on young people's choices:

'Another thing is, if I go to college they will ask the teachers here about me. I might end up with nothing. Now I'm regretting it, shouldn't have mucked about ...' (Ravinder, quoted in Archer and Yamashita 2003: 60)

Hopeful Reactors might, in this way, see themselves as negotiating quite a different terrain of risks, threats and possibilities from those experienced by other young people. Their descriptions conveyed 'a powerful picture of the uneven distribution of risk' (Vaughan and Roberts 2007: 97).

By contrast, for Passion Honers, the route into work and training is characterised more by a sense of purpose and coherence between the intended career and personal attributes. Their choice of career is woven fairly readily into their autobiographical accounts, in the sense of accounting consciously for where they have been and where they are going, such that 'pathway participation, interpretation and construction shaped their pathway selves' (p. 98). Confident Explorers display the same sense of certainty and purpose, but in their case this enables them to construct themselves as *producers* of their own lives' (p. 100), with the capacity to adapt and change plans and to construct a range of possibilities for themselves in a positive sense.

The final group, the Anxious Seekers, are described as being 'ill equipped' to negotiate just those alternatives that seem to excite Confident Explorers. For them the idea of 'choice' is more likely to be associated with wrong turns and a loss of options. Perceptions of failure and lost opportunities tend to lead to a rather restricted and 'paralysed' sense of self which undermines the whole notion of transitions and progress in careers or other aspects of life.

These researchers conclude that 'we need a broader understanding of pathways beyond transition-to-labour-market' (p. 103), not least because this concept tends to over-simplify and objectify the range of mechanisms and processes which young people will actively negotiate. The normative model of a seamless transition between education and adult careers tends to shape this kind of conceptualisation and underplays the importance of other considerations, such as the impact of 'social structure' and the 'ways in which young people's actual journeys are determined by such factors as class, gender and ethnicity' (Raffe 2003: 16). Thus, another study has found clear links between class, ethnicity and the structuring of possibilities and expectations. The sense of 'not being good enough' leads to an acknowledgement that certain aspirations are simply unrealistic and that it is important to avoid putting oneself into a position where one will risk 'failure' (Archer and Yamashita 2003: 59). These constraints are not just dependent on personal attributes, but are also associated with 'place' and 'reputation'. Being from a particular area, and having a certain type of accent, will mark young people as being different. Complying with normative expectations (like dressing smartly for interviews) might mean 'hiding' your real identity. For some young people, especially black young men in this study, this means establishing and asserting identities and a sense of self-worth in other ways:

> it may be safer (in identity terms) ... to not even attempt to be socially mobile, but rather to accept [your] limits and thus, not try to become or act 'all smart' and/or middle class. (Archer and Yamashita 2003: 61)

In this way, absenting oneself from conventional expectations and routines can be transformed from an acceptance of failure and inadequacy into a positive assertion of an alternative, strong, identity:

> The pull of 'bad boy' male peer groups was very strong and sometimes 'opting out' of continuing in education was one of the only (acceptable) ways to break away. (Archer and Yamashita 2003: 61)

These identities become positive options and offer affirmation by way of 'enjoyment, friendship, fun and power/status'. Other factors also impacted on this sort of choice, such as racism and the ways in which this shapes experience and expectations, both in day-to-day interactions and in the absence of role models – such as 'black men in professional ("suit") jobs' (p. 62). The metaphor of space is used to demonstrate the ways in which young people appeared to be making positive choices about themselves and who they were, albeit choices that were clearly 'bounded' by the 'limits' which had framed their lives. The language of failure may tend to underestimate the extent to which these choices and the actions associated with them are seen as positive and affirmatory rather than simply being about passive acceptance and an adaptation to perceived failure and inferiority. From this, then, the notion of 'normal' or conventional transitions through adolescence becomes increasingly difficult to sustain, except to the extent that 'normality' is seen as a situated concept, whereby ideas of conformity and achievement are redefined according to quite specific criteria and indicators. If this is the case, then the theoretical models we apply must be capable of accounting for diversity and variable identities, without imposing a uniform (and essentially normative) explanatory framework that fails to do justice to young people's own sense of self and community.

Situated normality: an established concept

Sociologists have for a long time been concerned with the problems associated with characterising and explaining the lifestyles and choices of young people. Merton (1957), for example, made a sophisticated attempt to classify and trace the kinds of patterns observable in their aspirations and behaviour. At its core, his typology relied on a distinction between 'goals' or ambitions, on the one hand, and the means by which these could be achieved, on the other. The consequence of this interplay between the two variables would be one of a range of possibilities in terms of young people's pathways through the adolescent years (and possibly beyond).

Thus, for example, if a person shares the dominant goals of a given society and both possesses and exercises the institutionalised (socially accepted) means to achieve these, then that person is demonstrating social conformity. In practical terms, then, white, middle-class children achieving good school results and going on to prestigious university courses would meet the criteria for this model.

However, a number of other patterns of adjustment and adaptation are possible, including, for example, 'innovation'. Young people in this group might be comfortable with the dominant social goals and indicators of 'success', but they might then adopt other than acceptable means to achieve these aims. As a result Merton noted

Table 2.1 A typology of young people's lifestyle choices

Mode of adaptation	Culture goals	Institutionalised means
Conformity	+	+
Innovation	+	−
Ritualism	−	+
Retreatism	−	−
Rebellion	±	±

Source: Adapted from Merton, 1957: 140

that in the United States 'contemporary … culture continues to be characterized by a heavy emphasis on wealth as a basic symbol of success, without a corresponding emphasis on the legitimate avenues on which to march towards this goal' (Merton 1957: 139). Because of this 'innovators' might understandably respond to this impasse by resorting to alternative means, such as acquisitive criminal activity. Merton also suggested that it would be likely that there would be a distinctive class bias towards the consequent patterns of behaviour, due to the more limited opportunities available to the 'lower strata' to achieve financial success through the labour market:

> Specialised areas of vice and crime constitute a 'normal' response to a situation where the cultural emphasis upon pecuniary success has been absorbed, but where there is little access to conventional and legitimate means for becoming successful. (Merton 1957: 139)

This framework seems to offer a ready-made explanation for the incidence and concentration of particular types of crime (essentially property-related) among certain groups in the population. However, it appears to be rather less plausible in this respect in terms of its ability to account for other types of criminal activity (such as acts of criminal damage or violence). Nor, for that matter, does it help to explain why young people with access to conventional routes to success should sometimes commit offences.

Nonetheless, as an explanatory tool Merton's model is a very helpful starting point in our attempt to conceptualise and account for the patterns and variations in 'normal' behaviour among young people. The idea that adherence to conventional norms may act as a prompt to engage in unacceptable forms of behaviour and that this may be the result of 'rational' choices prompts some intriguing possibilities. Crimes committed by the young, for instance, may thus be perfectly intelligible in a context of social inequality, oppression and unattainable (by conventional means) aspirations. Webster's (2006) analysis of 'race', youth crime and justice indicated that there remained a strong commitment to socially acceptable goals among marginalised groups and Craine's (1997) ethnographic analysis showed that 'alternative careers' in the hidden economy may be a response to perceptions of 'triple failure'. In this instance, young people were observed to be constructing viable, but essentially illegal, career pathways for themselves having:

'failed' educationally, 'failed' to secure post-school employment, 'failed' to 'get into' working-class adulthood through employment, even after participation in a succession of government schemes and special programmes. (Craine 1997: 148)

The illicit alternatives offered the opportunity to achieve not simply in material terms, but also in the important symbolic sense of being 'good at' something. Indeed, illicit ventures might offer the possibility of much greater rewards than other options (Webster *et al.* 2004: 20). Thus, we can perhaps account for some of the criminal behaviour of the young in terms of the social pressures and conflicting expectations they might experience and the constraints which exist on the means available to 'achieve' in socially acceptable ways.

Merton's explanatory framework can also be utilised to account for other forms of adaptive behaviour by young people. Drug and alcohol misuse might thus be accounted for as a form of 'retreatism', representing a combined rejection of conventional aspirations and acceptable behaviour.

As Merton emphasised, he was primarily concerned with the organisation and implications of social structures (1995: 519), rather than with the precise mechanisms by which 'individuals' initial departures from the norms crystallize into deviant careers'. It is particularly significant that this model assumes that there is an underlying dissonance between a *universal* culture of 'economic success and upward mobility' (the American Dream; France 2008: 36) and *differential* access to the means to realise these aims, which is skewed against those 'in the lower reaches of the social structure'. There is something about this portrayal which is inherently plausible, especially in a context where globalisation has taken hold and media images of the trappings of the 'good life' appear to be increasingly pervasive and homogeneous.

As Newburn (2007: 178) acknowledges Merton's ideas went on to exert 'enormous influence', propelling a series of criminological studies which became authoritative in their own right (see Cohen 1955; Cloward and Ohlin 1960, for instance), and leaving their 'footprints everywhere' (Newburn 2007: 179). This may be partly accounted for by the explicit recognition of class and inequality in this analytical framework – something that is immediately attractive to those pursuing radical explanations of youth crime and deviant behaviour. The link between a denial of opportunity and offending appears to place the onus for putting things right squarely on the shoulders of mainstream society and government. A society which encourages certain kinds of aspirations and, indeed, celebrates them, must also be prepared to take responsibility for ensuring that all its members are provided with the means of achieving these goals.

Unfortunately, for Merton, however, these tensions are 'endemic' (Downes and Rock 1982: 101). The nature of the process of 'Americanisation' had (and has) at its core a tendency to promote 'infinite aspirations', which by definition cannot be attained by everyone. Merton's typology did not, however, suggest that a denial of these opportunities would meet the same adaptive response in every case, because this would clearly run counter to the immediately observable evidence of different lifestyles and outcomes. For some, indeed, the achievement of material or social success might even be rejected as a desirable goal, leading to either 'ritualism' or 'retreatism'. Although Merton (1957) acknowledged that he was not offering motivational accounts of the choices people make, this did indicate that young people had available to them a repertoire of options and 'pathways', of which resorting to acquisitive forms of deviant behaviour was only one. Structural accounts such as his are extremely helpful in providing an insight into the underlying contextual and social drivers of young people's lifestyles and actions; however it is also clear, as he recognises, that the processes by which these outcomes are realised also need to be accounted for effectively.

Adapting and criticising Merton: structure and action

Over a significant period, Merton's attempt to provide a theoretical framework for explaining conformity and deviance had 'been enthusiastically embraced' (Featherstone and Deflem 2003: 471). Inevitably, though, and associated with the influential role it has had, much criticism has also ensued. This has tended to be of two kinds: comments on its oversights and omissions and questions as to its explanatory value. Because Merton had always aspired to provide structural accounts of social systems, his relative neglect of the processes which give rise to such outcomes should not be unexpected. Nonetheless, this has enabled others subsequently to express concern at this apparent shortcoming. For instance, the question of intentionality is left unaddressed and so we have no basis on which to determine the mechanisms which account for the patterns of behaviour specified. Do young people adapt to their circumstances and inherent social tensions through a process of rational choice, or can their 'adaptive' behaviour best be accounted for deterministically, as the inevitable consequence of a particular conjuncture of circumstances and attributes? A number of widely-cited studies (see for example, Cohen 1955; Cloward and Ohlin 1960) have attempted to address this question, seeking to account for the outcomes posited earlier by Merton. Cloward and Ohlin (1960: 45), for instance, pointed out that the observable patterns of change and 'adaptation' among young people – and 'delinquents' in particular – were not uniform and predictable because the 'transition' to adulthood could mean a confirmation of 'stable criminal roles' or a 'shift to law-abiding adjustment'. Yet other young people could 'shift' from one form of deviance to another, such as 'drug addiction or alcoholism'. In this way, the passage of time would seem to allow for young people to move between the structural roles specified by Merton.

Cohen (1955) also attempted to account for the routes taken by young people, especially those in disadvantaged communities, whose aspirations to 'middle-class goals' (Rock 2007: 10) could not be met. As Newburn (2007: 197) has observed, using language redolent of Merton's reference to the 'American' way of life, Cohen sought to unpick the implications of the 'problems of adjustment' facing some young people for whom conventional routes to achievement and success were closed off. Feelings of 'shame' and failure could only be dealt with by way of establishing alternative social forms and indicators of status and value – hence we can see the emergence of what came to be termed 'delinquent subcultures'. What this implied, as Cloward and Ohlin also seemed to agree, was that in the face of a denial of the opportunity to achieve in terms of dominant ideals, not only would young people adapt their behaviour, but they would also be likely to develop alternative cultural forms with their own 'opportunity structures' (Merton 1997), around which their 'deviant' activities would be organised. In terms of the original theoretical proposition, this generated two further problems: firstly, it seemed that, not only did young people 'adapt' their lifestyles to deal with the restriction of opportunities, but they also seemed to modify their 'goals' in order to avoid the consequences of rejection and failure. Cohen, for example, referred to short-term and hedonistic aspirations taking the place of longer-term 'career' aims. And secondly, while their behaviour could be judged 'deviant' according to dominant social norms it could no longer be seen in these terms in the 'subcultural' setting where it in fact becomes conventional.

This issue, in turn, has given rise to some of the other critical views expressed about Merton's theory of 'anomie and strain' (Featherstone and Deflem 2003: 472). Proponents of 'labelling theory', have notably, questioned the use of terms such as 'delinquency' and the ways in which these have become utilised to classify and then control young people:

One of the strongest of the criticisms has attacked the apparent assumption that delinquency is primarily a working-class phenomenon, and the analytic preoccupation of these authors with the delinquencies of working-class youth. (Schur 1973: 92)

A preoccupation with the problems of non-adaptation to conventional norms and goals seems to direct our gaze away not only from the question of the legitimation of these goals themselves, but also from the matter of the wrong-doing of those who ostensibly comply with respectable standards.

In this way, it seems, the implicit challenges posed by Merton to the 'American' way appear to have become subverted by way of an undue preoccupation with the behaviours and lifestyles of those whose behaviour did not conform with normative expectations. For some critics, such as Quinney (1970, 1974), this was simply missing the point. A one-sided focus on the attributes and activities of one section of the community merely served to perpetuate a series of ideologically-based assumptions. These, in turn, offered justification for established methods of behaviour management and control, in the apparent interests of the common good. Associated with this process were other important dynamics, such as the tendency to problematise 'deviant' behaviour also in order to incorporate discriminatory and oppressive tendencies, especially in terms of ethnicity and the 'racialisation' of criminal justice (Downes and Rock 2003: 359).

In reality, according to this perspective, both the partial attempts to explain and account for 'problem' behaviour and the means then used to deal with it should be viewed as part of a complex network of social control and reification on the part of dominant interests (Newburn 2007: 252). We should, instead, concentrate our efforts as analysts on developing effective critiques and counter-arguments that could be directed towards the repressive system, it could be argued (see my own attempt at this; Smith 2007).

Yet concerns have emerged about the validity of a crudely oppositional stance towards attempts to account for the experiences and actions of young people. It is suggested that while the unjust workings of an oppressive system should be a legitimate focus of inquiry, this does not of itself obviate the need to understand and account for young people's behaviour, especially where this is harmful to themselves or others. This is a position perhaps most closely with 'Left Realists', whose close attention to the nature and experience of crime in communities has attempted to balance these alternative foci of concern:

> From a left realist perspective, crime is a real problem for ordinary people that must be taken seriously, and central to their crime control strategy is the proposition that crime requires a comprehensive solution: there must be a 'balance of intervention' against both crime and the causes of crime. (Hopkins Burke 2008: 155)

One source (Webber 2007: 102) has gone as far as to suggest that the Left Realists have consciously sought to reintegrate Merton's ideas into a contemporary model of thinking about and responding to the problem of crime. Namely, that we need to understand both the 'social causes of crime' grounded in 'anomie' and the emergence of 'subcultures'; and the machinery by which offenders are identified, categorised and controlled. This allows us, among other things, to reinstate our concern to understand and 'appreciate' the experiences, aspirations and life choices of young people who are marginalised. In other words, their distinctive attitudes, beliefs and characteristics can be brought to the fore in relation to attempts from the outside to account for and respond to their (problem) behaviour. Webber's view is that the key challenge here is to develop frameworks for understanding 'action' rather than specific constructions of behaviour such as 'crime': 'The reification of crime as the thing to be explained is a narrow focus indeed, and excludes the wider contexts in which action takes place' (Webber 2007: 115). Behaviour needs to be both contextualised and demystified:

> Ever since the age of 13 I was wise enough to know what was going on in the streets ... For example, if a young person bumps into a bunch of boys and they force him to steal: if he refuses he gets beaten up; if he does it, he's free to go (so it's also about the young person's safety) ... Having money problems is another example: in the society we're living in, youths want the latest Nike trainers or the latest camera mobile phones ... At home young people may feel it's their responsibility to put food on the table ... (Fadipe and Gittens-Bernard 2005: 227)

'Drifting' into crime: anomie in action?

One of Merton's critics was David Matza, who was particularly concerned at the omissions of structural accounts of anomie and the lack of appreciation of the personal and inter-personal processes which led young people to make choices about identity and lifestyle. Matza is attributed with an awareness of the multi-faceted nature of young people's allegiances and circumstances (Webber 2007: 101), which raises significant questions about those typologies that appear to be too rigid and deterministic.

According to him Merton could be criticised first on empirical grounds, especially for his failure to take account of the shortcomings of official crime figures which appeared to overstate the level of concentration of offending among poorer communities (Matza 1969: 97). Not only did this create an over-stated sense of 'difference' between classes, but it also tended to underestimate the substantial variations within the 'working-class', in particular (p. 99), and theoretically problematic outcomes such as 'social mobility'. To understand the differential impacts of context, circumstances and contingent events, more nuanced theoretical models would be needed. Matza's concern with prescriptive models of conformity and deviation is linked with his scepticism about the processes by which certain characteristics become manifest: 'Did sociologists ever really believe that persons "caught" deviation? Not really; they simply acted and wrote as if they did' (Matza 1969: 102).

His attempt to disturb apparent tendencies towards theoretical rigidity is evident in several respects. The tension between behaviour and identity is articulated, for example, in his account of the attribution of the 'delinquent' label and the extent to which young people themselves might identify with this. Arguing in favour of 'soft rather than hard determinism' (Matza 1964: 27), he suggested that most people were 'neither wholly free nor completely constrained', although some were 'freer than others'. Thus, reflecting the pattern of lived experience, involvement in offending or anti-social behaviour is not a constant feature of someone's life but is rather something in which s/he is 'casually, intermittently and transiently immersed' (p. 28). As a result, it makes sense to think in terms of a 'provisional identity' (Matza 1969: 166), to which an individual may be more or less committed and which is subject to change and renegotiation:

The image of the delinquent I wish to convey is one of drift; an actor neither compelled nor committed to deeds nor freely choosing them; neither different in any simple or fundamental sense from the law abiding, nor the same; conforming to certain traditions in American [sic] life while partially unreceptive to other more conventional traditions … (Matza 1964: 28)

For him, the degree of 'commitment' to a particular deviant identity held by a given individual may be dependent on their exposure to certain lifestyles or behaviour patterns. Thus someone who only associates with 'thieves' may be more likely to be 'affirmed' as such (Matza 1969: 166). This process is likely to be intensified in the event of their apprehension 'for doing a banned thing' (p. 169) whereby an external confirmation of one's emergent 'identity' is also provided. However, as Matza acknowledges, criminal careers are not set in stone – even where offenders repeat their infractions – and so 'the process of becoming deviant remains open' (p. 196).

In reinserting the question of 'will' and subjective choice into the process of identity formation, conformity and non-conformity, and concrete actions, Matza has thus posed significant challenges for structural accounts of young people's behaviour in general and their 'delinquencies' in particular. In order to operationalise his own conceptual framework, he questioned a number of key elements of previous work, such as the 'delinquent subculture', which was dismissed as simply a reworking of prior 'positivist assumptions' about youth and crime (Matza 1969: 33). It is more appropriate in his view to think in terms of a 'subculture of delinquency', which is not just a play on words but also an attempt to capture the sense of collective 'possibility'. This:

> is a setting in which the commission of delinquency is common knowledge among a group of juveniles. The size of the group varies – as a rule of thumb, let us say twice the number engaged in those delinquent acts requiring collective effort. The exact number is unimportant. What is important is publicity. (Matza 1969: 33)

Augmenting this general state of awareness about the feasibility and possible outcomes of certain types of activity, Matza suggests that certain other processes can be observed in the transition from possibility to concrete outcome. Significant among these is the aspect of 'neutralization' (p. 60), not least because it reconnects us with the concept of 'norms' and their place in determining the acceptability or otherwise of certain forms of behaviour. Importantly here 'Norms may be violated without surrendering allegiance to them' (p. 60). Thus, in the way that dominant norms are pivotal in determining fixed and continuing forms of adaptation for Merton, in Matza's case they become 'conditional' and negotiable even if they are generally respected. Actions are justified and sanctions inappropriate in the young person's view where it is possible to advance alternative forms of legitimation, such as 'the primacy of custom', a denial of personal 'responsibility' or a prior 'sense of injustice' (p. 61). It is interesting in light of this to reflect on the evidence from the *Edinburgh Study of Youth Transitions* that being a victim of crime is positively associated with subsequent offending: 'The more often victimization is repeated, the more strongly it predicts delinquency' (Smith, D. 2004: 3).

Even at this point, however, Matza assures us that the commission of a 'delinquent act' is not certain, but it is simply that the conditions for this outcome have been established. Here, he breaks decisively from determinist arguments by suggesting that the 'missing element which provides the thrust or impetus by which the delinquent act is realised is *will*' (1969: 181; original emphasis). He then goes on to undermine his own case somewhat by suggesting, deterministically, that there are other factors which might 'activate' the will to commit infractions (p. 188), such as 'desperation'.

While this apparent equivocation on his part has been the subject of subsequent criticism (Downes and Rock 2003: 148), the important contribution here is to create a sense of uncertainty about the processes by which young people become involved in certain forms of behaviour (which may or may not be 'delinquent'; see Newburn 2007: 230). This provides a more contextual and contingent basis for the depiction and analysis of young people's actions and 'trajectories'. It certainly appears to offer a more plausible basis for accounting for the well-established empirical evidence that 'delinquent activity' is 'a temporary state' (p. 231). Young people are neither engaged in unacceptable behaviour all day every day, nor are they for the most part likely to sustain their offending careers into adulthood, at least according to conventional and official accounts of criminality.

We have not, it should be noted, quite broken free from commonsense assumptions about crime and who should be the object of concern in terms of the propensity to offend. In other words, Webber's concern to account for behaviour first – and only then to consider the processes by which it becomes criminalised in the minds of perpetrators and agents of criminal justice alike – needs to be once again acknowledged: 'Crime and deviancy are secondary to the processes that lead to action ...' (Webber 2007: 115).

A changing world: contingency and choice?

These reflections on the work of Matza and Merton certainly do not purport to offer a comprehensive account or commentary on the available range of theories of delinquency and young people (see Hopkins Burke 2008; Muncie 2009). Rather, they are used here as particularly significant attempts to account for aspects of young people's behaviour. While Merton emphasises the role of 'structure' and offers plausible explanatory accounts of its impact, Matza focuses instead on the processes by which young people become predisposed to certain forms of action and then make choices in light of this. Young (1999; 2004), for one, does not seem to regard these accounts as incompatible; instead they offer perspectives on different aspects of the same phenomenon. Others, however (Yar and Penna 2004), have suggested that criminological explanations need to recognise and adapt to changing times, whereby 'theoretical and empirical' (p. 543) observations must offer plausible insights into what is happening in the present. This suggestion has, indeed, been reflected in contemporary attempts to account for young people's choices and actions.

The transitions between 'modern' society and its successors appear to reveal a process of 'fragmentation' (Hopkins Burke 2008: 80), with the result that 'whole tracts of the former industrial working class now appeared superfluous to the requirements of society ...' (p. 81). In consequence, the phenomenon of 'social exclusion' has become more pervasive and embedded, principally affecting particular sections of society, including young people, ethnic minorities, and those on low incomes and in insecure forms of employment.

In light of these developments, there has been some pressure to re-evaluate previous assumptions about the dynamics and meanings of youth crime (Yar and Penna 2004). For example, as society has become more diverse and segmented, it might seem that explanatory accounts themselves must develop greater degrees of flexibility and specificity. Uniform and universal explanations of behaviour have become less satisfactory as they have been faced with increasing levels of nuance and detail. Situated and almost spontaneous accounts have now become more prominent (Hayward 2002). A life course which is no longer predictable or certain may, in turn, prompt an approach to 'risky decisions' which is of the moment and represents what is seen as a short-term solution to the lack of 'control' and an absence of more conventional incentives or opportunities. Explicitly building on the ideas of Matza and Merton, Fenwick and Hayward (2000: 31) argue that 'contemporary theoretical criminology offers something new'. They suggest that 'crime' itself has become a commodity like any other and the decision to 'transgress' is simply a 'lifestyle choice'. Even those who have given up offending would appear to acknowledge its immanent attractions:

'When you're shoplifting you get a wee buzz. I sometimes miss that'.
(Sarah, 27)

'I miss the buzz, being honest with myself, I suppose I do'.
(Vicky, 27)
(both quoted in Barry 2006: 124)

In this sense, acts of transgression need to be appreciated for their 'subjective' and intrinsic qualities, rather than as necessarily instrumental and purposive. Feelings such as 'excitement' (p. 36) can be seen as 'central' to a range of 'deviant practices', whose rewards are immediate and their consequences unconsidered. The examples of drug use or football hooliganism:

serve to illustrate the point that youth crime is best understood in expressive rather than utilitarian terms. Individuals are seduced by the existential possibilities offered by criminal acts – by the pleasure of transgression – and not necessarily by, or only by, the immediate material or practical benefits. (Fenwick and Hayward 2000: 38)

This account may, it is suggested, help us to understand why criminal behaviour among young people is socially dispersed and is not exclusive to particular social groups. It may also help us to understand why it is that not all of those who are excluded or marginalised become offenders; and that those who do, do not necessarily all offend in the same way.

Despite this, Fenwick and Hayward do recognise the need to contextualise the changing shape of deviant behaviour in some way and they attribute much of its contemporary character to the influence of 'consumerism'. The acquisition and experience of 'new' goods and 'sensations' become key drivers of young people's motivations and thus their actions; this, in turn, is driven by a recurrent sense of 'dissatisfaction' and boredom with the present. Unlike Merton's adaptive model, this is a generic condition of the young (and possibly others, too), rather than a feature simply of those whose aspirations are thwarted or diverted by a lack of opportunity or access to resources. In an ironic twist, the attractions of offending are themselves intensified by the way in which crime 'is being packaged and marketed to young people as a romantic, exciting, cool and fashionable cultural symbol' (p. 44). There does seem to be a lack of clarity here as to whether it is the attraction of infraction that is seen as the prime motivation or, rather, the activity which it constitutes, irrespective of whether it is an offence; but the central point is that the consumerist ethos itself opens up increased possibilities of, and creates enthusiasm for, criminal behaviour. In this way, the dynamics of 'fragmentation' and the emergence and increasing dominance of the consumer culture driven by market forces combine to enhance the likelihood of certain types of activity, prompted by a need to take control and feel good, in the moment. As this becomes the prevailing mode of existence, so too do the moral and structural inhibitors fade into the background. Young people are less likely to be constrained by social norms or cultural institutions and are no longer offered the kind of moral certainties which might have applied in earlier, more ordered, historical eras.

At the same time – as with the commodification of crime through film and electronic media – they also increasingly encounter mixed and ambiguous messages. Essential truths are increasingly elusive and formerly respected institutions become increasingly suspect, the unreliable arbiters of right and wrong. At the time of writing, for instance, recent scandals involving rapacious bankers and excessive expense claims by MPs are illustrative of a loss of moral authority among conventional institutions. In Muncie's (2009) view, this suggests that the very categories according to which we classify people and their actions become transient and negotiable. They are to be 'created' rather than 'given':

> postmodernism implies an abandonment of the concepts of 'crime' and 'youth' and the construction of a new language and mode of thought to designate and explore objects of censure and codes of conduct. (Muncie 2009: 153)

If this is the case, then formal categories such as 'crime' and 'young offender' lose their explanatory power to a significant degree. We would be better advised, it seems, to consider behaviour in its own right, rather than as representative of a broader socially constructed category. We may also find that we can gain a greater degree of insight by considering the 'narratives and accounts derived from young people themselves' (Muncie 2009: 153).

We may still feel that this loss of certainty and explanatory power has created real problems in trying to account for patterns or structural influences on beliefs and actions; however, this kind of explanatory frame does help to expose certain conventional assumptions about crime and who commits it to critical scrutiny. At the same time, it also reveals the considerable importance of taking close notice of the explanations and 'stories' offered by young people themselves, as Barry (2006), among others, demonstrates. For her, offending is a feature of 'transition' and of the necessity of asserting control and establishing a sense of identity and place in a context of uncertainty and relative powerlessness. Thus, individual accounts and histories assume real importance in the task of gaining a detailed understanding.

Towards a theoretical framework?

The aim of this chapter has not been to rehearse comprehensively the great variety of alternative theoretical accounts of youth crime and deviance; rather, it has been to introduce certain contrasting accounts which may pave the way for some tentative conclusions about the key elements for an explanatory framework. It has also provided a useful backdrop for subsequent considerations of what is already 'known' about young people's routes into (and out of) offending and anti-social behaviour and how far that knowledge can be justified or applied.

Merton's account, firstly, has drawn attention to the importance of structures and the ways in which young people's choices and adaptations are framed, according to dominant expectations and norms. Interestingly, and importantly, his model does not presuppose any element of criminality in the behavioural consequences of their attempts to reconcile 'means' and 'goals'. In other words, this kind of approach provides a basis for making sense of social action, without necessarily imbuing it with any moral connotations whether positive or negative.

Matza, on the other hand – and perhaps ironically – more readily adopts the language of 'deviance' and 'delinquency', even while trying to offer an account which is 'appreciative':

Once observed in their natural habitat, once their nefarious activities are put in proper context, once the subject is fully appreciated, the deviant person comes into proper, human focus. (Matza 1969: 40)

Although Matza himself has been identified as a critic of Merton (Young 2004: 555), it may be more productive to consider their approaches as being complementary; one identifies the importance of taking account of the structural location of subjective choices while the other seeks to elaborate the processes by which such choices are made 'in context'. These considerations, in turn, are given further impetus by the relatively recent attempts to account for behavioural choices as a feature of rapid social change and decentring. In other words, the culmination of a process of structural change has meant that the kind of choices and the process of 'drift' identified by Matza are now believed to take place within an increasingly complex and atomised moral framework (Ferrell 1994). Moralities and modes of organising one's decisions – firstly about what is 'right' and then about what to do in relation to that precept – may originate at the level of overarching and pervasive (even global) social forms, but at the point of realisation they are constructed in relation to relatively narrow and constrained points of reference. As we shall see, these conclusions, tentative as they may be, pose very substantial questions for attempts to describe and account for the 'crimes' of the young against an apparently uniform and uncontentious template of what is generally socially acceptable and what is not. Importantly, then, attempts to account for and make sense of the behaviour of young people must be distinguished from those characterisations which uncritically overlay notions of crime and deviance upon them.

Whether or not something is defined as a 'criminal' act may have a bearing on young people's choices (Presdee 1994), but this is very different from seeking to explain or predict levels and types of delinquency in terms of their identifiable characteristics or external influences.

Chapter 3

Becoming 'criminal': what does the evidence tell us?

The search for explanations

Having tried previously to set out some possible frameworks for understanding young people's choices and adaptations, it may be helpful here to move on to consider the available evidence and the messages which have been gleaned from it. Given the persistence of our interest and indeed 'fears' about what young people do and who they are (Pearson 1983), it is not surprising that these questions have attracted extensive interest from researchers and other commentators. What we should also acknowledge at this point, of course, is that it is this very concern which has tended to frame investigative activity of this kind. In other words, the starting point has often tended to problematise young people and their behaviour, treating this as a challenge which needs to be addressed or a threat which must be controlled. This tendency has a number of consequences; notably, that it focuses attention on young people and what they do as an apparently legitimate cause for concern. In the process, other valid questions become secondary and receive relatively little attention; for instance, there is a tendency to acknowledge the problematic nature of terms such as 'crime' and 'delinquency', but at the same time to relegate these to ancillary status. In one example, there appears to be a considerable degree of ambiguity in the juxtaposition of concerns about the effects of 'labelling' with a highly detailed account of the achievements of an intensive supervision and surveillance programme in reducing re-offending:

A degree of arbitrariness seems inevitable, and there are growing concerns that the targeting of particular groups is resulting in a labelling of a sub-group of offenders as 'innately criminal'. While risk management provides a theoretical basis for intensive community programmes, these difficulties and concerns suggest that any emphasis on this model needs to be constrained to ensure that risk is seen alongside other social principles and priorities ... (Moore *et al.* 2006: 220)

Concerns about the ways in which young people come to be categorised as offenders and in what circumstances thus sit rather awkwardly with a preoccupation for explaining (and then responding to) the conceptually and methodologically distinct phenomenon of their criminality. In short, there is an analytical disjuncture between the socially constructed nature of youth crime and young offenders, on the one hand; and attempts to explain these as if they are specific and exclusive characteristics of certain individuals, on the other. Furthermore, the links between assumptions about the essential nature of youth crime and criminality and what Muncie (2009: 3) refers to as 'populist assumptions and dominant political discourses' only compound the problem facing us when we come to ask questions about the extent of youth crime, who is responsible for it, and why? Muncie (2009: 3) maintains 'that we should ask instead, who says this is a social problem – and why do they say so?'

Despite these caveats which we should always have at the back of our minds, the aim of the present chapter is to explore some of the copious evidence that we do have about young people's offending, their levels of criminality, and the causes of these.

Such evidence has tended to fall under, or be attributed to, a number of conceptual categories, such as:

- individual characteristics;
- psychosocial features;
- population-wide influences. (Rutter *et al.* 1998b)

Others have sought 'risk factors' associated with delinquency in a series of distinct 'domains': family, school, community, and personal or individual factors (Communities that Care 2005).

The usual suspects: families and communities

'I blame the parents!' (*Daily Telegraph*, 6 April 2009) is almost a mantra in contemporary society. It is certainly the case that there is a well-established strand of empirical research which has sought to identify and determine the extent of the relationship between children's experience of family life and their subsequent offending behaviour (Wilson 1975, 1980; Sampson and Laub 1993; Buchanan and Hudson 1998; Communities that Care 2005).

Collectively, these findings seem to suggest that delinquency can be associated with a series of family and parental characteristics, including conflict, poor supervision and parents' own 'deviant behaviour and attitudes' (Communities that Care 2005: 12). Attempts to quantify and explain the relationship between parenting and 'delinquency' date back some time (e.g. Wilson 1962). Early studies appeared to show a strong correlation between certain parental and family attributes and offending by young people. These attributes included 'father's occupation, size of family, adequacy of school clothing, school attendance, and parental contact with school', as well as 'parental criminality' (Wilson 1975: 249). Thus, both parental and family characteristics (such as size and employment status) and 'parental behaviour' (Wilson 1974) could be associated with young people's anti-social behaviour. It should be acknowledged perhaps that even these early studies did not seek insular or simplistic causal explanations, linking family circumstances to wider concerns:

> it is futile to expect changes in parental behaviour in an unchanged social situation ... Middle-class child-centred behaviour is not operable in conditions of the slum. A debate concerned with preparation for parenthood or education of parents may be more appropriately focused on families who have scope for a change in style of living. (Wilson 1974: 253)

Subsequent studies from elsewhere also attempted to maintain this linkage. Sampson and Laub (1993), for instance, tried to establish a model which accounted for both direct and indirect effects on delinquency, enabling a connection to be made between family processes and antecedent factors such as poverty. Thus while 'family processes of informal social control' were identified as being responsible for 'a significant share' of the variations in offending behaviour by adolescents (p. 133), these processes could, in turn, be shown to be linked to the effects of 'poverty'. In concluding their discussion, Sampson and Laub (1993: 134) also expressed the hope that 'future research will address further the connection we have emphasized between poverty and mediating family processes' in contextualising and explaining youth offending. In other words, their view was that it would be unwise to attempt to overemphasise or isolate certain types of explanatory factor – such as family behaviour – given the detailed and complex social setting, of which poverty is a particularly significant aspect. These conclusions echoed the earlier work of Bronfenbrenner (1979), who had developed an 'ecological' model of human development that was similarly concerned with the interactive and social nature of the influences on growth and behaviour.

Other work in this area, however, has seemed to incorporate an implicit assumption (or assumptions) that the causes of problem behaviour can be disaggregated and identified and 'treated' independently (see Buchanan and Hudson 1998, for example). Such relationships may be demonstrated from early childhood, it seems. There is, apparently:

> a clear association between parenting practices characterised by harsh and inconsistent discipline, little positive parental involvement with the child, poor monitoring and supervision, and behaviour and conduct problems in early childhood. (Barlow 1998: 92)

This kind of conclusion is closely associated with the idea of an intergenerational transmission of deviant or 'anti-social' attitudes and behaviours. 'Continuities' can seemingly be identified across at least three generations (Smith and Farrington 2004). A number of factors appear to be associated with the repetition of problem behaviour in subsequent generations, including parental conflict, authoritarian parenting and parental anti-social behaviour. These associations are further developed into a hypothesis based on the notion that like attracts like. The 'selective seeker' hypothesis (Patterson 1998) suggests that children whose development is adversely affected by failures in parenting will reflect this in their adaptive decision making: 'Given their limitations, children actively seek settings and persons that maximize payoffs' (p. 1265). The antisocial children of antisocial parents will, in turn, seek out antisocial partners, it is suggested. Thus 'disrupted socialization is likely to promote the continual display and reinforcement of antisocial and coercive behaviors in different life settings over the life course' (Smith and Farrington

2004: 242). This will then create the conditions for a subsequent and continuing intergenerational transmission of problematic attitudes and behaviours.

Recent attempts to detail comprehensive accounts of the factors associated with youth crime have retained the central emphasis on family and parental characteristics. These are believed to comprise:

• pre-natal and perinatal factors;
• poor parental supervision and discipline;
• family conflict;
• a family history of criminal activity;
• parental attitudes that condone antisocial and criminal behaviour;
• low income, poor housing and large family size. (Communities that Care 2005)

Cumulatively, these elements appear to be linked to 'four interlocking models that continue to exemplify the adverse influence that families can exert on children when under stress': neglect, conflict, deviant behaviour and attitudes, and disruption (p. 12).

However this emphasis on family processes and outcomes has not been exclusive, especially in those reviews which have sought to provide comprehensive accounts of the factors associated with youth crime (Rutter *et al.* 1998b; Communities that Care 2005). As a result, schools and communities are also considered, to the extent that they too may be associated with differential rates of youth offending. Thus, patterns of increased 'risk of involvement in crime' are found to be evident among the populations of 'disadvantaged neighbourhoods' (Communities that Care 2005: 15). It is not just disadvantage, though, that is associated with an increased likelihood of offending. 'Community disorganisation and neglect' (p. 16) and other signs of instability, such as a 'high turnover' and the absence of a 'sense of community', also seem to be pertinent (p. 17). Of course, it may not appear coincidental that such characteristics seem to mirror the destabilising influences observed in families also.

Similarly, the organisation of schools and the nature of the school experience seem to have variable relationships with the levels of offending by young people:

A measure of 'school process' based on structure, organisation and functioning was found to be significantly linked to misbehaviour, low achievement and truancy after controlling for intake factors ... high levels of punishment and low levels of praise by teachers were significantly linked to delinquency. (Communities that Care 2005: 15)

The nature of recorded crime by young people also suggests that peer influences may be important it seems. 'Young offenders tend to commit delinquent acts in small groups rather than alone' (p. 21) and so it would appear that there may be a 'peer group' effect on the decision to offend. This may be linked to the previously cited 'selective seeker' phenomenon, whereby 'antisocial children and young people gravitate into each other's company' (p. 21). This observation is supported by wider assessments of the nature of children and young people's friendships and how these impact on their behavioural choices. Certain types of interaction are associated with particular patterns of behaviour. For example: 'Antisocial children ... are known to engage in large amounts of talk with their friends – talk that is deviant even when the children are being videotaped in the laboratory' (Hartup 1998: 151).

Analysis of 'friendship clusters', however, also highlights some of the complexities of trying to establish or prioritise causal links (Dishion *et al.* 1995: 147). Geographical proximity, school experience and similarities in family backgrounds all seem to be associated with the formation of 'antisocial peer groups'. Although these factors are to be consistently found together, the direction of the relationship and its dynamics are much less easily specified (Hartup 1998: 154). Causes and effects appear to be 'interactive', rather than simply additive.

At the same time, there is evidence that other 'protective' factors may operate to modify the likelihood of young people becoming involved in crime, including strong and positive family relationships (not necessarily with parents), good experiences of education, moving away from 'high risk' neighbourhoods, or forming friendships with non-offenders (Rutter *et al.* 1998b). This array of possible factors associated with the onset, persistence and desistance from offending suggests that it is unwise to focus unduly on one (or even a few) of the possible causes, such as 'bad parenting'. Not only is this likely to be inaccurate, it is also likely to be associated with those stigmatising processes which single out and discriminate against individuals who have been identified as potentially problematic. To the extent that such assumptions become embedded in social and organisational practices, they may indeed go some way to promoting the very behaviours they seek to anticipate and prevent (Lemert 1967). Nonetheless, such approaches to the challenge of classifying and addressing delinquency are undeniably popular (and sometimes populist) – as Wilson (1980) has reminded us, the opportunities for misdirecting ourselves are significant:

> Lax parenting methods are often the result of chronic stress, situations arising from frequent or prolonged spells of unemployment, physical or mental disabilities among members of the family, and an often permanent condition of poverty … If these factors are ignored and parental laxness is seen instead as an 'attitude' which can be shifted by education or by punitive measures, then our findings are being misinterpreted. It is the position of the most disadvantaged groups in society, and not the individual, which needs improvement in the first place. (Wilson 1980: 234)

Offender characteristics: individualising explanations of crime

Although families are often the starting point for many of those concerned to explain the incidence of youth crime, accounts grounded in this one domain appear to be insufficient on closer inspection. Widening the net to include social networks, and peer and neighbourhood influences, seems to account for some of the additional variance in criminal careers, but does not provide convincing explanations for some of the persisting variations in young people's trajectories and levels of involvement in delinquent activity.

Gender, for instance, has readily been identified as a significant factor in influencing levels of involvement in 'youth crime', although it seems to be a moot point as to whether it is the fact of being male that constitutes a 'risk factor', or being female that acts as a 'protective factor' (Communities that Care 2005: 22). Nonetheless, it is suggested that the 'risk factors' to be found in young people's 'backgrounds' are similar, regardless of gender, but despite this young women are consistently observed to be less frequently represented in official crime figures. At the same time, 'self-report surveys' also reveal that girls and young women are less likely to be involved in criminal activity. However, these observations are modified by the recognition that the 'sex ratio' has declined in the recent past – that is, while males are still significantly more likely to get into trouble, they do not outnumber females to the same extent as previously. At the same time, the ratio will vary depending on the type of offence, with boys and young men being 'much more likely than females' to be responsible for serious acts of violence, while the disparity is much less for theft and other property offences (Communities that Care 2005: 22).

Age, too, appears to be a significant factor in determining the levels of young people's involvement in crime. For females the peak age is around 15 and for males it is 18. While these peak ages have varied over time (Rutter *et al.* 1998b), there is a clear trajectory to criminal careers in general which suggests that they are to a large extent an adolescent phenomenon. On the other hand this is not a uniform pattern, because as well as gender other factors – such as offence type and 'co-offending' – can be seen to interact with age as variables (Mastrigt and Farrington 2009).

These well-established, clear and consistent variations in the levels of involvement in offending by young people may also be taken to suggest that personal characteristics in general should be taken into account in formulating explanations. Thus, for example, it is believed to be not merely the passage of time which determines the level of criminal activity, but the change processes related to ageing. This kind of approach has culminated in 'developmental' or 'life course' models of the 'trajectories of crime' (Sampson and Laub 2005: 13). It is proposed that social and contextual influences are under-pinned and inter-twined with individual characteristics, both biological and psychological. Further it is suggested that these various components of the larger picture are likely to have a variable, time specific quality; some may operate from the first years of a child's life, while others may only operate at particular points or up until certain 'turning points', such as marriage (p. 14), occur. To the extent that these factors will also vary independently according to age and other characteristics, it may be assumed that explanatory frameworks are likely to be both complex and, probably, somewhat less than comprehensive. These accounts seem to be closely influenced by broader accounts of adolescence which seek to articulate similarly multi-faceted explanations for the variations in young people's characteristics and behaviour (Coleman and Hendry 1999; Smith *et al.* 2003, for example). Some, indeed, have gone so far as to try to quantify the different contributions of different types of causal factor to delinquent outcomes. One twin study concluded that:

> The best fitting model suggested that 18%, 56% and 26% of the variance in delinquency among both boys and girls is associated with additive genetic, nonshared environment, and shared environmental factors, respectively. (Taylor *et al.* 2000: 433)

57

The suggestion that genes and physiological make-up have some part to play is not new of course (Hopkins Burke 2008: 98) and a fairly wide range of characteristics has been adumbrated as having a relationship to young people's propensity to offend. These include direct genetic influences, physiological processes and 'altered biological states' (Hopkins Burke 2008: 106). These might derive from substance use or perhaps diet or food additives.

Early life experiences as well, such as problems in developing secure attachments to care-givers, might have a significant impact in terms of establishing the pre-conditions for subsequent antisocial behaviour. 'Disorganized attachment' (Smith *et al.* 2004: 104) seems to be associated with a number of longstanding problems as children grow up, and this may well be particularly 'relevant ... in understanding severely maladaptive or antisocial behaviours in later life' (p. 105). The combination of genetic influences and early life experiences is believed to result in a series of individual characteristics which have 'an established role in the development of antisocial behaviour' (Rutter *et al.* 1998b: 13), namely hyperactivity, cognitive impairment, temperamental attributes such as 'impulsivity' and a 'lack of control', and a 'distorted style' of understanding social situations and others' behaviour. Hyperactivity, for instance, has reportedly been shown to be associated with subsequent criminal careers. ADHD (Attention Deficit Hyperactivity Disorder), as it has come to be known, has been said to have 'a strong genetic component' and this has also been repeatedly linked to persistent antisocial behaviour (Communities that Care 2005: 18). While it is bound up generally with 'poor social functioning', it is significant for:

> its continued ability to predict juvenile convictions among 8–10 year old boys after controlling for other conduct problems [which] placed ADHD towards the start of a developmental sequence that could lead some children to become persistent and violent offenders. (Communities that Care 2005: 18)

In passing, it is worth noting that the categorical term 'ADHD' is itself contested (Timimi 2005) and so its purported association with youth crime may not be as clear cut as this review of 'risk factors' indicates. Indeed, it is noteworthy that the review itself goes on to acknowledge that 'Hyperactivity, impulsivity and cognitive impairment ... are so closely related' that there has been some confusion as to whether or not we should treat them as 'one or several' influences.

Nonetheless, cognitive impairment and 'low intelligence' do also seem to be consistently linked with subsequent offending. Because this finding has been replicated in relation to self-reported offending, it has been concluded that this is not because those with lower intelligence ratings are 'more likely to get caught' (Communities that Care 2005: 19).

Thus it seems that there is an array of individual characteristics with a variety of origins which can be associated with an eventual involvement in youth crime. Others may well operate as protective factors too, such as 'high intelligence', an 'outgoing disposition' or strong attachments to 'one or both parents' (p.23). The processes which lead towards, or insure against, future offending have been recognised as 'complex' though (Rutter *et al.* 1998b: 13). It is not clear how the various factors will interact among themselves or with other types of influence, originating in the family or wider context. In addition, there seems to be a degree of confusion in many of these accounts as to the range of behaviours they purport to explain. There are clear differences and indeed different trajectories depending on whether we are concerned with violent offending, drug use or property crimes for instance. We are thus faced with a diversity of outcomes as well as a diversity of inputs. Studies have claimed, for example, that there are different biological and personal characteristics associated with violent as opposed to non-violent offenders (Piquero 2000: 410).

These levels of complexity suggest that effective explanatory accounts within this kind of 'positivist' epistemological perspective on youth crime (Muncie 2009) must develop a high degree of sophistication if they are to make any real contribution to our deeper understanding, and indeed, as is their general aspiration, to being able to address and prevent the problems associated with the crimes of the young. It may be, for example, that we need different explanatory models to account for different 'trajectories of crime' or alternative patterns of offending. 'Persistent offenders', for example, appear to follow different offending pathways from others, but they can also be distinguished according to a range of other characteristics (Arnull *et al.* 2005). Does this then suggest that there are fundamentally different processes operating according to the nature and intensity of young people's offending careers? Or might it just be a matter of degree? In other words, the influences on their offending behaviour may simply be more substantial and act more intensively upon them. Those who would argue for a comprehensive approach to understanding the development (and, indeed, cessation) of delinquency have been naturally inclined to suggest that a common basis for understanding is achievable:

> Although at first it may seem counterintuitive, our fundamental argument is that persistent offending and desistance – and hence trajectories of crime – can be meaningfully understood within the same theoretical framework. (Sampson and Laub 2005: 13)

The search for intellectually coherent explanations of young people's pathways into (and out of) crime is therefore at the heart of explanatory models which argue for a degree of uniformity and predictability about antisocial behaviour and its perpetrators. What they have in common is held to be more important than what differentiates them.

Developmental and 'life-course' criminologies: squaring the circle?

Despite Wilson's cautionary note, it is clear that increasingly sophisticated attempts to explain youth crime and to develop the machinery for predicting and responding to it are deeply embedded in most contemporary social systems. The emergence of 'developmental criminology' as a recognised strand of research and theory has been significant, to the extent that it has sought to overcome earlier difficulties in accounting for crime while also becoming increasingly influential in terms of its incorporation into the thinking and practices of those institutional interests responsible for reducing the levels of offending in society. To some extent also this kind of account is attractive because it coincides with widely held public perceptions (and, indeed, personal experiences) to the effect that adolescence *is* a very distinctive life stage with its own highly specific demands and 'strains' (Agnew 1999). Conflict and stress are believed to be inevitable aspects of youth (see Chapter 1) and therefore these are susceptible to generalised explanations which may explain certain regularities, such as the persistence of the peak age of offending in the mid to late teens. These assumptions coincide too with broader theories of adolescence that associate behavioural and emotional changes with certain key events, such as puberty at one end of the spectrum, and 'settling down' (marriage, employment and fixed accommodation) at the other. Theories of 'storm and stress' have been applied to adolescence for a long time (Coleman and Hendry 1999: 208). In contemporary societies, there is no doubt that 'in the course of the adolescent period an individual will experience a wide variety of events, changes and transitions, some of which may be stressful in themselves' (p. 210). Many of these events are, additionally, distinctive to adolescence and do not occur, or do not occur with the same level of intensity, at other points in the life cycle. It might seem, therefore, that young people are inherently prone to experiencing some of the demands and pressures which will lead towards antisocial activities and this is reflected more or less directly in the crime statistics, in terms of both rates and the types of crime committed (Coleman and Hendry 1999: 183; Hopkins Burke 2008: 223).

Thus, for instance, both 'age' and the 'mechanisms of desistance' can be seen as invariant features of young people's distinctive patterns of criminal activity (Laub and Sampson 2005: 17). These factors are said to retain their influence even in the light of observable differences, such as the 'enormous variability in peak ages of offending' for example. Even allowing for these variations it seems that age has 'a direct effect on offending', with the result that there is a general tendency for offending rates to fall as young people grow into adulthood.

Equally, there are observable 'turning points' which seem to act consistently in the same manner to promote 'desistance'. These:

> all involve, to varying degrees, (1) new situations that 'knife-off' the past from the present, (2) new situations that provide both supervision and mentoring as well as new opportunities of social support and growth, (3) new situations that change and structure routine activities, and (4) new situations that provide the opportunity for identity transformation ... (Sampson and Laub 2005: 18)

Thus an 'involvement in institutions such as marriage, work and the military' can be shown to have independent effects on young people's continuing propensity to become involved in criminal activity.

These patterns, according to Sampson and Laub, are the strongest predictors of 'offending careers' in evidence. In other words, irrespective of their background circumstances and characteristics, young people's profiles of criminal activity have strongly similar shapes (p. 25). Those who are purportedly at a 'high risk' do appear to offend more frequently, but as they grow older their levels of delinquency decline in exactly the same manner as those who are identified as being at a 'low risk' of offending. If this is the case, then searching for the risk (and protective) factors associated with youth crime must focus on those factors which are *specific* to this age group to a greater extent than those which are constant and would tend to imply a much greater degree of continuity in offending behaviour. Coleman and Hendry (1999: 210), for instance, offer a typology which distinguishes between 'normative events, non-normative events and daily hassles'. Normative events, such as physiological changes or school transfers, affect all young people; non-normative events, such as poverty, family breakdown, illness or school exclusion, affect individual young people to varying degrees at unpredictable points in time; while 'daily hassles' represent persistent occurrences which may have a cumulative but largely unattributable impact, such as victimisation or bullying. This framework helps to add a degree of depth and detail to 'developmental' accounts of delinquency.

Sampson and Laub (2005) are also critical of what they see as simplistic developmental accounts which represent the 'dominant (and unreflective) interpretation in criminology'. They equate such assumptions to 'traveling by train – one gets on a trajectory and ends up at a later point directed by the plan set down at the beginning ...' (p. 42). Thus, in their view, it is unwise to give too much weight to accounts of criminality which rely on genetic origins or early family experiences. They believe instead that 'the concept of *emergence*' (p. 43; original emphasis) offers a unifying principle, which brings together different strands and influences in the genesis of offending behaviour, including 'group' characteristics, 'time-varying events', and 'human agency'. This sort of model helps to account for individual variations, within- and between-group differences and changes related to particular patterns of experience, or key 'turning points' (p. 43). This phenomenon is summarised conceptually as one of 'situated choice'. Decisions are not only grounded in human agency, they are also bounded by the structures and contingent events within which they are located and by which they are constrained.

These conclusions represent both a modification and extension of Sampson and Laub's (1990) earlier observation that, against a backdrop of the 'indirect' effects of 'poverty' and structural inequalities:

> Although 'child effects' are clearly present, a full understanding of delinquency ... requires that we also come to grips with the socializing influence of the family as reflected in disciplinary practices, supervision and direct parental controls, and bonds of attachment. (Sampson and Laub 1990: 538)

Differences at the individual level may be significant, but they are certainly not enough to account for the diverse outcomes that have been identified. Nor can they realistically explain the regularities between general patterns of persistence and desistance, in their view.

As opposed to the generic model advanced by Sampson and Laub, some developmental accounts have attempted to distinguish between alternative pathways (Moffitt 1993; Rutter *et al.* 1998a), proposing two alternatives, in particular, the 'life-course-persistent' and the 'adolescent-limited' groups (Moffitt 1993), although the true extent of this distinction has also been questioned (Nagin *et al.* 1995). Nonetheless, it is suggested that the presence or absence of risk factors, especially from early in life, can be associated with ongoing patterns of involvement, persistence and desistance. Rutter *et al.* (1998b) have concluded that these are important distinctions, reflected in the findings of a number of longitudinal studies, and that 'persistent recidivist offending often has its roots in disruptive behaviour first manifest during the preschool years' (p. 307). This in turn leads to the suggestion that this particular trajectory is 'influenced' by individual characteristics with significant biological or genetic components. On the other hand, wider social and interpersonal influences may be more significant when we come to account for antisocial behaviour which 'arises in adolescence rather than early childhood' (p. 214). Participation in 'delinquent peer groups' may be a predisposing factor, for instance. In other aspects of young people's behaviour too, early onset appears to be indicative or predictive of different pathways, with a younger involvement in drug-taking likely to result in a 'serious, non-recreational' use of addictive substances later on (Communities that Care 2005: 20).

The problem for 'life course' criminologies, though, is the precise nature of the relationship between associations and causes. While certain patterns can be articulated – such as the prevalence of (recorded) offending during the teenage years or the links between early onset and a deeper and more persistent involvement in offending behaviour – the more detail is provided, the less certain the connections appear to be. Operationalising the available evidence in the form of reliable intervention tools is highly problematic, as even committed 'developmentalists' would recognise:

The technical difficulties of incorporating risk and other factors into reliable assessment scales remain formidable. This is especially the case with attempts to identify young offenders most likely to develop into chronic serious or violent adult offenders. (Communities that Care 2005: 106)

This challenge becomes even more daunting if we factor in an emerging recognition of the differential nature of influences on young people (Coleman and Hendry 1999), the uncertain nature of the interactions between different factors (and different types of factors) (Rutter *et al.* 1998b: 378), and recent attempts to incorporate the dimensions of 'contingency' and human agency (Sampson and Laub 2005). In the end perhaps we should take a step back and remind ourselves of the concerns expressed presciently by Beck (1992), who foresaw this kind of development in the empiricist project, with the 'disintegration of the certainties' of modern society being paralleled exactly with a 'compulsion to find new certainties' (p. 14) on which to base our judgements and actions. Indeed, Sampson and Laub sum up the problem with the 'logic of prediction' quite neatly:

one gets the sense from 'early interveners' that it is just a matter of time before risk factors are measured well enough (from the human genome?) that the false positive problem will become ancient history. From the perspective of our theory, this is simply wishful thinking, and we predict continued heterogeneity in criminal offending over the life course no matter what the childhood classification scheme of the future. (Sampson and Laub 2005: 41)

Groups and gangs: a developmental case study

As we have seen, developmental criminologies have become highly influential as they have sought to elaborate increasingly detailed and sophisticated explanations of young people's pathways into and out of crime. At the same time, a number of their inherent limitations have become apparent, suggesting that they may be both empirically and conceptually flawed in certain respects. In order to explore these issues a little further in concrete terms, it would be helpful to consider the example of young people and 'gangs'. This has been a subject of recurrent and sometimes acute concern to policymakers, practitioners and criminologists alike, and therefore considerable effort has been invested in attempting to make sense of the phenomenon (Hallsworth and Young 2008).

For many working within the language and practices of developmental approaches, the primary concern is to identify those 'risk factors' which, in turn, are believed to account for 'serious and violent delinquency' (Howell and Egley 2005: 36). Therefore, it has been claimed that recent research has produced three key findings in this respect. Firstly, the predictors of eventual gang membership can be discovered in 'all five of the risk factor domains (family, peer group, school, individual characteristics and community conditions)'. Secondly, these factors have a cumulative impact, such that the more there are in the individual's background, the greater is 'the likelihood of gang involvement'. And thirdly, the more domains in which risk factors are identified, the more likely is gang membership also. Explanatory models thus need to account for the ways in which these cumulative factors interact and lead towards an eventual participation in gang-related activities. One of the principal sources of this form of explanation derives from the US-based Rochester Youth Development Study (Thornberry et al. 2003). This study found that 'gang members suffer from deficits in multiple developmental domains' (p. 183) and that the 'cumulative' effects of these deficits is particularly influential: '61% of the young boys and 40% of the young girls who have deficits in all seven domains were gang members' (p. 183). The nature and timing of the risk factors point persuasively towards a 'life-course perspective' which locates the origins of gang involvement in the interaction between early influences and 'dynamic' variables acting in the present (p. 187).

Relevant influences may be said to emerge at successive 'stages', with each predisposing a child to a greater likelihood of gang involvement subsequently:

> Taken together, concentrated disadvantage at the community level, family problems, and certain child characteristics lead to early childhood problems (aggression and disruptive behaviour), and each of these four variables in turn increases the likelihood of delinquency in childhood and gang membership in adolescence. (Howell and Egley 2005: 341)

So it is that disadvantage, punitive parenting and characteristics such as impulsivity point towards the emergence of further predisposing influences at the next stage – 'school entry'. Pre-existing traits such as aggression and disruptive behaviour may lead to a 'rejection by prosocial peers' and an exposure to other antisocial peer pressures.

By the 'later childhood stage', it seems, further 'risk factors (causal variables)' will begin to make their presence felt, such as a mutual reinforcement of delinquent behaviours, early criminal activity, and 'weakened bonds' with integrative institutions such as schools and community organisations (p. 342). At the same time, external factors will continue to be significant, including 'poor-quality schools' and high rates of exclusion from formal education. Other relevant factors interestingly include 'personal victimization' which also appears to be associated with subsequent precursors of gang membership such as 'violence and aggression' (p. 345).

These authors conclude that the multiple risk factors identified are part of a 'developmental sequence' (p. 347) originating with an 'accumulation' of indicators of possible risk in early childhood (p. 347). Others, too, have suggested that the proper focus for intervention is the point at which there is an 'initial escalation of delinquency' in order to address the 'conditions that foster gang development' (Esbensen and Huizinga 1993: 583). While there is clear evidence of a common belief among these sources in the 'causal' effects of antecedent factors (Howell and Egley 2005: 342), this has been modified by reference to the motivational factors which might be important for young people themselves, such as 'friendship', personal safety and, occasionally, the chance to make money (p. 345). Thornberry *et al.* (2005: 184) propose other possible motivating factors, such as the offer of 'fun and action' and 'glamour', that are based on the personal accounts of 'gang members'. However, these qualifications of the orthodox developmental model often appear to be quite limited and do not provide a real alternative to deterministic explanations. They simply complement pre-existing 'causes' and only come into play once the possibility of an involvement in delinquency and gang activity has been established. The mechanics of the interaction between the two sets of factors are left unexplored by these accounts:

> the insights from observational studies would suggest that the gang holds a special status for its members. For some it is seen as playing the role of a surrogate family; for others it constitutes an alternative life-style. However, the processes through which it plays these roles have not been documented. (Thornberry *et al.* 2005: 203)

These limitations have prompted substantial criticism from some quarters. Pitts (2008) challenges the developmental frame of reference on a number of grounds, both implicitly and explicitly. Firstly, he suggests – as do his developmental counterparts that levels of gang membership and activity have increased substantially ('This increase is alarming'; Thornberry *et al.* 2005: 2) in recent decades, which suggests that involvement cannot be reduced simply to risk factors located within individuals and their family lives. Secondly, the definition of the term 'gang' is far from straightforward and has, itself been the subject of 'definitional entrepreneurialism' (Pitts 2008: 13) which might, coincidentally, 'open up many new opportunities for researchers' while at the same time importing a degree of blurring and imprecision into our understanding of the term. These indications of social change on the one hand, and definitional uncertainty on the other, both contribute to a degree of doubt as to the explanatory value of 'the risk factor paradigm' (p. 33). As has been observed, the predictive qualities of risk factor analysis are themselves suspect, given that many if not most 'delinquents' do not fall into the supposedly 'high-risk group'. This in itself gives grounds for extreme doubts about the 'causal' nature of prior conditions as far as gang membership is concerned. As Pitts goes on to observe, somewhat ironically, where gangs do not operate or are not open to the young person concerned no amount of predisposing factors will lead to membership (p. 34). For him, these flaws are crucial, and reveal the essential limitations of this kind of explanation when trying to account for social variations and the 'complexities' of young people's lives and circumstances.

Indeed, he goes on to observe that most social scientific accounts of the emergence of gangs and the involvement of young people are inadequate, because they focus disproportionately on 'the moral character, proclivities or deficiencies of criminal individuals' (p. 106). He is, in turn, concerned that all such versions of gang formation and activity 'fail to recognise the power of the machinery of intimidation and coercion at work in gang-affected neighbourhoods, and the choices it necessitates for the young people confined there' (p. 106). The limitations of causal accounts grounded in quantifiable risk factors become clear, in this respect. Membership of gangs appears to be a 'choice' but one which is not dependent on individual characteristics, rather on the context and the moral and coercive pressures which are brought to bear on those affected:

> The idea of involuntary affiliation describes most accurately the bind in which increasing numbers of young people in the poorest neighbourhoods in Britain find themselves. (Pitts 2008: 109)

In this light, it is also worth reflecting on the way in which developmental accounts appear to map out a differential life trajectory for those young people who become gang members compared to others who – with the blessing of society – establish other collective groupings and shared activities. In fact, the processes of affiliation and group formation seem on the face of it to be rather similar across the terrain of 'youth' in general:

> In summary, the role of friendship groups increases during adolescence as young people's ability to form more mature relationships increases ... Friends act as a source of support, provide mutual activity involvement and influence. Friendships at this age are distinctive, in that they usually occur between young people of the same age, educational background and interests, whose current life experiences are similar ... (Coleman and Hendry 1999: 154)

This rather rose-tinted account of the positive experience of adolescent group formation does, of course, contrast with Pitt's darker vision of 'cultures of conflict, coercion and control' (2008: 109), but the processes of social integration and contextualised choices may be much the same. As peer relationships begin to supplant those organised around kinship ties, it is not surprising that these should be shaped by the context as well as local expectations and pressures.

It might, however, still seem rather paradoxical from a developmental perspective that young people who have been identified in relatively early childhood as displaying 'aggressive, inattentive and attention-seeking behaviours' (Howell and Egley 2005: 341) are capable of collaborating on any level to form a functional social group, albeit one that displays high levels of 'antisocial' activity and may be characterised by mutual antagonism and instability.

Accounting for youth crime: the need for a broader canvas

The example of gang involvement and activity helps to illustrate both the pervasiveness of developmental explanations of youth offending and many of their shortcomings. Indeed, these limitations are widely embedded in attempts to make sense of the crimes of the young. They can variously be elaborated under the headings of causality, the meaning of 'crime', and the nature of 'choice'.

Causality

Many positivist or developmental accounts appear to be somewhat confused over the nature of the causal relationship between 'risk factors' and antisocial or delinquent behaviour. Despite the kind of caveats which are issued (Rutter *et al.* 1998b; Communities that Care 2005) to the effect that there is 'no single factor that can be specified as the 'cause' of antisocial or criminal behaviour' (Communities that Care 2005: 7), many such studies tend to lapse into the language of cause and effect rather too easily. Even where attempts are made to introduce a greater sophistication into their portrayals (Thornberry *et al.* 2005, for example), it seems that the inclination to over-explain patterns of behaviour and outcomes is embedded in this perspective. This is where Matza's (1964, 1969) work acts as a kind of corrective, 'normalising' deviance and locating it in context, subject to a variety of influences such as contingency, control and opportunity.

The meaning of 'crime'

It is also unclear from many developmental accounts as to whether they can appreciate the distinction between trying to explain forms of behaviour, which may have an absolute quality, and accounting for 'crime' which is socially determined and 'negotiated' in practice (Cicourel 1968). It seems that 'risk factor' models suffer from a fundamental flaw in seeking to account for individuals' and groups' propensity to act in breach of socially-defined norms and rules. Merton's (1967) typology presents a clear challenge to this way of thinking, given that the 'adaptations' of young people may involve a conscious and deliberate rejection of the dominant norms and definitions of their behaviour ('rebellion', for instance).

Associated with this skewed logic is a tendency to concentrate on the 'crimes' of certain social groups – often those from ethnic minorities and poorer communities – as if they represent a special type of infraction or 'pathway' which is both unique to them and more problematic than the questionable behaviours of other segments of the wider population.

The nature of 'choice'

Determinism is another strand which seems to prevail within the 'risk factor paradigm', despite the relatively poor predictive capabilities of the explanatory models elaborated (Pitts 2008). This appears to be especially the case where attempts have been made to generate ideas of life 'trajectories' established in the very early years of life and typically to associate these with some kind of 'deficit' model. Thus normative phrases such as 'poor parenting' (Communities that Care 2005: 9) achieve scientific respectability, despite their pejorative and non-specific qualities. Matza (1964: 181), by contrast, is keen to reassert the concept of 'will to crime', in order to allow for the complexities of young people's lives and the element of choice in deciding whether or not they will act in certain ways. Pitts attempts to capture the nature of this kind of process by offering us the paradoxical phrase 'involuntary affiliation' (2008: 109) to account both for the situational constraints and the element of commitment (or 'opting in') when young people join 'gangs'.

In conclusion, we need to acknowledge here that we must problematise 'crime' and the processes by which it is 'constructed' and attributed to certain individuals, groups and behaviours, just as much as we must focus our attention on the contexts, circumstances and characteristics which set the scene for young people's own situated choices and actions, which may (or may not) be defined as antisocial or criminal.

Chapter 4

Constructing crime and creating delinquents

The problem of definition

Up to now, we have been primarily concerned with reviewing the processes associated with young people's identified characteristics and behaviour and the theoretical frameworks within which these have been discussed. In other words, the focus has been on young people and what it is about then that influences what they do, especially where this is deviant or breaches conventional social norms. However, this is only one side of the coin, because such explanations tend to incorporate an assumption that what constitutes delinquency is essentially fixed and timeless. It is a 'given', acting as a constant benchmark against which behaviour may be judged. Therefore, a critical analysis of the relationship between young people and criminal justice is required to problematise this kind of assumption. How is it that certain types of behaviour come to be categorised as antisocial or criminal, and how is it, equally, that some young people come to be associated with that behaviour? How are 'young offenders' produced, in other words, by the interplay of ideologies, structures and systems and the lives of young people themselves?

The starting point for this kind of discussion is not, therefore, the specific young person, but the methods and mechanisms by which social order and disorder are constituted and deviant populations characterised. The processes by which certain groups are demonised or 'othered' (Garland 2001) are particularly important, if we are to understand how youth crime and youth justice are constructed and take the forms they currently do.

The initial question, then, for these purposes relates to the origins and meaning of the idea of crime. It is not an objective term since certain types of behaviour can at different times be defined as criminal or not and as we know it is subject to an ongoing process of definition as it comes to be applied *in situ*, and as the outcome of contextualised social interactions (see Cicourel 1968, for example). How the term comes to be applied specifically to young people – and becomes 'youth crime' in the process – is at this point only a subsidiary question. The primary focus is on the issue of crime itself as a mechanism for organising the social and moral order and creating important distinctions between legitimate and illegitimate activities and lifestyles. It is only subsequently that any consideration will turn to the interaction between these processes of establishing social order and norms and the population (and subsections of it) defined by age and attributes variously assigned to young people, juveniles, adolescents, teenagers or 'youth'. As will become clear, the material consequences of this coincidence of powerful social constructions may be quite dramatic, giving rise to a number of moral certainties and commonly accepted truths, while at the same time being based on interlocking but variable constructs. This may also give the appearance of unity and coherence to a range of dynamic and changing forces that are inherently unstable and contested. We are thus brought face to face with the realisation that the kinds of knowledge and 'objective' evidence we have about young people and their crimes depend on a series of assumptions and contingent social realities which are themselves open to debate and transformation. This, as we shall see later, is a fundamental tension, leading to calls to adopt different ways of characterising and responding to the 'delinquencies' of the young.

Discourse and crime

Although the starting point for this discussion could be the material origins and basis of social order, it is equally helpful to begin by reflecting on the contemporary concern with the nature of 'discourses' and the ways in which these operate to construct and order our social lives. This has become an increasingly prominent element in current debates about how systems of meaning and social processes are organised and maintained (up to a point).

In order to account for the way in which social order is constructed and (to an extent) maintained, it may prove helpful to turn to the type of argument developed by authorities such as Gramsci (1971) and Foucault (1979, 1980). These sources are important for their contribution to our understanding of the processes by which the underpinning logic and necessity of social systems is established and sustained. Their accounts suggest plausible ways of making sense of the mechanisms of social cohesion and control which make contemporary forms of organisation appear 'normal' and justifiable. Gramsci's formulation of the idea of 'hegemony', for example, offers a means of capturing the logic of authority, control and regulation. The social relations in place at any one time therefore appear to be the natural order of things and to provide an inbuilt rationale for existing forms of dominance and subordination:

> Social control ... takes two basic forms: besides influencing behaviour and choice *externally*, through rewards and punishments, it also affects them internally, by moulding personal convictions into a replica of prevailing norms. Such 'internal control' is based on hegemony, which refers to an order in which a common social-moral language is spoken, in which one concept of reality is dominant, informing with its spirit all modes of thought and behaviour. (Femia 1981: 24; original emphasis)

Social control in this sense is distinguished from pure force, and depends to a large extent on a ready acceptance of the ideas and principles underpinning the prevailing form of social organisation. Control depends on 'consent' and on the recognition of the legitimacy of the way institutions are ordered, including schools and other sources of social and moral leadership. This means that there is a form of logical coherence to the ways in which norms, rules and conventions of behaviour are organised, which appear to be the natural consequence of the 'way things are'. And so, there is also a degree of consistency between the way in which social relations and the rules of everyday behaviour operate and the more formal and authoritative regulatory systems and machineries which are incorporated in structures of law and governance.

It is in this sense that much of the organisation of day-to-day life depends on a particular type of 'order' (Hall *et al.* 1978: 202). That is to say, although there is a capacity within the machinery of the state and the establishment to resort to the direct use of force to retain control, this is not the option of first resort, being inefficient and in the end self-defeating, and thereby losing its claims to legitimacy. Rather, control is maintained through mechanisms of 'cohesion':

73

In this respect, Gramsci argued, the state had another, and crucial, aspect or role besides the legal or coercive one: the role of leadership, of direction, of education and tutelage – the sphere, not of 'domination' by force, but of the 'production of consent' … The legal system – the site, apparently, of coercion – also had a positive and educative role to play in this respect … (Hall *et al*. 1978: 202)

As Hall and colleagues observe, 'society clearly works better' (or more efficiently at least) when the population accepts the logic and desirability of the established order and recognises the legitimacy of existing rules and processes – that is to say, where the people 'learn to discipline themselves…'. Clearly, there are certain identifiable points in history where this type of consensual arrangement and willing acceptance of state authority breaks down, as in early twentieth-century Italy, which was the central focus of Gramsci's writing; but, nonetheless, for most of the time it does seem to have a central part to play in maintaining stability and order.

'The Law', then, becomes the primary vehicle for representing and maintaining the consensus around what is acceptable in thought and deed (Gramsci 1971: 246). It is the mechanism by which the common good is specified, in terms of setting limits to behaviour and constructing abstract notions of infraction and criminality. By virtue of its apparent 'neutrality' (p. 195) and its representation of an apparent common good external to individual interests, it performs a powerful 'educative' (p. 247) function 'and tends to create a social conformism which is useful to the ruling group's line of development' (p. 195). While it may be working essentially in the interests of a specific (dominant) social faction, the law is nonetheless more effective as a means of securing widespread consent and cooperation, to the extent that it is 'autonomised' (Hall *et al*. 1978: 206). By appearing impersonal and by relying on principles of equal rights and impartial administration, the law is highly effective in practical terms in securing popular support, even where it tends to operate against the interests of large sectors of the general population.

In this way a very specific and historically situated form of social organisation becomes reified, making an arbitrary set of social relations and structures appear normal and routine. This is the basis of legitimacy and represents the ideological process of organising and sustaining a sense of inevitability and necessity about a specific form of social order. The tendency of this kind of order to work better for some interests than others is masked by its apparent neutrality and fairness. Thus, ironically, according to Anatole France (1894), '[t]he law, in its majesty equality, forbids the rich as well as the poor to sleep under bridges, to beg in the streets, and to steal bread'.

As Muncie (2009: 123) points out, this kind of critical analysis has been replicated in the work of criminologists as well, with the recognition by Kitsuse (1962), in particular that the starting point for an ananlysis of crime is (or should be) the process by which certain idealised forms of (mis) behaviour become defined as illegal or deviant:

> Accordingly, deviance may be considered as a process by which members of a group, community or society (1) interpret behaviour as deviant, (2) define persons who so behave as a certain kind of deviant, and (3) accord them the treatment considered appropriate to such deviants. (Kitsuse 1962: 248)

In his view, it is the first of these elements which requires a shift of emphasis among analysts, such that behaviour cannot simply be assumed to be deviant by definition. The source of and impetus for such definitions are also a matter of concern for those intent on understanding the underlying character of the criminal justice system.

Although the rule of law can be seen to be a powerful organising force, in terms of its ability to secure consent and encourage compliance, we should not overlook some of the tensions which arise. In practice, legal sanctions are not applied consistently and indeed moral disapproval is also a much more contingent process than might be inferred from a strict reading of law's hegemonic impact. There is a disjuncture between the underlying principle – to which there may be a fairly general adherence – and its application in context. As Kitsuse observes, deviant 'forms of behaviour *per se* do not activate the processes of societal reaction which sociologically differentiate deviants from non-deviants' (p. 248). Instead, perhaps, we must look to the symbolic and overarching effect of the law and criminal justice as a way of securing a broad commitment rather than uniform compliance.

This observation helps too when we come to the task of accounting for acts of non-compliance or resistance, which could not be possible if the ideological force of legal forms were universally effective. Thus it is possible to be both an 'offender' and at the same time to respect the principle of the legitimacy of the criminal law and its sanctions – that is to say, those who come to be treated as criminals may themselves accept the definition and thereby come to see themselves ambiguously as 'in the wrong' and in need of correction, despite their ready involvement in what are recognisably illegal activities. The empirical consequences of this paradox are evident in the kind of responses to their own behaviour sometimes advanced by young people in trouble with the law. They are, in effect, willing adherents to the dominant discourse of conformity and deviance, embedded in the language of law and justice. This kind of ambiguity is observable in research evidence which is based on young people's own accounts of their behaviour and their attempts to 'reform' themsleves. Thus, for example, in the developing area of restorative justice, conventional discourses of 'apology and forgiveness' (Hayes 2006: 378) continue to dominate proceedings. The measure of success in such encounters between 'offender' and 'victim' is often viewed in the form of 'apology and forgiveness' based on the young offender's acceptance of responsibility and a demonstration of 'shame and remorse' (p. 376). In some studies, more than half the young people involved in restorative 'conferences' were found to have apologised to the victims of their reported 'crimes' (p. 377). In other words, this seems to demonstrate that young people who are seen to have infringed legal norms are frequently ready to acknowledge that they are in the wrong, to take direct responsibility, and to seek to make amends. This, of course, is often taken as a measure of the success of restrative models of practice in youth justice, but it is also indicative of the extent and influence of conventional constructions of law, justice and transgression.

Similar evidence of self-blame and recrimination can be found among young offenders with established drug problems (Chui *et al.* 2003). While some may have had a purely instrumental view of the need for compliance with the law (that is, to avoid coercive sanctions against them) others appear to have decided to internalise the logic of wrongdoing and irresponsible behaviour:

> If I only look back before I started heroin and stuff like that, because when I was about sixteen I though 'I'll never touch that, never ever'. If I look back I would say 'I would never rob a house', which I never thought I would do. (young person quoted in Chui *et al.* 2003: 271)

For this individual the moral and personal guidelines had now become clear and this statement represents his attempt to reinstate a sense of responsibility and social acceptability for himself.

Even for 'looked after' children and young people, who are perhaps thought to have a more compelling explanation for behaving anti-socially than most, their own accounts seem redolent of the prevailing sense of what is acceptable and what is unacceptable:

> You know I was just fighting or nicking stuff, drinking. I mean I was getting absolutely drunk when I was 12 ... When I went into care it sort of stepped up a level ... you've got two choices, get in trouble with the people you live with or get in trouble with staff ... it's an easier life going out and getting arrested ... I knew it was wrong, I do know right from wrong. (young person quoted in Taylor 2006: 86)

These comments from young people involved in the criminal justice process do suggest that there is a consensus about the proper boundaries between lawful and unlawful behaviour which extends even to those who are found to be responsible for criminal activities. However, they also clearly illustrate the danger of taking an overly functionalist view of the meaning and impact of the dominant 'discourse' of crime and antisocial behaviour. Those who are involved in crossing the line themselves demonstrate that there is a degree of fluidity and indeed ambivalence about levels and the extent of a commitment to common standards. Equally, of course, we must also reflect on whether or not this means that notions of crime and responsibility should be seen as monolithic or all-pervasive. They may perhaps incorporate deep-rooted contradictions, as represented by the apparent desirability of acquisitive and competitive behaviours in a capitalist society, for instance. Perhaps it is best to think of discourses of law, order and conformity as persuasive but not conclusive?

The iron fist? Material realities of authority and control

While discourses are clearly important according to this analysis, in that they establish a common understanding and 'organise' consent (Gramsci 1971), they may be seen more appropriately as acting in a complementary fashion to other mechanisms of social control. This is not to suggest that they have no material force themselves, rather it is to question whether discourses and their underpinning belief systems are sufficient to maintain particular forms of social order. As we have already acknowledged, discourses cannot be seen as commanding a universal commitment or compliance not least because of their own inbuilt tensions and contradictions. So, the problem arises of how such conflicts are resolved and reflected in lived experience. What, then, is the relationship between ideas, in the form of organising principles and systems of thought, and practice, in the form of the concrete realities which manifest themselves in day-to-day life?

Althusser (1971), for example, distinguishes sharply between the logic of control and the mechanisms which support its realisation. 'Ideology' provides the basis for commonsense understandings which constitute social conventions and shared norms while these are maintained and propagated through a series of institutional structures that give social relations their material reality. Importantly, these structures themselves are organised and depicted according to the same sets of ideas and assumptions which inform the prevailing 'discourse'. These are constituted in the form of 'Ideological State Apparatuses' (Althusser 1971: 36) which permeate all aspects of social life. These include the family, the legal system, religious organisations, the media, educational provision, culture and the political system. It must be acknowledged that this is an esentially functionalist position which takes the view that all such apparatuses share common characteristics and serve the same purposes – and that not all accounts of the social would agree with this by any means.

Nonetheless, it offers a plausible account of the machinery by which consensus and social order may be maintained. These 'ISAs' are held to incorporate a common logic and to be underpinned by similar principles and interests. Thus notions of individualism, rights and responsibilities are to be found embedded in each of them in ways which are consistent but applied somewhat differently in each context. They are organised according to the same principles and these are replicated in the ways in which they operate and are experienced. Therefore roles and expectations are clearly demarcated within the family, just as the formal education system reflects a preoccupaton with promoting and 'celebrating' individual achievement. Althusser believes that 'the School-Family couple' (1971: 146) is a crucial alliance in sustaining contemporary social forms. They construct a sense of the natural order of things, as well as providing the everyday machinery for its sustenance.

Donzelot (1979), for example, has developed a persuasive analysis of the changing place of the family in the social order and of its transformation as a vehicle for replicating and enforcing wider social norms and behaviours. Specific forms of intervention in the family can be seen, in his view, as concrete manifestations of the 'procedures of social control'. Thus, the modern family is not so much an institution as a *mechanism*. It is through the disparity of the familial configurations (the working-class and bourgeois polarity), the variances between individual interests and the family interest, that this mechanism operates. Its strength lies in a *social architectonics* whose characteristic feature is always to couple an exterior intervention with conflicts or differences of potential within the family: the protection of poor children which allowed for the destruction of the family as an island of resistance; the privileged alliance of the doctor and the educator with the wife for developing procedures of savings, educational promotion and so on. (Donzelot 1979: 94; original emphasis)

This is one example of the ways in which historical developments have operated through the family and its changing forms to maintain and enhance a particular way of life and set of social relationships according to Donzelot. But it does not (and cannot) be seen as an isolated process. It is effective because it forms part of a wider network of relationships and institutional mechansms that share and perpetuate common beliefs and principles. These are backed up, in Althusser's terms, by 'Repressive State Apparatuses' (1971: 136), but these act as a reserve power that may only to be drawn on when ideological mecanisms and consent cannot be relied upon. Indeed, while repressive institutions can act as guarantors to the maintenance of existing social relations, they too depend for their effectiveness on a certain level of credibility – that is to say, an ideologically-based legitimacy. Pure repression is the consequence of a failure of hegemony rather than a reflection of it.

We can think perhaps of 'repressive' actions being carried out in many settings, even those which are ostensibly 'ideological' institutions such as the family, the school or the workplace. However, they cannot be used systematically or repeatedly without undermining the legitimacy and the logic of the institution itself. It may be at least partly for this reason, for instance, that corporal punishment has gradually been extinguished as a form of practice within schools and to a large extent families as well.

Instead, those institutions which are essentially 'repressive' – such as the armed forces, police, prisons and the legal sytem – do not operate purely through force and other coercive measures. They also depend on popular consent and compliance to be able to operate credibly and effectively. The argument presented by Donzelot, Althusser and others is that these aspects of social control are mutually supportive and cannot operate coherently or effectively without each other. They also depend to a great extent on the mutually reinforcing sense of legitimacy that each accords the other, both implicitly and explicitly. In this sense, then, the logic of control is mirrored by the machinery which exists to give it substance and to reinforce it.

Cohen (1985) is another exponent of this form of analysis. He argues that systems of justice and wider social institutions act in complementary fashion, with each taking its cue from those around it as to its purposes and structural relationships. He suggests that in this way the 'normal' institutions of society become legitimate vehicles for the maintenance of social control, illustrating this argument with a number of specific examples:

> The family having a delinquent living with them is seen as a 'remarkable correctional resource' for the future. In Britain and Scandinavia a number of alternative systems of family placement besides salaried foster parents have been tried, for example 'together at home' – the system of intensive help in Sweden in which social workers spend hours sharing the family's life and tasks. (Cohen 1985: 79)

Other previous examples of such practice have used the offender's 'own family' as the vehicle for enforcing compliance and regulating behaviour. Parents and other family members may be 'parties to the behavioural contract and are expected to play an active role in retraining their errant child' (1985: 79). Just in case we are led to assume that these are now merely historical examples, we should bear in mind contemporary forms of practice such as the Acceptable Behaviour Contract which has become a popular device for securing conformity in contemporary Britain. Thus, we find that parents are seen as important contributors to the management of ABCs, and indeed they are believed to be essential players in the task of securing good behaviour. In one scheme investigated, the use of ABCs was believed to have been:

> made parents aware of their child's behaviour and forced them to tackle it. 'Now parents have to take notice. In the past they were just sent a letter by the council which they probably igored.' (Islington local authority housing officer). (Bullock and Jones 2004: 40)

Indeed, it has been argued on a number of occasions that the family has played a central role as a vehicle for social organisation and the dispersal of discipline in the modern era. Rose (1999: 128) describes a process of 'familialization' which he traces back to the nineteenth century, whereby the arena of personal relationships could be infused by the social control objectives and ordinances of the state. As he suggests this was not simply an ideological process, but one in which new realities were established and new mechanisms developed for the administration of control functions. In this way, the family becomes established as an ambiguous entity, enshrining the right to personal and private lives on the one hand, while on the other acting and being expected to act as the focal point for translating the requirements of the wider society in terms of conformity and public order into individualised and 'targeted' behavioural requirements. As we have seen, Donzelot (1979) has articulated a similar analysis of the roles and functions of the modern family. Here as well it is seen as a vehicle for 'governing' individual behaviour and setting common expectations and boundaries for its members. Again, in his view, one of the great strengths of the family as a vehicle for social control is its varied and (to some extent), contradictory nature. It is constituted both as a means of organising behaviour and shaping character and as a way of encouraging certain forms of solidarity, aspiration and ambition. Barrett and McIntosh (1982) have similarly argued that the family is peculiarly defined by its dual and apparently contradictory functions of containment and control versus protection and nurture. Donzelot argues that it was a peculiar challenge for developing societies in the twentieth century to reconcile these competing aspects of the family, in order to ensure its functionality for dominant interests:

> the problem ... was to be, not the defence or abolition of the institution of the family, but the resolution of the questions that arose at the two trouble spots of the juncture between family and society: (1) How to cope successfully with family resistances and individual deviations in the working clases in such a way that the necessary intervention does not generate excessive advantages or overly harsh repression ...; (2) How to achieve the maximum harmony between the principle of family authority, its egoisms and specific aspirations, and the procedures of socialization of its members ... (Donzelot 1979: 94)

Of course, the achievement of 'modern' states during the twentieth century was to develop processes and structures for articulating and intervening with the family to achieve (more or less) these intended outcomes. This is characterised by Donzelot (1979: 151) in the form of a 'mission', whereby 'educators' and 'social assistants' are sent by 'judicial' authorities to do 'what is necessary' to ensure that parents fulfil their responsibilities towards their children and that the use of custodial measures is avoided wherever possible. In the process of constructing this edifice for intervening in the family, he argues, there also emerged a specific set of practices and terminologies to categorise families and their behaviour, in preparation for, and in order to provide a formal justification for the actions of state welfare agencies. Some are thus characterised as 'unstructured families' while others may merit an intervention because they are 'rejecting or overly protective' and a third category are simply 'deficient' (p. 152). Donzelot further suggests that these depictions represent a translation of 'widespread living conditions' (p. 157) into sets of behaviours and characteristics which can be constituted as problems in terms of the agencies involved. The focal point of attention and the site for intervention thus become the family and its pathological characteristics. In turn, the test of its capacity and commitment to change is the level of conformity it demonstrates to the agencies which are legitimately constituted to make judgements and decisions about it.

As a product of this level of attention, Donzelot concludes (p. 227), the family becomes almost an extension of 'the disciplinary continuum of social apparatuses'. It may not be a particularly effective vehicle for the transmission of socially accepted norms and behaviours, for the reasons of internal stresses and contradictions, but this is what is expected of it and these are the criteria against which it is judged. In the contemporary era, the anticipated role and performance of the family can be gauged by the regularly expressed mantra: 'I blame the parents' (see Chapter 3). This is usually expressed in light of some failure – to protect children, to set appropriate standards for them, or to exercise 'control' over their behaviour. The family in such cases has demonstrated its failure to achieve a sufficient standard of functioning, simply by virtue of the (apparent) outcome highlighted. Other social factors and influences fade into the background to be replaced by a monolithic concern with parental responsibilities and deficits. This is reflected not just in public opinion and political rhetoric, but also in some aspects of the legislative framework ('parental responsibility' is a concept enshrined in law by way of the Children Act 1989, for example).

The materiality of power

The previous sections have explored two aspects of the dynamics of power and control as they impact on young people – namely, ideology and discourse – and the mechanisms through which these power relations are realised. At this point, then, it will be helpful to move on to try to capture a sense of how these elements combine to constitute the 'materiality' of social control, especially as it impacts on young people. In order to develop explanatory frameworks for this, it is difficult to look beyond the work of Foucault (1979) and Cohen (1985), both of whom have offered persuasive accounts of the processes by which sources of legitimate authority are established and then utilised in specific contexts in order to establish and promote conformity.

Foucault's work has been highly influential in this context, because it seems to offer a plausible account of the ways in which the expression of power *in situ* is not accidental but represents the very specific culmination of a range of influences and interests. For him, power and knowledge are entwined in an inseparable relationship and that they are mutually 'constitutive' (1979: 27). This relationship is not necessarily fixed or static, but it infuses all aspects of society:

> power is not exercised simply as an obligation of a prohibition on those who 'do not have it'; it invests them, is transmitted by them and thorough them; it exerts pressure upon them, just as they themselves, in their struggle against it resist the grip it has on them. (Foucault 1979: 27)

This suggest that it may be unhelpful to think in terms of concentrations of power, expertise or authority in particular locations. Rather, its relations and the logic underpinning it are to be found at all levels of society and in all social transactions and relationships. The notion of 'resistance' introduced here suggests that Foucault does not believe that all such relationships are uni-directional or 'top-down', because at each level and within each of their constituent parts there is the possibility of questioning and challenging. At the same time, there are clearly discernible regularities which appear to be situationally and historically specific, so that interactions at the individual level can be seen to reflect a broader pattern of social relations.

Thus it is possible to distinguish between different eras, and their corresponding modes of punishment and control, moving from the dramatic and explicit use of the 'spectacle of the scaffold' (p. 32) in pre-modern times to a much more sophisticated and precise formulation of the 'mechanisms of power' (p. 222) in modern societies. Individualising systems of rights and laws produce the appearance of a universal and commonly applicable framework of rights and justice and *inter alia* that sets 'limits on the exercise of power' (p. 223), while on 'the underside of the law' there is 'a machinery which is both immense and minute which supports, reinforces, multiplies the asymmetry of power ...'. The universal application of a 'fair' system of legal norms and sanctions provides the implicit justification for another complementary set of mechanisms for identifying, assessing, categorising and controlling those who do not comply with its requirements. The one depends on the other and the consequences are clear. Foucault identifies the emergence of new models of justice in the mid-nineteenth century which were infused with this logic and represented in concentrated form 'all the coercive technologies of behaviour' (p. 293). Not only were indivudal offenders subject to minute scrutiny and precise systems of classification, but in consequence very specific and personalised forms of surveillance and control were also to be specified for them. On the establishment of one penal colony at Mettray in 1840, he observes that the staff there were 'technicians of behaviour', responsible for organising and supervising all aspects of the inmates' lives:

> Training was accompanied by permanent observation; a body of knowledge was being constantly built up from the everyday behaviour of the inmates; it was organized as an instrument of perpetual assessment ... in this very work, provided it is technically supervised, submissive subjects are produced and a dependable body of knowledge built up about them. (Foucault 1979: 294, 295)

I have argued elsewhere that this kind of technological framework of thinking can be found to be replicated very closely in contemporary legislation (Smith, R. 2001) and the example of the Intensive Supervision and Surveillance Programme (ISSP) may help to demonstrate this kind of 'logic of power' in action. The ISSP has been developed as a response to certain perceived gaps in the portfolio of disposals for young offenders (Moore *et al.* 2006), and in particular to provide 'effective' community-based sentencing options for serious and persistent young offenders. As such, the ISSP is constituted as a highly-intensive intervention which combines a range of elements designed to 'bring structure to offenders' lifestyles, while systematically addressing the key risk factors contributing to their offending behaviour, such as educational deficits, weaknesses in thinking skills or drug misuse' (Youth Justice Board 2010). We can see from this, and from the level of intensity (25 hours' contact time per week for the first three months at least), that the lives and activities of the young people concerned are to be closely circumscribed, presumably with the aim of habituating them to forms of (conformist) behaviour that are predictable and manageable. It is interesting, too, that this framwork is explicitly related to a number of perceived shortcomings in their previous lifestyles or circumstances, with the word 'deficit' being applied directly in the case of presumed educational limitations. A lack of structure is thus associated with those other aspects of their lives which demonstrate behavioural lapses, knowledge gaps or inadequate skills levels. Once this connection has been made, it becomes a matter of pure reason to compensate for these deficiencies by imposing order and normalising routines, as much in the young person's interests as those of the wider law-abiding community. It is thus no surprise that in its implementation researchers have found that:

> The key features of the ISSP model can be summarised as follows:
>
> - An intensive programme initially targeted at young people who were persistent offenders and had high criminogenic needs. This was subsequently modified to include serious offenders at risk of a custodial sentence.
>
> - A multi-modal programme tailored to the risk factors facing each young offender, with a strong educational emphasis.
>
> - A disposal seen by sentencers as sufficiently demanding and tough to be used as an alternative to a custodial sentence.
>
> - A combination of intensive help and strict surveillance, with prompt breach procedures in the event of non-compliance. (Moore et al. 2006: 88)

These authors go on to say that this approach to young offenders 'fits very well into' the overall framework of what has been described as the 'new youth justice' (Goldson 2000), notably because of its combination of elements of supervision and surveillance. A generic model of structured activities and close control could be aligned in this way with a detailed understanding of the specific characteristics and behaviours of individual young offenders – a 'tailored' package in effect.

Of course we must be careful of inferring precise practical consequences from original policy intentions and so it is also helpful that Moore *et al.*'s (2006) study is able to offer considerable detail about the implementation of the ISSP model on the ground. The first 'fully fledged' ISSP projects were implemented by the Youth Justice Board[1] in July 2001 and there were 41 schemes in place by the end of that year, with national coverage achieved by October 2003 (p. 88). The approach adopted was a 'devolved' model (p. 118), allowing local Youth Offending Teams to opt for different combinations of programme elements and delivery mechanisms. Some adopted 'pre-existing models of change' such as the US-originated 'Youth Advocate Programme'. Interestingly, this programme is reported as offering a 'wraparound' form of intervention aiming to identify and respond to the whole range of needs faced by young people and their families and incorporating local services and resources to respond to these as required. Another scheme attempted to use 'Multi-Systemic Therapy' as its operational model, informed more by behavioural strategies aimed at the family, although Moore *et al.* (2006: 119) conclude that this is less well-suited to the 'structure and demands of ISSP'.

Whichever delivery model was adopted, the YJB[1] required all schemes (except bail ISSPs) to cover five core areas, including: education and training; offending behaviour; interpersonal skills; family support; and restorative interventions. Of these, education elements and offending behaviour work were the most consistently provided by ISSPs, while other frequently occurring components included 'constructive leisure' activities and interpersonal skills training. Implicit in much of this is the notion of shaping individuals' actions and attributes to normatively defined models of behaviour which are 'constructive' or 'acceptable' and so the programme modules follow a fairly standard framework of expected elements and desirable objectives. At the same time, the rhetoric of a 'tailored' approach to each young person appears to dictate a more sensitive and nuanced array of activities and resources geared towards specific needs and circumstances. Thus:

> Many schemes adopted a 'holistic' approach, matching interventions to each young person's strengths, while also involving the young person in the decision-making process in order to encourage their continued engagement. (Moore *et al.* 2006: 125)

In practice, however, this study identified 'large numbers of young people on ISSP' whose needs were not being accommodated by the programme, however much staff tried to work 'on a one-to-one basis'.

The structure of the ISSP also required that alongside the supervisory element of the programme surveillance should be a core feature, incorporating electronic tagging, 'human tracking' or a combination of methods. In practice, this element of the programme was associated with a high level of 'non-compliance' (p. 134) and formal 'breach' – that is, return to court for a failure to comply (this applied to nearly three fifths of all participants). This approach to transgressions of programme rules is believed to be the product of a progressive tendency in England and Wales 'towards tougher enforcement of community penalties', which in turn is indicative of a widespread 'low-tolerance' policy agenda (p. 187).

So in effect close scrutiny of finely-graded interventions serves a number of complementary purposes in the form of the ISSP. It exerts a direct and explicit control of behaviour through its use of surveillance, compulsory attendance and mandatory activities; it provides a framework for supposedly individualised and calibrated intervention programmes; it develops a rationale grounded in notions of normal and socially useful attributes and activities; and, based on these elements, it establishes the baseline for rigorous maintenance of programme boundaries and tight enforcement in cases of infraction. A failure to comply and a refusal to take up the opportunities offered by ISSP can only be taken, in these terms, as confirmation of the initial pre-programme prognosis; these are 'persistent' and ultimately incorrigible individuals for whom coercion and containment are the only realistic options, in the wider interest of community safety. This seems to provide further justification for the historically well-established belief that there is and always will be a consistent group of persistent offenders who are between them responsible for a great proportion of recorded offences and who are not responsive to anything less than the most coercive forms of treatment. There is thus a 'self-fulfilling' aspect to programmes such as ISSP, to the extent that they offer a filtering mechanism to confirm what we already 'knew'. Moore *et al.* (2006: 220) are concerned at the implications of this development, linking the empirical challenges of 'defining persistence and seriousness and ... identifying high-risk offenders' to the consequences of applying programmes 'arbitrarily' and the process of 'intensification' which they see as a feature of the contemporary youth justice system, especially in light of the further observation that interventions like ISSP are self-justificatory. Failure to comply is simply taken as confirmation that we were right to be worried about the young person concerned in the first place. They conclude with the warning that:

> While risk management provides a theoretical basis for intensive community programmes, these difficulties and concerns suggest that any emphasis upon this model needs to be constrained to ensure that risk is seen alongside other social principles and priorities, such as justice and rehabilitation. (Moore *et al.* 2006: 220)

If close scrutiny and control become self-sustaining ends in themselves the rehabilitative potential of such programmes is likely to be severely compromised if not lost altogether. They argue instead for a reassertion of 'a careful balance' between welfare and justice models of intervention (p. 222), a compromise which the present author has already reflected upon with a degree of scepticism (Smith, R. 2005).

Ideology and practice in youth justice

The aim of this chapter has been to sketch out some of the deeply embedded ideologies and processes within youth justice which, in combination, shape the ways in which criminality among young people is defined, identified and managed. It is difficult to avoid giving the impression of holding to a purely deterministic view of the relationship between ideas, systems and practice in this context, so it may be more helpful to frame the argument in the form of tendencies, capabilities and possibilities. It is clear, for instance, that the contemporary youth justice system is populated by competing and changing sets of beliefs and orientations to intervention, as Muncie (2002) has commented. In his view, youth justice is 'an amalgam' of at least six strands of ideology and practice, namely: just desserts; risk assessment; managerialism; community responsibilisation; authoritarian populism; and, restorative justice (p. 156). This accumulation of aims, objectives and practices is partly attributable to legislative changes which have, in effect, piled new responsibilities and requirements on top of old ones rather than replacing them. Instead of resolving the inherent contradictions – or at the very least recognising them – if anything this sort of approach cements them in place. Thus, for example, 'in the formulation of policy the emphasis on inclusionary crime prevention is used to mark a significant departure from punitive justice, yet a commitment to an ethos of individual responsibility and penal custody is retained and seems actively to promote exclusion' (Muncie 2002: 157) (see also Chapter 5). Muncie also seems to be hinting at a further refinement of the analysis offered, in the sense that contradictions at one level of ideology and practice may themselves be accounted for by a form of meta-analysis which sees them not as opposites but as variants on a common theme. Thus, as I have argued elsewhere (Smith, R. 2009), both 'welfare' and 'justice' models of youth justice turn their forensic gaze towards the young person and away from other potentially problematic questions, such as the very definition of crime itself. Both also hold an essentially individualistic view of the 'offender', her or his 'victim', and the behaviour which has given rise to the concerns of the justice system. Again, as Muncie argues, this means that there is scope for the conflation of competing arguments around common systems of problem identification and management:

> In the guise of 'modernization' welfare, justice and rights have been eclipsed by the imprecise science of risk assessment and the statutory responsibility to meet performance targets. (Muncie 2002: 157)

In the process, explicit attempts to align 'welfare' and 'justice' objectives can be seen to recur in the formulation and revision of youth justice policies over time (Smith, R. 2007), most notably in recent years in the White Paper 'No More Excuses', in which any analytical, procedural or practical distinction was simply swept away:

> Preventing offending promotes the welfare of the individual young offender and protects the public. (Home Office 1997: 7)

Thus, it is argued, it is always in the best interests of young people to pursue measures to prevent them offending, and to deal with any offences they do commit purely in terms of the best way to ensure such behaviour is not repeated. The inadequacy of this line of reasoning is manifest, for example, in the case of a young person in poverty who steals food for her/himself and her/his family; however, it is clearly an attractive argument.

The capacity of such forms of elision to effectively 'organise' the way we think about young offenders and youth crime and 'smooth over' disjunctures is their strength – and yet recognising the nature of this achievement also reveals the problematic nature of conventional assumptions about the subject and how it is constituted.

Note

1 As part of a wider programme of cuts, the abolition of the Youth Justice Board was announced by the Ministry of Justice on 14th October 2010 to a mixed reception. The consequences of this in policy terms remain uncertain at the time of writing.

Chapter 5

Recruiting young 'criminals': material practices

'Pathways' and 'thresholds'

Previously, we have considered the ways in which ideological frameworks and the logics and mechanisms of control have informed the processes of establishing criminality and justifying the imposition of penal sanctions in general terms. In many respects, as we have seen, these are self-fulfilling formulations which rely on their own formal products to justify the decisions and actions emerging from within the criminal justice system. So, the imposition of a criminal sanction in itself serves as validation for prior beliefs and categorisations of the behaviour to which they are applied, and indeed, of the perpetrators of that behaviour. Classically, this is the achievement of the ASBO which acts as both a classificatory tool and a form of legitimation for specific measures of social control, despite its reliance on standards of 'evidence' which fall well short of those required for a criminal conviction. Once in place, though, the ASBO acts both as confirmation of the unacceptable nature of a young person's activities and as a mark against her/his character which justifies continuing attempts to impose conformity on him/her.

Signifiers of undesirable behaviour and characteristics such as this therefore produce a cumulative effect and act to distinguish certain individual members of the population from 'normal' society. In doing so, though, they also act as tools for the recruitment of these individuals into another recognisable category – that of 'offenders' or outlaws. Following on from this, it becomes plausible and indeed logical to think in terms of the characteristics which members of this group have in common and to begin to draw inferences based on these. It will thus clearly be of interest here to consider the manner and contexts in which these classificatory processes come to operate. We are therefore prompted to reflect on young people's 'pathways' into crime, and the ways in which they are, individually and collectively, identified as potential, and in due course, actual offenders, appearing as such in the 'official' statistics.

In order to address these concerns here, I will adopt an approach that is organised around the currently popular term of 'social exclusion', which itself can be understood in several different ways. Firstly, it is a term recently popularised by government and other opinion formers to describe and (partially) account for the mechanisms by which certain groups and categories of the general population become disadvantaged and exposed to the possibility of poor 'outcomes'; and which prompt certain types of social policy intervention. And yet social exclusion can be interpreted critically as a process in which those very hegemonic interests (government and its powerful allies in the policy world) are implicated and take a positive role in creating and sustaining excluded groups through their own practices, which expose them to various forms of oppressive action. The treatment of refugees and asylum seekers might be a case in point in this regard.

Accordingly, the aim of this chapter is to provide an account of these alternative characterisations of 'social exclusion' and its dynamics, specifically in relation to the processes by which young people – and certain groupings within this wider category become 'recruited' as criminal actors and therefore become legitimate targets for certain forms of intervention.

Social exclusion: the authorised version

To begin with it will be helpful to reflect on the emergence and application of the term 'social exclusion' as an organising concept and explanatory device in public policy circles in recent years. It has, of course, become very closely associated with the New Labour project, but it has also wider resonances and is likely to continue to have a bearing on discussions of social welfare and criminal justice irrespective of anticipated changes in the political order. For this reason it will be beneficial to consider the way in which the term itself has acquired hegemonic (see Chapter 4) significance, at least for the time being.

It has been suggested that the notion of 'social exclusion arose in Europe in the wake of prolonged and large-scale unemployment that provoked criticisms of welfare systems' for their failure to resolve satisfactorily endemic problems of poverty and disadvantage (Loury 2000: 226). It is thus understood as a generic phenomenon associated with the weakening of traditional social ties, the loss of a sense of community and mutual responsibility, and the persistence of inequality and discrimination despite the best efforts of modern welfare systems. The notion of exclusion is felt to have come to prominence first in mainland European countries such as France and only subsequently to have been exported to the UK and other anglophone states. The European Union and its predecessors are believed to have had a key role in developing an understanding of the concept alongside policies to promote the 'inclusion' of those adversely affected (Hantrais 2000: 188). Suspicion of the EU and its earlier manifestations may be one reason for the UK's reluctance to accept the value of such notions as inclusion and exclusion, and this perception may well have been associated with the long-running (1979–97) Conservative administration's view that an undue emphasis on state interference in people's daily lives would be unhealthy and unacceptable. In any event, there was clearly a change of tone with the advent of the New Labour government in 1997, with both a much more interventionist tone to its utterances and a more positive view of Europe and its institutions. 'Social exclusion' suddenly became an extremely attractive organising principle. It was quickly incorporated into the Blair government's repertoire of explanatory devices and policy targets. Very soon after coming to power (in December 1997), New Labour established the Social Exclusion Unit which was to have a strategic relationship to all government departments. It was located in the Cabinet Office, 'putting it at the heart of government', and from that point on it focused on a range of implicitly connected issues, including 'deprived neighbourhoods, 'drug use', 'teenage pregnancy', 'school exclusion' and the 'reintegration of ex-offenders' (Young and Matthews 2003: 7). In this formulation, social exclusion takes the place of poverty and material deprivation as a central explanation of poor social outcomes and at the same time establishes itself as a linking theme which ties together a variety of identifiable manifestations of its effects.

The Social Exclusion Unit itself defined it as a 'shorthand term for what can happen when people or areas suffer from a combination of linked problems such as unemployment, poor skills, low incomes, poor housing, high crime, bad health and family breakdown' (Social

Exclusion Unit 2001: 1). In this generic use, the idea of social exclusion served a number of practical functions in blurring a series of contentious political questions. It helpfully (for government, at least) avoided the invidious task of directly blaming anyone for initiating the process, either by way of contributing to their own problems or by acting in such a way as to discriminate against certain groups. Indeed, it tended to gloss over the problem of attributing causation altogether. At the same time, it also contributed to a strategy of agglomeration, whereby manifestly different groups and communities could all be said to be suffering from the same exclusionary effects; the challenge of determining whether or not one group was 'more deserving' than another was thus side-stepped for the time being. This is not to suggest that these problems did not subsequently re-emerge or that notions of blame and responsibilisation had disappeared from the agenda. Rather, the development of this framework formed part of an initial strategy of securing consensus around a set of ideas that everyone (or nearly everyone) could be encouraged to support and buy into. Social exclusion therefore offered a core theme in the development of a 'third way' in UK politics and social welfare (Powell 1999: 14).

The use of an umbrella term like this also led to a number of other consequences in terms of the way social problems were categorised and solutions articulated. There emerged an implicit belief that there were common causal links between the various categories of exclusion and that therefore the kinds of solutions to be developed could themselves be generalised and delivered in a standardised manner. In an era of sound bite politics, and indeed following through the logic of an integrated approach, we were repeatedly told that 'joined-up problems' require 'joined-up solutions' (Coles 2003: 298). As far as the Social Exclusion Unit was concerned, this recognition was breaking new ground:

> Above all, a joined-up problem has never been addressed in a joined-up way. Problems have fallen through the cracks between Whitehall departments or central and local government. And, at neighbourhood level, there has been no one in charge of pulling together all the things that need to go right at the same time. (Social Exclusion Unit 1998: para 7)

The language of inter-related problems and integrated responses became prevalent across welfare policy as a whole and drove much of the thinking and action of the New Labour government in the early years, spanning the late 1990s and early 2000s. Given that by its initial working definition social exclusion could straddle a very wide range of key welfare issues, it is probably significant that the early activities of the Social Exclusion Unit encompassed particular topics which conveyed a sense of thematic unity. The unit's initial approach was to carry out a series of investigations and produce major reports on the subjects of: truancy and school exclusion; rough sleeping; poor neighbourhoods; teenage pregnancy; and young people who were not in education, employment or training. Coles (2003: 298) suggested that this selection was attributable to 'the intention of the government to focus on early routes into, and forms of, social exclusion'.

As he went on to demonstrate, this choice of initial topics generated a large quantity of quite startling evidence about the 'excluded' and their characteristics. However, this may also have served to deflect attention from the processes by which these groups become excluded as we shall see. Thus, for example, the report on children and young people out of school highlighted an apparent explosion in the number of those excluded during the 1990s (see also Smith, R. 1998). Not only did this immediately take on the character of a large and growing problem, but the detailed evidence also shifted attention onto specific subgroups of the school population. As a result, it was noted that over 'four out of five' of those permanently excluded were boys, that school exclusions were geographically concentrated among certain schools, and that African-Caribbean students were far 'more likely to be excluded than their white peers' (Coles 2003: 298). It appeared also that absenteeism in the form of truancy was concentrated in 'inner cities' and that there were identifiable 'links' between non-attendance at school and other 'poor' outcomes, such as a lack of qualifications, unemployment and offending. It seemed too that the problem could be effectively narrowed down to a 'hard core' of non-attenders. Although the focus later shifted to girls and young and young women, the SEU's investigation into teenage pregnancy found a similar concentration of 'problems' that linked early pregnancy and motherhood to a number of other factors, including limited qualifications, school non-attendance, and a 'disengagement' from the labour market. This concentration of overlapping indicators of course gave further sustenance to the initial working assumption that social exclusion could indeed be best represented as a 'complex, multi-faceted syndrome of disadvantage' (Coles 2003: 298) that would necessitate a systematic and integrated response.

Returning for a third time to the subject of young people, the SEU's fifth report dealt with the issue of 'NEETs' – that is, those young people who were not in employment, education or training (see Chapter 2). Once again:

The SEU report confirmed that being disengaged at the ages of 16 and 17 was indeed highly correlated to later experiences of unemployment. It was also closely linked to educational disaffection and disadvantage prior to the age of 16 ... involvement in crime and teenage pregnancy. (Coles 2003: 299)

Not only did this amount to a preoccupation with the problems of youth in the SEU's early work, but even when this was not the explicit focus – as with the concern for 'poor neighbourhoods' – the thematic links between different aspects of exclusion seemed clear:

the poorest neighbourhoods have tended to become rundown, more prone to crime and more cut off from the labour market. The national picture conceals pockets of intense deprivation where the problems of unemployment are acute and hopelessly tangled up with poor health, housing and education. (Social Exclusion Unit 1998: para 1)

These observations themselves chimed in well with the earlier work of the Audit Commission (1996) which found that youth offending could be linked with a range of predisposing factors, including 'inadequate parenting', a 'lack of training and employment', 'unstable living conditions' and 'drug and alcohol abuse'. Thus, individual and family shortcomings were located within a broader pattern of disenfranchisement and disengagement. Entire communities could now be seen to be effectively dysfunctional with various problems concentrated within them. This tendency also seemed to apply to the patterns of offending that the Home Office (1997) reported on at around the same time, claiming that 25 per cent of all youth crime could be attributed to a mere 3 per cent of young people.

The processes by which this pattern emerged appeared somewhat opaque, however. Hope (1998: 53) described a phenomenon of *'compound social dislocation'* by which an 'accumulation' of individual social problems – such as drug misuse, disrupted family lives and unsatisfactory educational outcomes – would effectively interact and therefore contribute to a spiral of decline. These would be associated with *'areas of concentrated poverty'* too, in which the denial of access to conventional opportunities would be another factor giving rise to the 'conditions' which 'bring together vulnerable victims and potential offenders ...' (Hope 1998: 52).

It seemed, then, that these were both the symptoms and consequences of a process of marginalisation and cumulative social disadvantage. The logical consequence in policy terms was to develop programmes to eradicate each of the individual symptoms and thereby bring to an end any possibility of an interactive negative effect. As a result, a series of programmes was put in place with specific targets, such as the Teenage Pregnancy Initiative, SureStart, Connexions, Education Action Zones and Youth Inclusion projects (Smith, R. 2003: 53). These, then, were the visible manifestations of a comprehensive 'joined up' strategy to combat social exclusion in all its forms. A degree of sophistication was introduced into this model of intervention, in that it focused on a series of inter-related 'universal', 'targeted', and 'individualised' initiatives that would act progressively more intensively as identifiable problems became more acute. In relation to youth crime, it incorporated both generic 'crime prevention' activities, measures tailored to 'at risk' groups, and direct responses to those whose behaviour had crossed the line and become socially unacceptable. However, each of these forms of intervention was connected by the logic of prevention and 'joined up' thinking. As a result, a strong note of approval was sounded in some quarters:

> Most pleasing of all is the adoption in government of the more holistic approach to youth policy academic researchers have been advocating for some time ... much of this interest seems to have been fuelled by a recognition of the long-term expense of vulnerable or 'troublesome' groups of young people if issues concerned with disadvantage and disaffection are allowed to spiral out of control. (Coles 2003: 302)

This model of policy making and practice has clearly persisted in government thinking, with the emergence of the *Every Child Matters* (DfES 2003) strategy and its 'five outcomes' against which all services for children and young people should be judged. Similarly, *Youth Matters* (DfES 2005) took a coordinated approach to services for young people as a given. Social exclusion and the series of coordinated responses to it therefore seem to have established a degree of longevity as models of explanation and action for policymakers and services concerned with improving the lives of young people and reducing the problems arising when things go wrong for them. Thus, it remains influential as a generic term to describe and account for social decline and disorganisation.

One 'think tank' believed to be influential with the Conservative Party, the Centre for Social Justice, continued to express this kind of analysis even as the wider political terrain itself appeared to be shifting, although the 'family' seemed to be emerging as the focal point of concern:

It is no coincidence that the highest levels of family breakdown are found in our most deprived communities and that these areas also suffer the highest levels of addiction, worklessness, crime and educational failure. (Centre for Social Justice 2010: 36)

It seems, then, that the contemporary reliance on the notion of social exclusion and the interlocking and interacting set of social problems it encapsulates is well established and provides a plausible and widely accepted account of what it purports to explain. On the other hand, as we shall see, its very circular nature creates some significant difficulties when we begin to think critically about the 'causes of crime'.

Social exclusion and youth crime: a critical view

The emergence of the concept of 'social exclusion' as both an organising and explanatory concept in relation to youth crime has been significant. However, it also gives rise to a number of key questions about the assumptions it incorporates, and the aspects of the phenomenon it leaves unconsidered. The idea of excluded groups or communities seems to suggest that there are certain characteristics or dynamics which impact only on them and that this marks them out as clearly different from the 'mainstream' or 'normal' society. Importantly, too, the idea of exclusion suggests that there are embedded in the social system certain processes and influences which are responsible for prejudging who is to be set apart in this way. In other words, the 'excluded' are essentially victims of more powerful structural determinants. In this case, it might seem reasonable to seek causal explanations in the actions and belief systems of these dominant elements, rather than in the products of these forces manifested in the circumstances and behaviour of those who are excluded. To turn the focus on them alone seems to reflect a preoccupation with symptoms, as suggested previously, rather than causes. There is therefore an immediate problem with the logic of the social exclusion thesis, as conventionally articulated, and by implication with the measures adopted to counter its impacts.

The failure to turn the spotlight on exclusionary mechanisms therefore seems to be a notable omission. Indeed, it is more than just an omission because it contributes to the problematisation of the very groups which are held to be 'excluded'. The implications of this are that they paradoxically come to be held primarily, if not solely, responsible for their own exclusion on the one hand, and that the requisite solutions involve changing their behaviours or attributes, on the other. In other words, the machinery for defining and responding to social exclusion is itself exclusionary. A critical perspective needs to take account of these dynamics rather than concentrating only on those who are the product of such processes. This is essentially the thesis advanced by Young (1999) in his depiction of 'The Exclusive Society'. Exclusion has become a central characteristic of late modern societies in his view, and as a result certain groups are not only 'othered' by the material forces at play, but also by the explanatory logics and interventions developed to address the problems of those defined as 'out groups'. As modern societies have moved from 'inclusive' models of functioning organised around ideas of mutual welfare and the common good, so they have become more divisive and more prone to seek out and demarcate individuals and groups on the grounds of 'difference' and deviance:

> The fundamental dynamic of exclusion is a result of market forces which exclude vast sections of the population from the primary labour market and of market values which help generate a climate of individualism. Such a situation has an effect both on the causes of crime (through relative deprivation and individualism) and on the reaction against crime (through economic precariousness and ontological insecurity). The exclusions which occur on top of this primary process are an attempt to deal with the problem of crime and disorder which it engenders. (Young 1999: 26)

There is thus a 'multiplier effect', whereby those who are firstly excluded by way of primarily economic and structural forces then become subject to a pathologising process of identification, scrutiny and control which compounds this impact. Conventional depictions of social exclusion are not wrong, according to Young, but they clearly do not tell the whole story. They may be based on a 'misperception', in his view (1999: 26), but these skewed assumptions are grounded in 'real' rather than imagined or socially constructed problems – that is to say, one of the impacts of exclusionary forces may be a greater likelihood of those affected acting in ways that are damaging to other members of the community and this cannot be wished away. On the other hand, attempts to control crime purely by dealing with its visible manifestations may themselves 'exacerbate the problem in a dialectic of exclusion' (p. 26). Because they are only designed to address symptoms, such forms of intervention are unlikely to have the impact desired and may add to the underlying sense of social distance experienced by marginalised groups. What may be in evidence here is an over-emphasis on what are termed 'weak' versions of social exclusion (Young and Matthews 2003: 18) at the expense of 'strong' versions. Whereas strong versions 'emphasize the role of those excluding', 'weak versions involve focusing on qualities of the excluded'.

Young and Matthews suggest that New Labour certainly espoused the weak version and this resulted in some notable anomalies in the ways in which the excluded were depicted. In particular, the shift in focus towards the groups concerned has had a distorting effect, in that it has removed others from the picture and provoked a preoccupation with those who are arguably on the receiving end of exclusionary processes. Instead of these processes, however, concerns become much more strongly centred on marginal populations and their attributes. Perhaps unsurprisingly, this also has consequences for the ways in which policies and intervention strategies are formulated. It becomes a matter of responding to the localised and visible manifestations of exclusion, and managing these populations, rather than rooting out and tackling underlying 'causes'.

Criticisms along these lines have been aired previously concerning government plans to address social exclusion among young people (Colley and Hodkinson 2001). The predominant difficulties appear to be related to the orientation of investigations of exclusion, initially undertaken by the Social Exclusion Unit but still evident in the work of bodies such as the more right-wing Centre for Social Justice. Arguing that the SEU's *Bridging the Gap* report was particularly influential in shaping government policy towards young people, Colley and Hodkinson (2001: 335) also suggest that the report itself incorporated 'fundamental contradictions', largely deriving from its partial analysis of the supposed problem:

> Despite appearing to re-instate a concern for the social, it [*Bridging the Gap*] locates the causes of non-participation primarily within individuals and their personal deficits. Yet it denies individuality and diversity by representing the socially excluded as stereotyped categories ... Deep-seated structural inequalities are rendered invisible, as social exclusion is addressed through a strongly individualistic strategy based on personal agency. (Colley and Hodkinson 2001: 335)

Indeed, they go on to argue that misconstruing the phenomenon in this way may well lead to the imposition of 'solutions' that may simply make the situation worse for some young people.

In its limited search for causes, the SEU appears once again to be quite selective. Two 'major' contributory factors are acknowledged – namely, educational shortcomings, and poor family circumstances. As with its other work, the SEU at the same time associated these with a range of other 'risk factors', including drug and alcohol misuse, criminality and, significantly, membership of ethnic minority groups. While these linkages might be taken as being suggestive of structural explanations, the 'weak' conceptualisation employed turned attention towards purported failings or inadequacies *within* the groups concerned, such as a family history of worklessness, negative attitudes to learning or a catalogue of unacceptable personal behaviours, which somehow appear to be inter-related and interactively causal (p. 338).

From this catalogue of individual and collective shortcomings, the emergence of a 'deficit' model of marginal groups cannot be far behind and is reflected in the view of Colley and Hodkinson (2001: 339) in 'the use of metaphors of descent and fall'. If we are constrained to search for explanations among excluded populations themselves, we are almost obliged to think in terms of their own 'deficiencies', such as laziness and lack of moral purpose and guidance. Such explanations are plausibly supported, of course, by those examples of young people who survive and even thrive, escaping the perils of moral decline and personal degradation through their own efforts. If *they* can do it so can everyone, goes the argument, picked up elsewhere by the populist media and politicians. The upshot of this process of selective investigation and analysis is an apparently coherent explanatory frame, centring on young people's:

> lacks and needs. As we have seen, their attitudes, values and beliefs are seen as key factors in reinforcing their non-participation [in mainstream society] and, therefore, as aspects of *self*-exclusion. Overwhelmingly, they are portrayed as deficient, delinquent, or a combination of the two, as are their dysfunctional families and communities. (Colley and Hodkinson 2001: 340; original emphasis)

At best, these young people are 'passive victims' with meaningless lives and no capacity for growth or change, but at 'worst, they are deviant perpetrators of criminal behaviour and drug abuse' (p. 341) who represent a major threat to the integrity and well-being of society in general. Their shortcomings and depravities are endemic and become associated with an idea of cyclical disadvantage which feeds off itself, leading to the establishment of a more or less permanent 'underclass' (Murray 1996) from which few will escape.

Far from promoting inclusionary measures, then, investigations and explanations of social exclusion appear to confirm and solidify ideas of separateness, difference and intractable deficiencies. Interventions may be designed to offer a 'leg up' to the lucky few who have the qualities and support networks to promote 'resilience', but for the remainder the task appears to be one of problem management, containment and control. Ironically, the very attempt to quantify and even understand social exclusion has resulted instead in accounts which have further underpinned that keen sense of difference and 'otherness' that distinguishes between respectable society and its unacceptable underside.

The logic of these arguments flows through into policy and practice, too, specifically in the kind of approach to assessment and intervention evident in the youth justice system. This is geared towards the identification of indicators of deficiencies, personal shortcomings and 'risk' (Smith, R. 2005, 2006), rather than towards those antecedent factors which might create the conditions for certain types of behaviour, or, indeed, for that very behaviour to attract a certain label such as 'anti-social' or 'illegal'. This orientation is manifest in specific tools in use in youth justice, such as the ASSET assessment suite. Completion of the ASSET documentation is mandatory in most cases where young people are referred for offending behaviour in England and Wales, and this is clearly skewed towards identifying 'risky behaviour' and providing a rationale for an intervention to manage such behaviour (Youth Justice Board 2010). As I have argued elsewhere, the 'general approach of ASSET can be summarised as a "tick box" exercise, with a heavy emphasis on the negative indicators of risk of offending' (Smith, R. 2007: 113). Once selected and subjected to processing in this way, the young person becomes liable to detailed scrutiny which, by its nature, focuses attention on those attributes and circumstances which are supposedly criminogenic or potentially harmful. The process itself appears to have been designed to operate in a confirmatory fashion, drawing on indicators of future risk in order to provide a rationale for the decision to criminalise a young person in the first place.

We know, however, from the available evidence that classificatory machinery such as this is highly flawed – both intrinsically and extrinsically. ASSET, for example, is only reckoned to achieve a 70 per cent success rate in terms of predicting future offending, even by its advocates (Baker *et al.* 2005). At the same time, this sort of strategy has wider implications which are frequently not recognised in the day-to-day operation of a supposedly neutral scientific assessment tool. The cumulative effect is that certain groups of young people are implicitly and sometimes explicitly 'targeted' (Smith, R. 2006: 103). As a result, the over-representation of black young people in the justice system comes to be seen as an unfortunate side effect of the process rather than something which is actually a product of institutional discrimination embedded in the process itself. The 'system' itself can therefore be viewed as a contributor and indeed a central player in the selection and recruitment of young people and frequently subgroups within the wider youth population as potential, current and future criminals. The very existence of 'targeted' interventions that will include young people on the basis of their risk of future offending can be seen as contributing to this process of 'splitting off' and marking out our criminal classes:

> Such processes of exclusion work negatively in at least three ways. First, they can contribute to young people's perceptions of themselves as 'offenders' and thus consolidate deviant identities ... Second, because children are 'objectively' identified as potential offenders, this creates the possibility for the community and criminal justice agencies to categorise them as criminal ... Third, the presumption of criminality may lead to children's rights being compromised. (Smith, R. 2006: 103)

Exclusionary processes: 'push' and 'pull' factors?

The previous sections have considered the concept of 'social exclusion' from rather different perspectives and crucially a tension has emerged between explanations which locate exclusion within a range of distinct and situated dysfunctional processes and characteristics which interact and magnify problems, on the one hand, and accounts which attribute the phenomenon to structural forces of which conventional mechanisms of explanation, classification and response are themselves a feature, on the other.

To help to explore this tension further and develop a clearer understanding of which is the more plausible, it may help here to consider further some of the ways in which social exclusion impacts on young people and contributes towards the establishment of criminal careers and identities.

Both perspectives seem to share a view of social exclusion as a process which, in turn, may indicate that we might be able to identify its impact over time and as young people move from childhood through adolescence. The idea therefore emerges of a kind of exclusion 'career' that can be linked in turn to the more commonly held notion of an 'offending career' (Berridge *et al.* 2001). This perception has prompted some to attempt to understand exclusion and offending in terms of distinct pathways and transitions which mark out the trajectory of young people's lives and the different influences and outcomes they are likely to experience (Johnston *et al.* 2000; Webster *et al.* 2004; Stephenson 2007). Divergent pathways are marked out for young people from early on, depending on factors such as schooling, relationships and family circumstances. Thus 'relatively successful transitions (for instance, involving regular employment and non-offending) invariably result from academic success' (Johnston *et al.* 2000: 24). In this account, the alternative of opting out of schooling is portrayed as a matter of conscious choice:

> School was perceived by many as irrelevant or too authoritarian and some fled its confines for the freedom and fun of 'hanging around' the streets or making trips to parks and woods in the area with groups of friends. (Johnston *et al.* 2000: 24).

The process of disengagement may be triggered by specific events or circumstances, but it seems to be a conscious process, a form of 'self-exclusion'. This, in turn, renders this group more liable to a number of other exclusionary and potentially criminalising influences it seems, including 'a fuller immersion in local, street-based networks and longer term disengagement from the opportunities provided by college and training schemes' (p. 24). Even so, a life of crime is not a certain outcome of this kind of emerging pattern and it is suggested that contingent 'life events' and contextual factors – such as the availability of 'youth projects' – will continue to 'play a key role' in shaping individual trajectories into and away from offending behaviour. The model of social exclusion developed in this and follow-up work (Webster *et al.* 2004) is of a series of contingent events that will shape but not determine the opportunities and choices available to young people, perhaps resulting in a greater likelihood of 'exclusion' and offending careers for some, but even so such outcomes are only provisional and are subject to subsequent developments which may themselves have a significant impact and result in a change of direction, often towards 'desistance' (Webster *et al.* 2004: 19).

Other researchers, focusing on the relationship between school exclusion and offending, seem to offer a rather different account of the process itself, suggesting that a number of factors independent of young people themselves should be emphasised, such as 'extreme social and educational disadvantage' (Berridge *et al.* 2001: 5). They note also that exclusion is a 'social process' (p. 6) and that 'there are many differences in the way in which schools 'respond' to behaviour which is believed to be problematic. They suggest that concentrating unduly on 'difficult behaviour' may have a distorting effect on such processes, failing to take account of individual 'learning and social needs' (p. 6).

What they identify is a complex and interactive process, during which identities are negotiated, determined, sustained or modified. The classroom and the wider school environment are particularly important sites for this sort of exchange in their view because they play such a substantial part in children's experience:

> The classroom is a complex social setting within which formal and informal rules operate, and in which individuals can act strategically to achieve certain goals. Young people have a sophisticated stock of knowledge about behaviour and the way in which this is likely to be perceived within the school environment … Relationships will also develop across time, and students will thus acquire a particular identity. Students perceived to be deviant can have this identity either affirmed, or alternatively, recast positively, through the interactions in which they engage. (Berridge *et al.* 2001: 7)

Furthermore, these transactions are supplemented by other contextual influences, including those of the family and peers outside the school as well as the wider cultural and social setting. Children who are already marked out as different in some way are perhaps more likely to be the subject of close attention, especially from official sources. Where they have had difficult prior experiences, they may find it hard to negotiate the expectations and pressures of a structured environment and they may also become a target for the attentions (welcome or unwelcome) of their peers. These, and possibly other sensitising factors may expose certain children to a greater likelihood of scrutiny and then censure should they appear to transgress behavioural norms. Of course, we should also note here that the existence of prior stereotypes may also be a factor affecting the processes of selection and sanction to which some young people are subject.

Berridge *et al.* suggest three ways in which exclusionary processes in schools might operate. They may be associated with a broader process of victimisation or 'labelling'; they may act as confirmation of a chosen pathway and exclusion may be something which the young person actively 'seeks out'; or they may be linked to 'unhappiness' and associated behaviours which the young person feels unable to change. Exclusion, then, does not follow a standard path but varies between young people, perhaps according to certain identifiable patterns although not in ways which are easily predictable given the number of variables at play.

The detailed study of school exclusion and its links with offending on which these observations are based appears to show that exclusion is indeed a process, within which certain recurrent themes emerge. These include being marked out as different, perhaps because of a change of school or perhaps because of a preference for certain styles of dress. In the case of one interviewee for the study, this appeared to be linked to discrimination on ethnic grounds in the experience of the young person concerned (Berridge *et al.* 2001: 21). What is clear from this study, though, is that those who had been permanently excluded from school had become associated with a pattern of persistent behaviour that was deemed unacceptable by school authorities. Some were upset about the exclusion and a number of young people were surprised by it (p. 29). Others, on the other hand, had welcomed it because 'it offered a legitimate reason for staying away' from school: 'It was what I wanted. I didn't think about the future, I was glad' ('Robert', quoted in Berridge *et al.* 2001: 29).

Whatever their reactions though, for these young people permanent exclusion marked an important fork in the road. It had both material and symbolic consequences. For those who were 'out of school' the consequences were perhaps predictable, in the sense that they began to 'hang around' on the streets and thus became more likely to 'get into trouble'. Of the relatively small proportion (8 out of 28) who transferred to another school, a number found themselves to be 'marked' almost from the start. Young people's unpreparedness for a new environment may be compounded by the fact that they are judged on reputation, which is established by virtue of the fact that they have already been excluded. The difficulties of starting again – hopefully with a clean sheet – are then compounded by the differential approach taken by schools. Some would appear more unwilling than others to accept excluded students and those that do will often have vacancies, precisely because of their existing challenges and the reputations that these schools carry. They may well have high levels of behaviour problems already and might also as a consequence be caught in a spiral of disruption, exclusion and escalating image problems, attracting the label 'delinquescent' to themselves:

> It is important ... that statistics relating to reintegration are considered in relation to the geography of the local schools' market. It is, of course, ironic that such 'destabilised schools' in 'destabilised neighbourhoods', already confronting formidable social problems, must nonetheless continue to import further problems as their capacity to deal with them is progressively undermined. (Berridge *et al.* 2001: 31)

Where young people cannot be reintegrated into the mainstream, they will typically be referred to Pupil Referral Units or other 'exclusion' projects (p. 33). Often such schemes will be welcomed by participants as a way to get back on track, with a more personal and respectful approach helping them to feel valued. However, it is also acknowledged that one probable (unintended) consequence of bringing 'together young people with high levels of need, a limited capacity for self-control and considerable illicit expertise' (p. 34) is an escalation of involvement with 'the wrong crowd' – and hence with behaviour that is likely to come to the attention of the forces of law and order. It seems that a combination of situational influences, 'pull factors' in terms of peer influence and a sense of belonging, and increased visibility, is likely to heighten the risk of criminalisation for young people going down this route. Stephenson (2007), too, has provided useful evidence showing the importance of the relationship between schooling, 'exclusion', and offending, recognising that some of the processes in play have very extensive historical origins and are embedded in structural arrangements as much as they are in more localised and specific interactions between people and systems. Pitts (2008: 88) also draws attention to the role of schools in escalating feelings of 'not belonging' and being 'marginalised' for young black students in particular. Their belief in and experience of institutional forms of racism seem to contribute to a form of 'stand off' and mutual rejection, whereby formal exclusion and personal disengagement are complementary responses to an impossible situation.

Schools and the wider educational process are not the only vehicle through which exclusionary dynamics are played out by any means, but they do exemplify the consequences of a series of interlocking influences and they are clearly of significance because of the part they play in contributing to the longer-term project of assessing, classifying and allocating more-or-less fixed social roles to the entire population of children and young people. They are also hugely significant because they encompass the ages of peak offending to a large extent and therefore might be expected to contribute in some way to the trajectory being followed by those who become involved with the justice system. On the face of it, it is no surprise then that well over half (60 per cent) of the permanently excluded young people in Berridge *et al*'s study were 'involved in crime' (2001: 47), leading the authors to conclude that 'permanent exclusion adds impetus to pre-existing youth offending careers' (p. 48) and that the associated problems of 'visibility-vulnerability' are particularly acute for African-Caribbean young people:

> This kind of overlap between educational and socioeconomic disadvantage, together with an absence of alternative community identities, indicates one route through which permanent exclusion from school can lead to offending. While this perception of the issue had particular resonance for some of the black students interviewed, elements of it were echoed by young white people and their parents, who felt strongly that permanent exclusion strengthened links with delinquent peers within the community and thus increased the likelihood that a young person would become involved in offending or that their offending career would develop. (Berridge *et al.* 2001: 49)

It is in this way that key exclusionary 'moments' – notably but not only involving educational systems – can be seen to be part of a wider process of preparing young people for the role of young offender, which may in the end be the most attractive and credible option open to her/him from a restricted range of choices (Pitts 2008).

Becoming young criminals: 'push' and 'pull'?

The concept of 'social exclusion' has gained and indeed continues to exercise considerable influence in analysis and policy making relating to youth crime as well as to a wider series of identified social problems. As a result, much effort has been devoted to making sense of what it represents and how it comes about in order to devise effective strategies to counter its effects. Conventional explanations have tended to concentrate on the observed association of a number of 'linked' indicators of social disadvantage and community dysfunction. Policy initiatives to address the problem have therefore tended to base themselves on this assumption. However, in doing so, they have equally tended to incorporate a number of unresolved tensions and potentially contradictory practices. In adopting essentially 'weak' forms of the exclusionary thesis (Young and Matthews 2003), they have been complicit in shifting attention away from structural factors and back onto the perceived shortcomings and malfeasances of the 'excluded' themselves, notably including many young black people for example. Inclusionary initiatives themselves compound the problem in a number of ways: by adopting a 'problem' focus, they almost inevitably pathologise individuals, groups and sometimes whole communities; by ignoring or minimising structural factors, they over-emphasise 'agency' and the possibility of individualised solutions; and, by shifting the focus in this way, they provide a pretext for holding individuals accountable when they fail to make the most of second or third chances to reintegrate. Those who fail to take the opportunities offered by Pupil Referral Units, for example, are believed to have only themselves to blame (Berridge *et al.* 2001).

These dynamics form part of a broader strategy of 'responsibilisation' it is argued (White and Cuneen 2006: 21), whereby historically well-established distinctions between 'deserving' and 'undeserving' elements of the disadvantaged population are further substantiated when young people fail to take advantage of the reintegrative pathways made available to them. In this sense, perhaps, the rhetoric and the dynamics of social exclusion are nothing new. They represent more accurately a reworking of longstanding debates about responsibility, blame, and the question of how to deal effectively with youth crime. Exclusionary processes are thereby held to be a necessary feature of the established social order, just as the search for explanations and solutions to the problem originating from this source cannot, by definition, acknowledge this very fact. It has been suggested that New Labour did come close to recognising this inherent problem in articulating the desire to be 'tough on the causes of crime' (Blair 1993), but also that it finally retreated to a preoccupation with 'agency' and the language of individual accountability, opportunity, and blame:

> All in all, the major theme of the discourse remains agency; it is interested in disciplining the underclass rather than genuine empowerment for them. (Young and Matthews 2003: 22)

Furthermore, the processes by which these groups are identified as the object of concern and the 'disciplinary' measures devised for them come, in time, to represent a further confirmation of the 'legitimacy' of the discourse of responsibility and control itself. Nowhere is this more clearly evident than in conventional assumptions about the relationship between school exclusion and offending.

Chapter 6

Doing 'justice'?

The youth justice system: fit for purpose?

Having considered some of the ways in which young people are prepared for or 'recruited' to the youth justice process as potential offenders, it will now be important to reflect on the way in which the system itself responds to those coming into its sphere of operation. As will probably be discernible from previous chapters, the present author (along with many others) has serious misgivings about the way that youth justice is administered in the UK, and particularly in the shared jurisdiction of England and Wales, and the discussion here is inevitably informed by these concerns. This is not a neutral and dispassionate account, but one which is underpinned by a strong sense of *injustice* and damaging and discriminatory outcomes for very many young people.

Despite this, it is important to recognise that the picture is neither uniform nor constant, and that one of the major challenges in providing meaningful accounts of the treatment of young people in trouble is to recognise and incorporate an array of dynamic influences in our attempts to arrive at explanations which can claim a degree of authenticity. In their different ways, for example, both Muncie (2002) and Pitts (2002, 2008) have recognised that the youth justice system is unstable and subject to rapid changes of emphasis that in turn can produce dramatic consequences in terms of embedded practices and the impacts on young people. Equally, some accounts have tried to identify 'critical moments', such as the killing of James Bulger and its aftermath (Jenks 1996), which have had quite fundamental consequences for the way in which young people are viewed and treated by the criminal justice process.

At this point, too, another tension emerges between those who would seem to argue that there are deep underlying and historically fixed regularities about the way in which youth justice is constructed and administered (see, for example, White and Cuneen 2006) on the one hand, and those who perhaps would place more emphasis on what appear to be substantial and highly significant changes of direction in the short term (see Pitts 2002, for instance) on the other. Of course, these perceptions are in turn linked to the kind of explanatory frame advanced by different commentators, and for some at least it may be that both perspectives are to some extent justified (Muncie 2002). The immediacy and dramatic nature of short-term changes which have already been well-documented (Smith, R. 2007) does not necessarily mean that deeper explanations do not still hold some value. And yet for most of those engaged in practice in youth justice – and for young people, themselves – it is what is happening now which assumes greater importance of course.

It may be helpful, if challenging, to attempt in what follows to sketch out both a 'contemporary history' of youth justice and a more extended account of historical patterns and apparent regularities, before seeking to resolve the emergent tensions in some sort of explanatory synthesis. In other words, I will try to explain how impressions of continuity and change may both have elements of veracity about them.

So, what's going on then?

It is an interesting time in which to be writing this (March 2010), because recent months have witnessed a very substantial fall in the numbers of young people in custody and this does not, as yet, have any clear explanation. Indeed, for the first time since the Youth Justice Board was established and the New Labour reform programme was fully implemented in June 2000, there has been a sustained reduction in this figure (Youth Justice Board, 3rd March 2010). It is too early to tell whether this is evidence of the kind of dramatic shift already referred to or a possible artefact of other changes, perhaps in the way policing targets and outcomes are specified. Nevertheless, it would seem at first glance to fit quite well with the kind of pattern laid out by Pitts (2002), who has suggested that recent decades have witnessed a number of such changes, inspired by a coincidence of factors such as contingent political influences, economic pressures, professional orthodoxies, media campaigns and public opinion. From the late 1960s onwards, there appear to have been a number of 'movements' in youth justice during which a particular 'paradigm' (Kuhn 1970) could be seen to dominate. These distinct periods of time cannot quite be neatly identified with specific decades, although it would seem that each may be associated with a particular era and the 'spirit of the age'.

Thus the 1960s were a period when 'welfare' was in the ascendancy and the socially liberal Labour government of the time had put in place a series of reforms to give substance to this aim. These reforms were themselves a form of 'backlash' against earlier forms of intervention which were perceived as institutional, oppressive and class-based (Smith, R. 2007). Approved Schools and Borstals were to be replaced with more amenable settings and custody was to be superseded by care. In the event, subsequent political changes derailed these aspirations and what emerged was a set of parallel mechanisms. As a result a substantial 'welfare' apparatus developed alongside, rather than in place of, punitive sanctions and with the result that there was a very sizeable growth in institutional provision for children and young people during the 1970s (Thorpe *et al.* 1980; Morris and Giller 1987). From this a substantial increase in the utilization of residential care was mirrored by a similar rise in the use of custody: 'In absolute terms, this has meant a staggering rise – almost 4,000 – in custodial sentences between 1971 and 1977' (Thorpe *et al.* 1980: 13). It was the culmination of this process which led to a recognition of the phenomenon of 'unintended consequences' (Haines and Drakeford 1998: 40).

It was at this point that a number of influential analyses prompted a serious rethinking of the meaning and impact of 'welfarism'. If anything, young people were being drawn into the justice system *because* they had become the target for welfare-oriented practices such as Intermediate Treatment. Perhaps prefiguring later developments, it seemed that the insertion of such benign forms of practice into the panoply of interventions might actually facilitate the transition from less intensive to more intensive and 'drastic' responses to young people's behaviour, 'with the result that delinquent careers are promoted, even accelerated' (Thorpe *et al.* 1980: 128). It seemed, indeed, that there was concrete evidence here to support the 'net-widening' thesis developed elsewhere (Austin and Krisberg 2002). Similarly, these trends also resonated with aspects of Foucault's (1979) depiction of an 'army of experts', whose activities were organised around notions of scrutiny, classification and graduated interventions.

As these concerns crystallised there emerged the beginnings of a new consensus, largely organised around the principle of 'do no harm'. In other words, if it was not possible to demonstrate that children and young people were benefiting from interventions then these should be avoided or minimised wherever possible. Hence, we can understand the motivation behind the titles of two of the most influential books of that era – *Justice for Children* (Morris *et al.* 1980) and *Out of Care* (Thorpe *et al.* 1980). Guided for once by the evidence, practitioners and policy makers began to find substantial common ground, influenced variously by principles of rights and 'natural justice' (Morris *et al.* 1980), 'radical non-intervention' (Schur 1973), the drive for efficiency savings in an era of financial constraints and an emerging interest in reparation, informal offence resolution and what has since become known as restorative justice (Marshall 1985, 1988). As a result, there was a clear and distinctive change of direction from the early 1980s onwards, reflected in law, policy and practice. The 1982 Criminal Justice Act reasserted the primacy of 'justice' as the basis for decision making by the courts in respect of young offenders; the DHSS (Department of Health and Social Security) Intensive Intermediate Treatment initiative of 1983 established the basis for 'alternative to custody' programmes; and the influential Home Office Circular 14/1985 provided a significant impetus to cautioning and diversion. Practitioners, in turn, enthusiastically adopted these policy tools, applying principles of 'systems management' (Stevens and Crook 1986; Smith 1989) at all stages of the criminal justice process. It was at this point that the idea of 'youth justice' professionals began to emerge in England and Wales, as a form of practice distinct and different from that undertaken in parent agencies – typically social services or probation departments. As Haines and Drakeford (1998) have acknowledged, the corollary of this was a downplaying of the significance of 'welfare' issues in an assessment and consideration of appropriate interventions for young people in trouble.

Nonetheless, a coherent and consistent approach emerged which had very dramatic consequences for the pattern of interventions and disposals in youth justice. Whereas in 1977 over 184,000 children under the age of 17 were cautioned or convicted for offences, this number had declined by 43 per cent to 105,000 by 1991 (Smith, R. 2007: 13). Equally dramatically, the proportions of this number dealt with in different ways were also transformed. Whereas slightly over half those processed in 1977 were cautioned, this had gone up to more than three-quarters by 1991. In parallel with these developments, there was a very substantial reduction in the use of custody for young offenders (Smith, R. 2007: 14), at the same time as the use of care orders also declined (Smith, R. 1995: 104). Children were much less likely to be institutionalised as a result.

As has been observed, these changes were not just the product of a greater readiness to deal with minor infringements informally. The entire ethos of juvenile (youth) justice appeared to be shifting:

> If there were no changes in courts' sentencing behaviour, then an increase in diversion would be likely to lead to a proportionate increase in more severe sentences. But this did not happen in the 1980s ... juvenile justice practitioners were not just successful in reducing the custody rate, they were even more successful in reducing the rate for a relatively older and more serious cohort of offenders. (Haines and Drakeford 1998: 60)

Radical change in the terrain of youth justice in the 1980s led to a huge sense of achievement among liberal practitioners and academics, but it was earned at some cost which was not always acknowledged at the time. As noted previously, it had been grounded in a deliberate de-linking of welfare issues from the core functions of the justice system. Children's 'needs' were no longer to the fore when reaching decisions about appropriate disposals; instead, it was the offence which mattered primarily. In addition, the reductions in the use of penal measures did not amount to a fundamental rejection of certain underlying assumptions about crime, justice and responsibility. The change strategy adopted concentrated mainly on taking control of key decision-making points and the machinery of pre-trial decision making as far as possible, rather than attempting to articulate a change in the underlying principles and rationale for the youth justice system. This distinction was evident at the level of practice, too, with practitioners concentrating predominantly on procedural measures to stem the flow of young people into the formal justice system, on the one hand; on the other, some did seek to advance new models of practice based on early notions of 'restorative justice' (Blagg *et al.* 1986). On the whole, though, traditional models of justice, blame, responsibility and punishment appeared to prevail – or at least to act as the benchmark against which interventions were to be evaluated (Smith, R. 1989).

While the thresholds for key decisions and outcomes had clearly shifted, the arguments about proportionality and the due process in which they were grounded drew on established notions of individual accountability and the sentencing 'tariff'. In this respect, the liberalisation of the 1980s was not immune to the effects of a subsequent change of mood or political climate. Indeed, this is precisely what happened in the early 1990s as has now been widely recognised (Jenks 1996; Goldson 1999; Smith, R. 2003). Although the killing of James Bulger has come to be identified as *the* critical moment in this change of direction, it was not the only event to influence the changing climate. For some time before this occurrence the mood had been darkening. Once again, it seemed that a combination of factors created a tidal wave that was moving in a particular direction. The 'strong' image of Margaret Thatcher no longer held sway in government and the prevailing sense of 'weakness' at the centre (Fionda 2005: 42) perhaps fuelled a belief on the part of ministers that they must 'act tough'. At the same time, a number of disparate events in urban communities prompted a new 'moral panic' (Brown 2005: 58). Because of this there was an apparent wave of 'riots' in Cardiff, Oxford and North Tyneside in 1991, there were concerted fears about 'joyriding' and its inherent risks, and there were particular examples – indeed almost caricatures – of young people's behaviour around which such fears appeared to coalesce and escalate. The North East of England appeared to be a 'hot spot' for such eruptions of unruly behaviour. 'Rat Boy' from Newcastle was the term applied to one 14-year-old believed to be responsible for at least 55 offences, who was said to be living rough in the tunnels beneath a housing estate (*Independent*, 7 October 1993). In another case:

> A 10-year-old Hartlepool boy made national headlines when he 'swaggered free' from court wearing an SAS mask ... leading to cries for clampdowns on ever younger criminals. (Brown 2005: 60)

This culmination of trigger events and political uncertainty, fuelled by a vociferous media and powerful voices within the judiciary, effectively guaranteed a reversal of the trends of the 1980s. From a point where it had been possible to envisage the progressive eradication of the use of penal custody for children there was a fundamental change of direction. By the end of the 1990s cautioning rates had declined substantially and custody use had gone up – by more than 50 per cent for 15–17 year olds – as well as re-emerging as a regularly used disposal for younger age ranges too. By the end of the decade, the 'repoliticisation' and 'repenalisation' (Goldson 1999) of youth justice were well embedded in rhetoric and practice.

It is less easy to identify dramatic changes in direction, or the emergence of a new 'paradigm' in Pitts' (2002) terminology, during the first decade of the twenty-first century, because patterns of practice and outcomes have become more stable, albeit at unacceptably high levels of punitive intervention (Goldson and Muncie 2006). Nonetheless, it may be possible to discern some changes in ideology and behaviour following the election of the New Labour government in 1997. At the time, as Pitts (2003) observes, the change of administration manifested a number of continuities, for instance in the political strategy of 'penal populism' and the implementation of certain measures already signposted by the previous government; thus, the already proposed Detention and Training Centres were simply re-branded as Secure Training Centres under the Crime and Disorder Act 1998. On the other hand, he also detects a change of emphasis, reflecting wider governmental agendas and preoccupations such as 'joined up services' (see Chapter 5) and micro-management. Any last vestiges of 'minimalist' thinking were swept away: 'Indeed, a central theme... is that more young offenders should be brought before the court, earlier, and more swiftly' (Pitts 2003: 92). In accordance with this line of thinking, measures of close control and surveillance also moved nearer to the top of the agenda. These provided the means, it was believed, for achieving the aspiration of the new government to make the 'prevention of offending by young people' a reality. Therefore young people in trouble have become subject to much greater levels of formal intervention at all stages in the justice process – much closer and more pervasive regimes of surveillance and control and much more explicit scrutiny for indicators of 'risk' and the likelihood of future (re)offending. While 'punishment' remains a powerful rhetorical device in the political repertoire, at the level of practice the primary emphasis appears to have shifted from retribution to management, control, and damage limitation.

Notwithstanding all this, there has been (until a dip late in 2009) a surprising level of consistency in the pattern of disposals to which young people have been subject, with the use of custodial measures remaining more or less constant from 2000 onwards. This perhaps helps to underline an important consideration of which we should constantly be aware in the field of youth justice and this is the perennial gap between rhetoric and reality. Whatever the claims made for the 'new' youth justice, the experience of young people caught up in the system remains much the same it would seem.

Taking the long view? 'Deep' accounts of youth justice

Some historians of youth justice have taken a longer view, arguing that it is important to seek out evidence of the more fundamental continuities and seismic shifts that underlie and shape contemporary events. For some it may be that we should be seeking out those aspects of human relationships – particularly intergenerational patterns of conflict – which seem almost timeless and can be traced back to the Middle Ages and beyond:

> In 1448 the dean and chapter at Exeter accused young people who had entered their cloisters to play games of scrawling on walls and breaking windows. In the 1590s there were similar complaints of boys breaking windows and disturbing services at St Paul's Cathedral in London. (Heywood 2001: 111)

For others, though, it may be that concerns about children and their behaviour are best viewed in light of fundamental changes in the organisation and structure of social relationships. Hendrick (2006: 4), for example, refers to the 'birth of modern childhood' in the nineteenth century which is closely associated with 'the impact of an evolving and completely new urban industrial capitalism' (p. 5). According to this analysis, the emergence of youth crime and exaggerated fears about it was historically specific and related to deeper lying concerns with social stability and threats to the emerging hierarchy of social relations. These dynamics have, in Hendrick's view, been crucial in determining the nature of social attitudes towards and actions against young offenders ever since. This is an important point of disagreement – between those who see intergenerational conflict and concerns about young people's behaviour as timeless and those who see these as situated and essentially determined by the specific social relations that obtain at any particular time.

These competing perspectives are largely found to be reflected in alternative accounts of the origins of youth crime and the changing nature of the strategies adopted to respond to the problems associated with it. This has been captured neatly by Cohen (1985) who posits three alternative views of history, social problems and social change. The first of these is described as 'uneven progress' (p. 15), whereby developments in criminology and criminal justice are seen as part of a continuing trend towards better understanding and better practice in addressing essentially fixed and timeless challenges, such as the deviant activities of children and young people. The third of Cohen's 'models' of historical developments in criminal justice he refers to as 'the "it's all a con" view of correctional change' (p. 21). According to this perspective the justice system achieves its objectives quite successfully as it does for the first model, but these objectives themselves need to be understood rather differently. They are no more or less than the maintenance of an unequal and exploitative social order, partly achieved through a process of mystification which persuades all but a few that the system itself is 'fair, humane and progressive' (p. 22).

These two models share the implicit assumption that there are fundamental aspects of social relations that will necessarily shape our approach to dealing with the problem of youth crime. It is the middle of Cohen's three models ('we blew it') that coincides more closely with our earlier account of periodic attacks of self-doubt and sudden realisations that current practice may be crucially flawed. Thus, the rejection of welfarism and its reliance on institutional care at the end of the 1970s was one such shift, occasioned by short-term evidence of failure and a loss of faith in conventional wisdom.

For those who would take a more historical view, however, there appear to be contrasting ideas about the underlying characteristics of the problem of childhood delinquency and, therefore, what to do about it. If it is a matter of 'nature' then continuing attempts to improve and modify measures of control and reform may be inherently justifiable – within limits. Childhood itself is more or less predictable and constant according to widely dispersed 'commonsense' perspectives:

> Within everyday rhetoric and many discourses of theory childhood is taken for granted, it is regarded as necessary and inevitable, and thus part of normal life – its utter 'thereness' seems to foster a complacent attitude. (Jenks 1996: 8)

For Jenks too this is not just a lay perspective, but also one which has informed much psychological and sociological thinking 'until fairly recently'. In light of such assumptions, then, the challenge for society and its institutions is to provide the best possible means by which children can be enabled to grow and develop, and to be socialised in order to take their place eventually as full members of society (see Chapter 1).

Childhood, then, is a natural state which is necessarily unfinished and untutored, and necessitates adult intervention in order to shape it appropriately. At the same time, the characteristics of this initial state of being are a matter of dispute and of unresolved contrasts. Children are alternatively 'innocent and untainted by the world' (Jenks 1996: 73) or a 'wilful material force' which harbours 'a potential evil' (p. 71). Such views of childhood remain close to the surface in popular consciousness it seems and it is equally clear that they can be held simultaneously without a sense of their essential incompatibility. At the time of writing, the controversy over the treatment of James Bulger's killers has just resurfaced, with his mother reported to have stated that 'the first duty' of a commissioner for children is 'to stand up for *innocent* little children' who are harmed by '*evil* monsters' such as the 10-year-old killers of her son (*Daily Telegraph*, 13 March 2010; my emphasis). To hold such contrasting views about children simultaneously requires us to undertake a further process of rationalisation to make sense of this disjuncture. Childhood must thus be seen in its natural state as an unfettered site of possibilities, incorporating the capability of extremes of harmful behaviour at the same time as it is similarly exposed to the potential for mistreatment in the form of exploitation and abuse. As a consequence, the obligations of the social institutions engaging with children must be to impose specific procedures and mechanisms to secure children's safety on the one hand and to shape and control their behaviour on the other. The challenges appear to be self-evident and so, too, it follows that we should be able to develop standardised forms of intervention to ensure the desired outcomes.

In line with this reasoning, we might expect the youth justice system at any one time to be the culmination of attempts to regularise and consistently enhance measures to predict, monitor and control children's behaviour (and their environments) in order to produce well-ordered, conforming members of the social whole. Ironically, though, this is just what we might expect if we were to apply the alternative analytical perspective which holds that such methods of control are contrived purely to ensure that the logic and practices of an unequal society are sustained and legitimised:

> This is what the reformed prison does. It renders docile the recalcitrant members of the working class, it deters others, it teaches habits of discipline and order, it reproduces the lost hierarchy. It repairs defective humans to compete in the market place. Not just the prison but the crime system as a whole is part of the larger rationalization of social relations in nascent capitalism. (Cohen 1985: 21)

Within this framework, then, we should expect to see contemporary youth justice systems informed by a common logic and predictable shared objectives independent of the specific measures in operation at any one time.

Certainly until very recently, modern youth justice systems had thus attempted to acknowledge and reconcile the apparent contradictions between polarised views of children's 'natural' state. While such models assume that children are essentially empty vessels – unformed and untutored apprentices for adulthood – contrasting assumptions about their innate characteristics have necessitated successive forms of accommodation between them. Hendrick (2006) argues that in Britain this has been a characteristic of the 'modern' state since Victorian times, reflected in key legislative measures such as the Children Act 1908, the Children and Young Persons Act 1933, the Children Act 1948 and the Children and Young Persons Acts of 1963 and 1969. Introduced by governing parties of different persuasions, these all incorporated attempts to assimilate the specific 'welfare' needs of children within the framework of a formal 'justice'-based system for dealing with their crimes. Although the exact balance between competing considerations altered periodically, both in law and practice, this relationship was maintained as a central component of the measures put in place to determine how to respond to young offenders in the context of their specific needs *as* children. Given the fundamental nature of the differences between 'welfarist' and 'justice-based' positions, though, it was perhaps not too surprising that this consensual approach increasingly came under pressure as the welfare state itself underwent radical changes from the 1970s onwards:

> The failure of Liberalism to protect welfarism in juvenile penal policy was caused by a complex set of factors, perhaps the immediate one being the technical and inherent difficulty in trying to match the punishment and welfare approaches into a single piece of legislation that would reassure all political interests. But there was another influential factor: the issue of governance among an electorate that was increasingly disillusioned with the promise and vision of the post-war welfare state. (Hendrick 2006: 11)

As the nature and practice of welfare-based interventions came into question across the spectrum of state services, those operating on alien territory – such as, increasingly, within the justice system – became particularly susceptible to renewed questioning. Thus, we should see the changes since 1980 not as a series of pendulum swings but as the playing out of a 'neo-liberal' process of reaction and retrenchment. 'Welfare' has finally lost its place in the repertoire of youth justice interventions to be replaced by an emerging form of 'authoritarian populism' (p. 13). In this context, the apparent liberalisation of the 1980s should be viewed as no more than a fortuitous anomaly, borne out of the coincidence of a number of policy and practice agendas. The fragility of this consensus derived from its essentially pragmatic character, ungrounded as it was in any form of sustainable alternative rationale to that of disciplinary control and the punishment of wrongdoing. Irrespective of the political affiliation of the party of government, this neo-liberal ethos has gained in strength in the period since then. As Hendrick (2006: 14) puts it, there had been up to this point a variable but well-established 'reconciliation' between the 'control, rehabilitation and punishment of young people' who were themselves located at some point along a 'spectrum of victim/threat/neglected/delinquent' whose elements always bore some relation to each other. Since the 1980s, though, that relationship has been ruptured and substantially recast both in policy and practice. This process could be epitomised by the way in which the welfare needs of young offenders were simply subsumed under the measures of control advocated by the incoming New Labour government in 1997:

> the Government does not accept that there is any conflict between protecting the welfare of a young offender and preventing that individual from offending again. (Home Office 1997: 7)

The idea behind this elision seems to be that any form of intervention which reduces the likelihood of a young person reoffending must be for her/his 'own good' (Smith, R. 2001: 23).

The consequences of this kind of rationalisation are reflected in a number of recent developments, such as, for example, the subsuming of issues to do with well-being and personal development under the umbrella of 'preventive' projects delivered under the auspices of the Youth Justice Board. 'Targeted' initiatives – such as the Youth Inclusion Programme – were specifically designed to draw in and engage those young people within communities who were identified as being most 'at risk' of offending for example (Smith, R. 2007: 48). Similarly, the priority accorded to the 'prevention of offending' offered *prima facie* justification for measures such as the Anti-social Behaviour Order, Acceptable Behaviour Contracts, and Individual Support Programmes. Any benefits to the young person which might accrue from such interventions would have no intrinsic value, but would simply be a by-product of the primary purpose of reducing the potential for subsequent offending.

Running in parallel to these measures at, or before, the entry point to the justice system we have also witnessed a dramatic increase in the use of custody from the early 1990s until late in 2009 at least. This, too, is a predictable consequence of the reassertion of the logic of control and deterrence. Irrespective of the evidence of their effectiveness (or lack of it), punitive sanctions coincide with the fundamentalist ideological drive towards treating (some) children as inherently dangerous and in need of containment. In the face of this onslaught, attempts to reassert the merits of a welfare-based approach to young people who offend may have limited purchase as they are out of step with the prevailing ideological climate.

Towards synthesis: the 'drivers' of youth justice policy and practice

Having acknowledged that there may be both short- and long-term influences on the structure and direction of systems and practices in youth justice, it may be helpful to move on to consider in a bit more detail the specific conjuncture of these factors at the present point in time (early 2010). This will hopefully provide the basis for a fuller explanation of the current state of play as well as the likely or possible direction of any foreseeable change.

Firstly, there does not appear to be any let up in the relentless pursuit of a populist agenda by political interests and in the months before a General Election perhaps that is to be expected. Any move which strays from the current orthodoxy appears hesitant and quickly becomes the object of 'commonsense' criticism. Thus, an apparent attempt to express more liberal, 'welfarist' views by the leader of the Conservative Party in 2006 quickly became lampooned by political opponents as a wish to see people 'hug a hoodie', (*Guardian* 10 July 2006). In an apparent reversal of a former party leader and Prime Minister's (John Major) statement that 'we should condemn a little more and understand a little less', David Cameron suggested that we should 'try and understand what's gone wrong with these young people'. Expressing even this limited deviation from conventional wisdom still had to be qualified however and so he also offered the caveat that 'Of course people who commit crime should be held responsible', adding that addressing the problems behind offending behaviour did not mean that 'we can't be tough when a crime is committed'. So even when attempts are made to reintroduce concerns about the welfare and circumstances of young offenders into the political arena and media spotlight, they are advanced cautiously and remain 'in the shadow' of the punitive agenda.

As a General Election grew nearer though, there were signs of a reversion to talking tough. Perpetrators of anti-social behaviour should be sent clear messages by way of imposing a sanction 'that impacts on their lives and makes them think again', said the Conservatives' Shadow Home Secretary in the summer of 2009 (*Guardian*, 14 July 2009). At the same time, the language from the then Home Secretary was predictably tough: 'We are determined to tackle youth crime and drive down anti-social behaviour which ruins lives and damages our communities ...' (DCSF Press Release, 6 January 2010). This kind of rhetoric seems to reach a crescendo at or around the time of elections, but it is no more than the most explicit form of what seems to be a consistent and clearly dominant 'discourse' in the sphere of youth crime. As is clearly recognised, this is not the sole discourse at play at any one time (Fergusson 2007) and nor is it without its contradictions (Brownlee 1998). We also need to exercise caution if and when we might seek to generalise from a particular geographical and political context (Hartnagel 2004; Muncie and Goldson 2006; Field 2007). However, the persistence of tough talk – and the way in which it seems to operate as a default position – is noteworthy because it establishes the baseline against which the range of youth justice practices and interventions is intuitively judged and therefore has a key role in determining exactly what goes on at the point where policy becomes practice. Paradoxically, though, 'talking tough' may intensify fears and exacerbate demands for increasingly punitive levels of sanctions against young people for their crimes and misdemeanours. While we are unable to determine the precise impact of coercive policies, in the short term at least:

> What is more certain is that in the interim continuing to 'talk tough' on crime is a high cost and high risk-strategy for restoring public confidence in the law and once embarked upon, the political costs of withdrawing from tough policies are so high that few politicians will wish to pay them. Ultimately, the evidence ... suggests strongly that the public will never be satisfied with tougher new regimes unless widespread misperceptions about leniency in sentencing are challenged and changed. (Brownlee 1998: 334)

Thus the 'reliance' on punitive rhetoric may only fuel fears about young people and their behaviour, while conveying the implicit message that there is never enough being done to clamp down on wrongdoing. More and harsher punitive treatment will always be next on the agenda, according to this argument. Muncie (2008) demonstrates that this trend is evident not just in the UK but also across a wide number of jurisdictions, in the developed world at least. What was initially perceived as a case of 'policy convergence' between two more or less neo-liberal states (the UK and USA) could actually be observed as a developing process on a much wider scale, encompassing much of Western Europe as well it seems. Muncie claims to be able to identify convergence at the various levels of rhetoric, policy and outcomes in youth justice across national boundaries, perhaps epitomised by the United States, and in some cases such as that of the UK drawing directly on American experience. As a result, the 'adoption ... of American experiments with curfews, naming and shaming, zero tolerance, dispersal zones' and a number of other schemes (Muncie 2008: 109) suggests direct evidence of 'policy transfer' (Jones and Newburn 2006). Of course, the alignment between UK and US policy and systems has long been attributed to a common commitment to neo-liberalism (Esping-Andersen 1990), but it would appear that other welfare regimes are not immune to such influences thereby suggesting a broader convergence of historical trends. Thus, for example, a number of European countries with reputedly 'liberal', welfare-based approaches to young offending are reported to be following the same, increasingly punitive trajectory, including the Netherlands and Belgium. Similarly, in France, the intensification of political rhetoric has been closely matched by changes in policy towards 'responsibilising' young people:

> The election of Sarkozy in France in 2007 was swiftly followed by a promise that re-offenders aged 16 and above would be treated as adults. Sarkozy's electoral success has been partly explained by his pre-election declaration ... that delinquent youths on poor estates were 'scum' that should be 'cleaned out with a hose'. (Muncie 2008: 109)

Shortly afterwards, the German government made a commitment to introduce 'boot camps' – another initiative modelled on practice in the United States. Muncie concludes (p. 110) that this and associated evidence are sufficiently persuasive to suggest a general mood across Western Europe, to the effect that 'punitive values associated with retribution, incapacitation, individual responsibility and offender accountability' have gained ascendancy at the expense of 'traditional principles' of support and reintegration for young people who offend. Muncie goes on to argue that it is possible to provide some empirical evidence of the consequences of this collective ideological shift. Changes at the rhetorical level are paralleled by identifiable consequences 'on the ground', specifically in terms of compliance (or not) with internationally agreed instruments such as the United Nations Convention on the Rights of the Child and the growing use of custodial disposals for convicted young offenders.

Thus, eight states have been criticised by the UN Committee on the Rights of the Child for similar failings in terms of a lack of separation between juvenile and adult systems and disposals, a process which elsewhere has been described as 'adulteration' (Muncie and Goldson 2006: 199). Of particular importance, too, is the finding that in virtually all states in Western Europe there is evidence in the Committee's view of discrimination against minority groups – such as travellers and asylum seekers – by and within the youth justice system. Here it would seem that there is substantive evidence of the process of 'othering' (Garland 2001; and see Chapter 5), whereby greater levels of punitiveness in general are interlinked with exclusionary and stigmatising processes which effectively 'target' certain identifiable groups at, or beyond, the margins of society.

As well as the systematic shortcomings identified by the UN Committee, Muncie (2008: 114) also draws attention to a trend towards increases in the use of custody and other secure institutions in some European states from 2004 to 2007. As he acknowledges, though, these patterns are not evident everywhere and they are often based on figures calculated in different ways. Indeed the evidence of a continuing and wide divergence in policy and practice reflecting different welfare 'regimes' apparently leads Muncie to express a rather ambiguous view about the possible impacts of 'global' trends in youth justice:

> Comparative analysis may reveal something of a 'globalized' emergent politicization of the 'youth problem', but also the continuance of a diverse range of 'localized' juvenile justice practices based on informal social controls, diversion, education and social protection. (Muncie 2008: 119)

While this apparent ambivalence may appear problematic, it does seem to coincide with the views of others concerned with the relationship between politics and practice, nationally and internationally. Hartnagel (2004), for example, observes that the pronouncements of politicians and media on the subject of youth crime in Canada tend to 'exaggerate the threat' and 'advocate punitive responses' to offenders, thereby contributing to the distortion of public 'knowledge' and 'opinions' on the subject (p. 370). At the same time, however, the realities of practice, once mediated by the necessity to make compromises and control costs, are somewhat different. Fergusson (2007) similarly argues that there are dangers in over-simplification; we should think in terms of 'multiple discourses' in youth justice that will interact in ways which may be complex and unpredictable. It would seem fuller appreciation of the origins and dynamics of these different positions is required in order to make sense of the ways in which they are played out in practice. While they are commonly grounded in neo-liberal thinking, for example, 'responsibilization' and 'authoritarianism' may incorporate quite different explanatory frameworks for the 'fundamental sources' of wrongdoing, and thus of the processes whereby errant behaviour might be changed (Fergusson 2007: p.181). Such competing assumptions along with others – such as 'managerialism' and residual notions of 'welfarism' – may well be articulated in policies and procedures which simply incorporate rather than resolve conceptual and practical conflicts. These processes have been mapped out by those such as Lipsky (1980) who have detailed the extent of discretion and informal rule making resting with 'street-level workers' (Fergusson 2007: 188). Thus practice in youth justice as elsewhere cannot be directly 'read off' from dominant ideologies, powerful interests or explicit policy drivers; it may be seen, rather, as a continual process of resolving the embedded challenges deriving from these different authoritative sources, which results in what are described as an unstable series of 'fudges' that will provide short-term material solutions:

> Whether this governance paradigm leads to a picture of horizontally organized multi-levelled implementation of policy or fudged policy determinations with messy outcomes depends on how *power* is understood to operate within it. (Fergusson 2007: 188; original emphasis)

This is an important consideration because it recognises that pre-existing relations of dominance and subordination, and of legitimacy and exclusion, cannot be discounted in trying to make sense of specific outcomes in youth justice, but equally, they do not tell the whole story. Field (2007) has also developed a similar line of argument through his examination of 'practice cultures' in youth justice in Wales. In this study a range of professional and judicial opinions was sought on their approach to the administration of youth justice, but there did not appear to be any sign of a consistent 'shift' to tougher and more controlling approaches to young offenders. There seemed to be a multiplicity of aims and objectives across the spectrum and variations in attitude or approach did not easily fall into predictable categories. As a result there were differences in the orientation to welfare interventions but these were quite nuanced, being distinguished according to whether they were a 'means to an end' (commonly, the view of police and magistrates) or 'an end in itself' (other participants). However, even those with pronounced 'welfare' aspirations did not see these as being entirely separable from 'justice' objectives (Field 2007: 326). It could not be concluded from these observations, though, that any one perspective had gained clear dominance; in fact in the areas studied 'addressing welfare problems' continued to be viewed as a legitimate and even desirable aspiration for the youth justice system:

> Generally, the aims and objectives of the practitioners in our interviews were too complex, fragmented and multi-stranded to be easily captured by talk of 'punitive' practice cultures. Even for magistrates and police officers – the groups most traditionally associated with 'tough' punitive aims – there remained a widespread acceptance that the welfare of the young person must be addressed because only by doing so would the risk of re-offending be reduced. (Field 2007: 326)

Indeed, Field suggests that there may not be a coherent youth justice culture at all; he contrasts the 'control without constructive support' which is a feature of the use of ASBOs with young people to a rather different and more complex set of practices embedded in the 'mainstream' youth justice system (p. 328). If this is so, then attempts to develop and articulate 'grand narratives' of youth justice and its history are fraught with difficulty and run the real risk of a deterministic over-simplification which neither does justice to the complexities of practice nor acknowledges the possibilities for change. On the other hand, we will continue to have difficulty on this basis in constructing plausible accounts of and explanations for inequality, injustice, discrimination and harms which might be attributable to embedded features of 'the system'.

Going round in circles? The tension between fragmentation and unity

Understanding youth justice as a product of history has always presented substantial challenges. It is a context within which competing ideologies are played out in practice, and these struggles are also replicated in alternative attempts to account for the justice system's development and trajectory as Cohen (1985) has so clearly demonstrated. While a close inspection of its workings appears to indicate a myriad of complex and contradictory objectives, policies and practices, a more detached appraisal seems to suggest that deeply embedded power imbalances, inequalities and unfairness lie at the core of the process. This in turn brings us back to the question of whether contemporary practices and outcomes are no more than at best a 'special case' of these underlying dynamics and structural relationships, or are they really 'new' (and not in the New Labour sense) and in a state of realignment?

Answers to these questions will have significant implications in the 'real world' of practice and policy development of course, because they inform the choices we make about the appropriate strategies we should undertake in our various roles. Must we perhaps pursue a strategy of 'radical non-intervention' (Schur 1973) or 'abolitionism' (Mathiesen 1977) on the basis that any form of active engagement only serves to legitimise our oppressive treatment of young people? Or is it more important to remain involved because this is more likely to benefit young people experiencing the unfairnesses of youth justice and may help to change things for the better? As Cohen (1985, p. 270) has observed: 'The choice in every instance is pragmatic and depends on our values'. However, he does go on to suggest that there are criteria which we can apply which might help to test the validity of such choices. For instance, we may ask whether or not particular policies, actions or classificatory systems are 'exclusive' or 'inclusive'. In the case of the ASBO, for instance, this would seem like a fairly easy judgement to make.

Chapter 7

Doing injustice

Where are we now?

Having previously considered the question of historical trends and influences, it is important also to think in terms of their practical consequences and manifestations. The shape and substance of contemporary practices are not accidental and they represent the unfolding of broader patterns of social interaction and structural change. It is therefore important to attempt to identify and evaluate just what is going on at any point in time. This is especially so for a field of human activity which is as heavily contested and as controversial as youth justice.

Material accounts of this kind are important, too, because they in turn shed further light on our analysis and unresolved questions which have emerged thus far. Much has been made, for instance, of the concept of 'othering' (Garland 2001) and we might expect to find concrete support for this proposition in the day-to-day operation of the criminal justice process. This exercise is important for two reasons at least. Firstly, it will help us to determine the nature of the relationship between practical outcomes and the kind of ideological and structural dynamics referred to previously. In addition, however, it will shed further light on what exactly the justice system does to young people who are caught up in it. In this way, it is important to remember that we are not just dealing with systems and patterns of social interaction, but also with the real impacts and lived consequences for those affected. In this way, the very real question of whether or not the youth justice system is 'fair' or 'just' becomes concrete and meaningful.

In order to explore these issues further, I will focus on three aspects of youth justice which relate to structural accounts but also reveal direct impacts. Firstly, then, the question of whether and to what extent the youth justice system is 'divisive' – creating and sustaining a sense of 'us' and 'them' – will be considered. Secondly, and extending this further, we will reflect on the extent to which it is 'discriminatory' against certain sectors of the youth population. And, finally, the human consequences will be addressed – how far is the youth justice system actually 'damaging' to young people? Drawing on our earlier analysis, it will also be argued here that the outcomes which can be identified through these analytical frames are not accidental or indications of mere 'collateral damage', but rather, they are fundamental to the purposes and achievements of the justice process. In other words, the harmful consequences of youth justice for some young people are seen, usually implicitly – and only rarely explicitly – as a reasonable price to pay for the maintenance of a particular form of social and moral order. In this sense, then, we will be generating evidence of routinised and accepted forms of 'injustice' which is the product of systemically unequal and unfair social relations. The aim of securing order and maintaining social control, both symbolically and practically, is never far from the surface when we address the workings and processes by which young people are 'brought to justice'.

Divide and rule?

The notion of 'bifurcation' (Bradford and Morgan 2005) has been prominent in youth justice for a considerable period of time (Bottoms 1977), although the form it takes has inevitably changed. In essence, however, the term has been used to depict approaches to youth and crime which seek to differentiate between minor and relatively unproblematic infractions or miscreants and those who are or become a serious cause for concern, perhaps because of the persistence of their behaviour or because of the gravity of the threat they represent. In the contemporary era, bifurcation can be identified as a form of practice realised through 'targeting' (Smith, R. 2006). Recent practices, though, have tended to adopt a differentiated strategy of targeting, moving from generalised indicators of concern through anticipatory classifications of potentially problematic individuals and groups towards specific programmes directed towards those who are 'known' troublemakers (Smith, R. 2007: 45). Such classificatory mechanisms were indeed central features of strategies to tackle social exclusion in the early 2000s (Social Exclusion Unit 2002).

Again, the idea that potential problems can be scientifically identified and then addressed preventively is not new, and can certainly be dated back to the Intermediate Treatment initiative of the 1960s (Smith, R. 2007: 48). However, the approach adopted became increasingly sophisticated over time, and it became an integral part of government strategy with the advent of New Labour. There was no doubt that this strategy fitted precisely with a number of core assumptions and policy goals of this particular administration, linked to ideas about social exclusion, on the one hand, as we have seen, and on the other informed by a particular view of the potential for a close calibration of social problems and 'managed' solutions for these once identified. There emerged a stream of initiatives aimed at those young people who could be identified as 'potential' offenders which involved a kind of narrowing down of the forensic gaze. Those geographical areas assumed to be most problematic or criminogenic were highlighted and within them groups – especially of young people – would be targeted depending on certain factors in their backgrounds. Concrete examples of this kind of problem identification strategy are in evidence (Hayden *et al.* 2007). Using a 'geodemographic classification system' named MOSAIC (p. 295), it has proved possible to specify with a considerable degree of precision those areas and 'types of neighbourhood' where recorded youth crimes are at their highest rates (p. 302), as well as other indicators such as the connection between levels of neighbourhood risk and particular schools. It seems, then, that we may have good enough tools at our disposal to predict the likelihood of offending peaks:

> Classification systems such as MOSAIC begin to offer us more complex pictures than deprivation indices and, as such, provide the starting point for planning a response and collecting or analysing further data to fine-tune this response. (Hayden *et al.* 2007: 307)

The use of such tools is claimed to offer us the basis for much improved planning and resource allocation that may be directed to those areas (and schools) with the greatest levels of 'difficult and sometimes serious criminal behaviour' (p. 308).

The logic of this kind of strategy clearly appears to have taken hold and it seems to be establishing the basis for further attempts to identify specific 'at risk' individuals. Indeed, this provides the rationale for a range of projects developed over recent years under the umbrella of 'youth inclusion'. Drawing on the broader evidence generated by the Social Exclusion Unit, certain geographical areas were identified as particularly problematic 'hot spots' (Smith, R. 2007: 175) and it was within these areas that young people 'at risk' of offending were sought out. Indeed a panoply of projects and strategies was put in place, under such headings as 'On Track', 'Positive Activities for Young People', 'Summer Splash', 'Youth Inclusion Projects', 'Junior Youth Inclusion Projects' and 'Youth Inclusion and Support Projects' – all recognisably different, but all sharing the premise that the best approach to tackling youth offending was 'early prevention' (Smith, R. 2007: 48). These initiatives were supported by quite sophisticated multi-agency partnership arrangements, initiated by the Youth Justice Board, and apparently designed to 'divert' potential young criminals into 'mainstream' activities and services. As I have suggested previously, these arrangements bore an uncanny resemblance to the kind of 'army of experts' predicated by Foucault (1979) whose purpose was to apply a forensic rationale to the identification of problem populations and apply a range of 'normalising' techniques in order to bring them into line and ensure conformity.

The Youth Inclusion Programme, established in 2000, was intended to target 'the most disaffected young people in the 13 to 16 age range' (Morgan Harris Burrows 2001: 1) and its starting point was the identification in each of the specified problem areas the 50 young people at greatest risk of offending, and providing them with a menu of wholesome alternative activities to occupy their time and reduce their likelihood of becoming involved in routine criminal behaviour. Such initiatives quickly mushroomed and by 2005 there were 72 Youth Inclusion Programmes, 124 Youth Inclusion and Support Panels, 400 Safer Schools Partnerships, and '125,643 at-risk children and young people participating in Positive Action for Young People' (Youth Justice Board 2005: 6) – strikingly rather more than the overall number of young people processed by the criminal justice system each year.

The approach espoused by the Youth Inclusion Programme appeared on the face of it to be highly promising, with a substantial decline in criminal activity recorded in those areas where young people had been 'targeted' in this way (Morgan Harris Burrows 2001). Subsequent, longer-term, outcomes were not so impressive, though, with crime levels actually increasing in project areas (Morgan Harris Burrows 2003: 14), even though arrest rates had fallen for the 'top 50' young people at risk of offending. These schemes were consistent with the broader objectives of government policy, being designed to utilise best evidence of those most at risk of offending in order to deliver intervention programmes which would reintegrate them in mainstream activities, thus achieving the core objective of 'inclusion'. Only the most intractable offenders could be expected to persist and this group would therefore merit more intensive and controlling forms of intervention. However the limited evidence of 'success', allied with additional concerns about the underlying implications of this approach, has given rise to a number of criticisms. Percy-Smith (2000) took the view that 'targeting' would be problematic because of the negative connotations of identification as a potential problem, while McLaughlin and Muncie (2000) have questioned the value of 'administrative' forms of practice which do not take account of the essentially problematic nature of indicators of risk and the underlying structural factors relevant to young people's circumstances.

Indeed the process of problem identification – 'targeting' – and subsequent focused interventions may be taken as indicative of a deeper strategy, achieving important ideological outcomes of much greater significance than their practical impact. Public concern and practical action could equally be directed towards those who are judged to be 'at risk', according to actuarial principles. Deeper structural influences and other forms of wrongdoing (state crime, media abuses, and corporate crime) are relegated to the margins of popular consciousness. Success or failure therefore becomes very narrowly defined and will be equally determined by the outcomes for a small group of young people, depending on how they respond to interventions specifically 'tailored' for them. Success and failure alike are also capable of being interpreted in support of the underlying assumptions and strategies. Young people are either 'diverted' appropriately away from further criminal activity or on the other hand they fail to take advantage of the constructive programmes offered and continue to offend, thereby justifying our initial concerns about their anti-social tendencies, apparently.

The foregrounding of the individual, and her/his response to intervention, obviates the need to understand deeper 'causes' of crime, too, according to Cohen (1985: 176): 'if we can control crime, we don't really need to understand the causes'. Ironically, also the focus on a narrow range of 'indicators' actually depersonalises the individual concerned:

A political decision to eliminate concern for the social background of the defendant involves much more than making those characteristics inappropriate ... By the same token, the offender is to a large extent excluded as a person. There is no point in exploring a social background, childhood, dreams, defeats ... (Christie 2000: 163)

Studies of targeted youth crime prevention have raised concerns along the lines set out above, even where they have been broadly supportive. Thus 'Several YIPs have mentioned as a difficulty the perception in the area that bad behaviour is being rewarded and the labelling effect on young people targeted. They are still perceived as being YIP kids if they present challenging behaviour even if this is no worse than other kids' (Adamson 2003: 11). This concern carries echoes of earlier discussions, to the extent that young people characterised as being 'at risk' are to some extent in the position of being 'invited' to accept a deviant identity (Matza 1969). They are being singled out as different and then engaged in project work on this basis, alongside others with the same figurative tag. While providers and agencies are sensitised on one side to further indicators of concern or manifestations of problem behaviour, so young people are alerted to the fact (or at the very least their awareness is being reinforced) that they are viewed as being on the threshold of criminality. The crystallisation of the young offender identity is, it seems, the product of an interactive process, whereby the 'label' must be both offered and accepted in order for the circle to be completed (Lemert 1967).

Detailed evaluations of early prevention schemes have illustrated some aspects of this process of identification, engagement, and subsequent trajectories towards successful or unsuccessful outcomes. Young people are clearly earmarked by referrers to one Youth Inclusion and Support Panel as being at 'very high risk of offending' (Walker *et al.* 2007: xii), but they should not have gone beyond the 'reprimand stage' of the justice system at the point of referral. They should exemplify 'four or more risk factors' in their lives, and their behaviour should be of concern to a number of agencies, and/or their parents. The children included in this study 'were usually aware that they had been referred to the YISP because they had been naughty' (p. xii)

Following referral, the role of the YISP is to secure the provision of 'appropriate services' and to 'monitor changes in risk and protective factors' (p. xiv). Programmes of intervention would typically focus on 'addressing risk factors' by using off the peg programmes considering issues such as 'crime and consequences' (p. xv). In other words, the interventions themselves would be organised around the implicit (and possibly explicit) assumption that young people might be likely to offend at some point in the future. This seemed to be associated with a selective approach to 'risk factors' – thus 'only those risks which could be addressed seemed to be noted' in individual support plans (ISPs) while others 'were simply left to one side' (p. xvi).

The process of engagement (or not) itself appears to have contributed to the determination of subsequent outcomes, and positive factors such as 'parental support', relationships with workers and the young person's commitment were associated with continuing participation while the absence of these factors was associated with lower levels of motivation and involvement.

Concerns arise, too, about the possibility of 'amplification' of deviance and the effects of 'labelling' (p. 102). Changes in behaviour and attitude seem to follow a conventional narrative path, reflecting young people's motivation, willingness to engage and recognition of their problems and ways of dealing with them. Others, though, are more or less committed to a pattern of further errant behaviour:

> Several key workers referred to cases where children had engaged in mainstream services, one-to-one interventions, and/ or activities, but had seemed unable or unwilling to change their behaviour and attitudes. These were described as serious cases where the child's problems were complex and deep-seated, and the children were unwilling to admit that they had done anything wrong or that they had any problems. (Walker *et al.* 2007: 148)

These accounts offer some indication of a pattern of behaviours and interventions which is characterised in a way that distinguishes sharply between compliance and non-compliance, polarising perceptions of young people (and sometimes their families) into opposing groups whose behaviour is either capable of being influenced and changed or 'entrenched' and set on a particular downward path. In this way, the processes of 'bifurcation' can be seen to operate in microcosm, in the way in which such interventions are organised and evaluated. The patterns of delinquency are as much embedded in the minds, discourses and processes of those administering youth justice as they are apparent in the identifiable behaviours and life trajectories of the young people concerned.

Division and discrimination

One aspect of the youth justice system that has been a recurrent cause for concern has been the over-representation of certain ethnic groups among the overall population entering the system (Feilzer and Hood 2004; Wilson and Rees 2006; Smith 2007). The routine practices described above may offer some insight into the ways in which apparently neutral processes and the decision-making apparatus are implicated in profoundly discriminatory impacts on these groups and individuals. In one YISP area, it is noted that there was a clear correlation between one of the 'risk' factors associated with the potential for future offending, school exclusion, and involvement with the YISP; on this basis, it 'was clear that many of the children referred to Brent YISP were at high risk of offending and antisocial behaviour' (Walker *et al.* 2007, 164). Thus, an apparently neutral and objective indicator of risk significantly shapes the profile of those liable to be referred for early intervention. At the same time, though, it is also noted that 'boys from a black background [in Brent] are six times more likely to be excluded compared to any other ethnic group' (Jakhu 2004: 13). It is unsurprising, then, that referrals to the YISP in Brent appear to have been sharply skewed. Only one referral in the study population was White British, while 'what appears to be starkly apparent is most referrals, some 67% are from a black (Caribbean/African or Black British) background' (Jakhu 2004: 13). In this way, the process of 'targeting' interventions also helps to classify young black people disproportionately as potential troublemakers.

It is worth noting at this point that the consequences of such decision-making processes – based on 'soft' information, human judgement, and speculation about the future – become 'real' for those involved. In the Brent study, for example, the selection of young people for the YISP appeared to crystallise and give substance to certain feelings among their parents, which contributed to the unfolding narrative of their lives:

A recurring theme among parents/carers was their feelings around receiving interventions from 'outside bodies'. Some commented how they felt they were … 'at the end of my tether' and were amiss as to what else they could do as parents to change the behaviour of the young person in question. They went [on] to share their feelings of being 'that parent' and many stated they blamed themselves for the 'failings of my child', and elaborated by saying they felt 'embarrassed'… 'shamed' ….

Further, some parents admitted they believed that the CSP [Children's Support Panel] ... 'was at the end of the line' ... believing if the CSP programme could not ... 'turn X around ... nothing can'. (Jakhu, 2004: 32)

As this narrative turns the focus on the perceived shortcomings of parents themselves and the delinquencies of their children, other factors – such as ethnicity, discrimination, and social context – fade into the background, thus effectively 'normalising' the route being followed by the young person towards the formal justice system.

The 'micro-politics' of classification and control revealed here are reported to be deeply embedded in contemporary welfare practices (Garrett 2004), but in legitimising a particular way of seeing and responding to young people this obliterates critical aspects of culture, identity, and context. Once we shift our attention to these aspects of young people's experiences a rather different narrative emerges. Indeed, there has been considerable evidence accumulated recently of systemic discrimination, on the grounds of ethnicity, which has been partly informed by the neutral and supposedly objective application of a 'risk factor' analysis to individual young people. 'Institutionalised racism' has been identified as 'endemic' in the practices of criminal justice agencies (Macpherson 1999) and this is revealed both in the experiences of young black people and the outcomes of the justice process. Thus, one very detailed study carried out on behalf of the Youth Justice Board found clear evidence of differential treatment, including:

- the higher rate of prosecution and conviction of mixed-parentage young males;
- the higher proportion of prosecutions involving young black males;
- the greater proportion of black and Asian males ... remanded in custody before sentence ...
- the slightly greater use of custody for Asian males;
- the greater use of restrictive community penalties for Asian and mixed-parentage males ...
- the much greater percentage of mixed-parentage females who were prosecuted. (Feilzer and Hood 2004: 27)

These variations were found to occur despite additional evidence indicating, 'broadly similar' patterns of offending between different ethnic groups (Smith, R. 2007). Such limited variations as there are do not point consistently in one direction (Armstrong *et al.* 2005: 19), so it seems reasonable to accept the conclusion that 'the answer to the question as to why black (young) people are over-represented' in the youth justice system has little to do with differential rates of offending (Goldson and Chigwada-Bailey 1999: 54).

Over time, studies have identified little change in the pattern of treatment of young black people in the justice system (Barclay *et al.* 2005; Jones and Singer 2008; May *et al.* 2010), despite the findings and subsequent policy changes emerging from the inquiry into the death of Stephen Lawrence (Macpherson 1999). There remains a persistent trend towards discriminatory practice at different points in the youth justice system, it is reported:

> mixed race offenders are more likely than whites to be prosecuted than to be reprimanded or warned. Black and mixed race offenders were also more likely to be remanded in custody than white defendants. At court, black defendants had a higher chance of being acquitted than whites. At the sentencing stage, mixed race teenagers were more likely than others to be given a community sentence rather than a (less serious) first-tier penalty. ... (May *et al.* 2010: vii)

And while custody rates do not appear to vary between ethnic groups, taking account of 'all relevant factors' the fact that black young people are more likely to be remanded in custody itself has a distorting effect in terms of custodial outcomes.

A number of plausible explanations have been offered for these differentials, which locate the 'responsibility' for the variance identified within alternative explanatory frames. These include demography; a 'differential involvement' in offending; the impacts on behaviour of social exclusion; and 'differential' treatment, meaning discrimination, by youth justice agencies (p. 4).

Like many other such studies, this one sets to one side the key question of the social construction of definitions of 'crime'; although with this caveat it does try to review possible explanations for variations in behaviour on the part of young people themselves on the one hand, and the wider impacts upon them of social factors and systemic forces on the other. It is noted, for example, that recent census figures have demonstrated a rather younger age profile among certain ethnic groups, including specifically those of 'mixed race' (p. 5), 'other' black groupings, and those from Bangladeshi or Pakistani backgrounds. This might offer one reason for these groups to come into contact disproportionately with the justice system, although it does not account very well for notable variations between these groups (Feilzer and Hood 2004). May *et al.* (2010: 5) also suggest that differential outcomes for black young people may simply reflect a 'differential involvement in offending', but they recognise that this 'is a highly contentious and contested issue'. In one way it seems plausible that collective experiences and cultural variations may well be associated with diverse patterns of behaviour, reflected in the activities of individual and groups. But yet again, the unqualified incorporation of this sort of assumption into our thinking leads to the unacceptable and unjustifiable conclusion that black young people are more likely to be 'criminals'. Official crime figures are likely to reflect process variations, so May *et al.* prefer to rely on self-report studies to address this specific question in more detail. Here it is apparent that most such studies 'do not support the idea that ethnic minority groups are over-represented in offending' (p. 5). Despite this, they go on to comment that these studies themselves are insufficiently sensitive in the main to be able to account for 'the experience of the criminally involved' within 'socially marginalised groups' (p. 6), which may, presumably, also reflect population-wide ethnic divisions also.

This rather ambiguous observation is connected with the third of the possible explanations considered in this particular study, which links offending with social exclusion and economic disadvantage. If offending – or at least certain forms of 'crime' – is associated with poverty and exclusion, then it is likely that it will be concentrated among the most disadvantaged groups which include Black, Bangladeshi and Pakistani populations (p. 6). In this sense, then, we should expect poverty-related offending to be concentrated among these groups, shouldn't we?

> Traditionally, criminologists have tended to resist the idea that some ethnic minority groups are over-involved in offending. However, the weight of criminological theory and research is that patterns of social exclusion must place ethnic minority groups at considerable risk of involvement in crime. Arguably the phenomenon in need of explanation is that young people from some of the most socially marginal ethnic minority groups, notably Pakistanis and Bangladeshis, have not historically been over-represented in offending. (May *et al.* 2010: 8)

If this is the case, it seems to provide a plausible defence for criminal justice agencies against the charge that they are behaving in an overtly discriminatory fashion in the process of identifying and processing young people for their offences. Ethnically disproportionate outcomes are, they might claim, to be expected, in the same way perhaps as gender imbalances are the consequence of behavioural differences ... apparently.

Despite this, the possibility remains that there are differential practices among the justice agencies, including the police (Bowling and Phillips 2002), and this was certainly the conclusion drawn by the Macpherson (1999) and Keith (2006) inquiries into the deaths of Stephen Lawrence and Zahid Mubarek.

The study by May *et al.* (2010: 90) explores this question further, concluding that 'styles of policing' did indeed vary 'across area and even between units within the same area', and as a result the impact of specific 'tactics' on levels of representation of different ethnic groups at the point of first contact with the justice system could be identified. What are termed 'highly proactive and adversarial styles of policing', which intentionally 'target' certain pre-defined groups of young people can be seen to produce distinctive patterns of 'over-representation of some ethnic minority groups in public order offences, drugs offences and driving offences' (p. 90). Importantly, from this perspective, 'the disproportionality that exists at the point of entry is largely preserved throughout the system' (p. 91). This conclusion is consistent with findings in other studies (Barclay and Mhlanga 2000: 2), although it does not entirely obviate the possibility that there may be 'at various points of the [justice] processes, differences that were consistent with discriminatory treatment' (Feilzer and Hood 2004: 27). Equally, external influences on patterns of discrimination and disadvantage do not cease to operate once young people are 'recruited' by the justice system, and there may well be interactive effects, as suggested by Bowling and Phillips (2002: 260) who point to the impact of variations in family circumstances and housing status on bail decisions.

Discrimination against certain ethnic groups appears to be demonstrated by the empirical evidence, then, although its precise mechanisms and impacts remain a matter of some debate. It poses some serious questions for those engaged in youth justice, then, since it appears that efforts to respond 'neutrally' and even-handedly may not be sufficient to counter external influences and pressures. Indeed, as we know practices which are grounded within an ideology of fairness, equal treatment and due process may well appear entirely justified and indeed blameless in our search for the 'causes' of discriminatory treatment. But perversely, it is this very quality which establishes the legitimacy of embedded oppressive institutional practices. To treat offenders more leniently on the basis of their ethnicity of background is likewise made to seem unreasonable, in the same way as positive discrimination more widely is called into question. By contrast, Bowling and Phillips (2002) appear to be arguing that it is incumbent on the justice system itself to do just this and to 'factor in' those features of the social landscape that are systematically discriminatory and therefore to take a proactive stance to counter them. In this light, a genuinely fair system of youth justice is one that acts to counter social inequality and unfair treatment elsewhere (see also Scraton and Haydon 2002).

Damage

As the previous sections have illustrated, youth justice and its mechanisms are characterised by a dynamic process of identification, selection, recruitment and 'othering', which is both divisive and discriminatory. The consequence, however, is not just one of symbolic differentiation, but is also reflected in the experiences and outcomes for young people who become 'criminalised' in this way (Hancock 2006). Indeed, there is considerable evidence now available of the very real 'damage' that is done to young people in the name of criminal justice and we should be doubly concerned about this given the earlier evidence that this impacts on certain groups of young people in particular. The consequences for wider social division and systemic *injustice* should not be underestimated.

Most dramatically, of course, is the consistent pattern of mistreatment in custody, resulting in a considerable number of avoidable deaths in the most extreme cases (Goldson 2002; Goldson and Coles 2005). Between 1990 and 2005, for instance, 28 children (under the age of 18) died in penal custody in England and Wales, prompting the observation that it 'is difficult to comprehend' how this could happen 'without a public inquiry into any of the deaths' (Goldson and Coles 2005: xi). By 2008, this figure had increased to 30 (Howard League, 2008), of which 29 were self-inflicted and one 'followed restraint by staff'. The deaths of children in custody are the (tragic) tip of the iceberg, however, as the Howard League for Penal Reform has discovered:

- in 2007, there were 1,007 self harm incidents among 15–17 year olds in prison;
- between November 2005 and October 2006, physical restraint was used 3,732 times on boys in prison;
- between January 2005 and October 2006, the forcible strip searching of boys took place 100 times.
(Howard League, 2008: 2)

These demeaning and harmful experiences are themselves located within a context which reflects an excessively punitive approach, it is argued. The Howard League has also reported that 'custody is not being used as a last resort' in England and Wales, comparing domestic practice highly unfavourably with a number of other European countries. These outcomes are associated, in turn, with other facets of 'social exclusion', such as being 'in care', having experienced 'violence at home', being excluded from school, or being sexually abused. It is certain, too, given what we have noted previously, that these young people will be disproportionately from particular ethnic backgrounds.

The negative consequences of the custodial experience are not simply those which are most clearly manifested in the form of physical mistreatment or harmful outcomes, they are also to be found more widely diffused: 'not surprisingly, the experience of imprisonment itself has been identified as having a deleterious effect on the physical and mental well-being of children' (Goldson 2006: 147). These ill-effects are diffuse, arising from a neglect of health needs; bullying; ill-treatment; racism; an invasion of privacy; extended periods of confinement; a lack of exercise; and poor diet among other things (p. 148).

Despite a very recent decline in the use of custody for children and young people (at the time of writing), the underlying argument remains consistent. The 'punitive spirit' appears to infuse the justice system at all levels and in all its facets and this remains distinctive to the UK, and to England and Wales in particular. Not only is evidence for this to be gleaned from what we know about penal practices, but this conclusion is also supported by the continuing disparity between rhetoric and practice in the government's approach to children's rights under the terms of the UN Convention on the Rights of the Child. The evidence of mistreatment of children in the justice system has been available from this source as well for a considerable period of time, and the response from successive governments has been dismissive. The approach to youth justice in the UK was identified as being clearly out of line with international standards and practices as early as four years after the country's ratification of the convention (Smith 2010a). Particular concerns were expressed about the implications of maintaining a very low age of criminal responsibility, and the potential use of an increasing array of penal facilities for children as young as 12 (Committee on the Rights of the Child, 1995: para 36).

Perversely, the incoming New Labour government appeared to take no notice of these concerns and proceeded to extend the range and depth of punitive sanctions at all stages of the youth justice process, from pre-criminal measures such as the ASBO and Curfew Orders (Jones 2001), through an intensification of community interventions, to a greater encouragement of the use of custody by the courts and by the use of administrative devices such as breach of community orders. Indeed, government policy has been clear on the point of strengthening the response in such cases. In 2008, ministers acknowledged that the 'decision to strengthen the courts' response to breach was deliberate Government policy' (Lord Chancellor and Secretary of State for Justice 2008: 32), and was intended to avoid the practice of allowing orders to continue with 'no additional penalty' following a failure to comply.

Perhaps predictably, research into the use of custody carried out for the children's organisation, Barnardo's, has shown that 22 per cent of children 'received their custodial sentence for breach of a community intervention' (Glover and Hibbert 2009: 4), including ASBOs and curfews. As the authors observe, it is the 'National Standards … relating to breach' which offer 'very little flexibility' to allow practitioners time to work with young people in order 'to promote compliance' (p. 14). In fact, the increased availability of community orders of various kinds has a direct consequence in terms of the use of custody; these orders, in turn, are both more widely used – and more intrusive – in terms of the impact they have on young people's lives. This study went on to identify a significant disparity between the ostensible provisions of legislation and policy and contemporary practice in terms of the use of custody: 28 per cent of children in the study sample had not committed a 'serious or violent offence' and 35 per cent 'did not appear to meet the custody thresholds' defined in law under the Powers of Criminal Courts (Sentencing) Act 2000. At the same time, the study also revealed that a considerable number of these children had prior negative experiences which could be expected to impact adversely on their well-being. The Barnardo's report drew the following conclusions:

young people serving custodial sentences are exceptionally vulnerable members of society – suffering disproportionate levels of disruption including inadequate parenting, abuse and neglect, learning difficulties and mental health problems – whose needs are often not met throughout their young lives ....

The Government wants custody for children aged 14 and younger to be used only as a last resort, yet ... a significant number of 12 to 14-year-old children ... were sentenced to DTOs [Detention and Training Orders] despite not meeting the criteria ... set out [for the use of custody] .... (Glover and Hibbert 2009: 24)

While custody is the apogee of the 'punitive' ethos which we have noted, what is demonstrated here is that custody and its operating principles of close control, behavioural monitoring, and embedded sanctions also permeate the practices of the youth justice system as a whole, reaching down figuratively and literally (in the case of breach action) into the outer fringes of the system at the point where young people first become singled out as being worthy of its attention. This is apparently in spite of (and in some cases it might even be triggered by) the apparent welfare needs and prior harms experienced by many of these young people. It is unsurprising that this should be seen as a matter of fundamental concern and illustrative of a persistent disregard of children's rights (Smith, R. 2010a), whatever the government may profess to believe about principles of minimum intervention and using custody as a 'last resort'.

What appears to be in evidence here is a consistent process of the incursion and infringement of children's rights under the guise of extending the 'responsibilisation' (Cuneen and White 2006) project throughout the population.

The extension of criminalising measures into the community by way of ASBOs and other measures of anticipatory or actuarial (Smith, R. 2006) control also raised serious concerns about the threat to children's rights. By pre-empting 'due process' and widening the net still further, these measures could be construed as part of a wider project of 'dispersal of discipline (Squires and Stephen 2005: 87) among children and young people.

To the extent that such measures place general restrictions on children's movements and interfere in the conduct of their family life, such measures can be recognised as breaching their rights in other ways too (Freeman 2002; Muncie 2009); not just those offered by the UN Convention on the Rights of the Child but also the protections of the Human Rights Act 1998: 'Curfews override parental discretion and ... seem incompatible with Article 11 of the European Convention on Human Rights, which affirms the right to freedom of peaceful assembly', irrespective of age (Muncie 2009: 345).

The failure to respect children's rights in the context of youth justice has become a matter of continuing concern for international observers, such as the UN-appointed Committee on the Rights of the Child. The committee has continually criticised aspects of policy such as the very low age of criminal responsibility maintained in the UK, but it has also repeatedly drawn attention to some of the concerns identified earlier, such as the endemic discriminatory impacts of the justice process and what it has identified as the excessive use of 'restraint' in secure settings (Committee on the Rights of the Child 2002: para 34) which we now know to have been associated with a number of deaths of young people in custody (Smith, R. 2010b: 13). Indeed, a picture of sustained measures was beginning to emerge at this point:

> The Committee is particularly concerned that since the State party's initial report, children between 12 and 14 years of age are now being deprived of their liberty. More generally, the Committee is deeply concerned at the increasing number of children who are being detained in custody at earlier ages for lesser offences and for longer sentences imposed as a result of the recently increased powers to issue detention and restraining [sic] orders. The Committee is therefore concerned that deprivation of liberty is not being used only as a measure of last resort and for the shortest appropriate period of time .... (Committee on the Rights of the Child 2002: para 59)

It has subsequently become clear that this active disregard for children's rights in the youth justice system is endemic. Little has changed in recent years to enhance the rights of children and young people in this sphere, despite initiatives such as 'Every Child Matters' (DfES 2003) which sought – albeit tentatively – to reassert the principle that the needs and entitlements of children and young people should be indivisible and should not be dependent on their ascribed status.

In its third report on the UK's 'progress', the Committee on the Rights of the Child (CRC 2008) expressed a continuing frustration with the lack of a response from government, noting 'with regret that some of' its previous recommendations 'have not been fully implemented, in particular .... juvenile justice' (para 6). Specifically, the committee reiterated the need for government 'to ensure that restraint against children is used only as a last resort and exclusively to prevent harm' (para 39), to put in place 'mechanisms for monitoring the number of cases and the extent of violence, sexual abuse, neglect, maltreatment or exploitation in … institutional or other care' (para 51), to implement 'a statutory right to education for all children deprived of their liberty' and, once again, to increase 'the minimum age of criminal responsibility' (para 78). Alongside these recurrent pleas a new recommendation was made at this point to 'conduct an independent review of ASBOs, with a view to abolishing their application to children' (para 80). Most telling, however, was the fact that that the specific recommendations of the CRC were contextualised by a broader criticism which may go some considerable way towards explaining the consistent shortcomings of UK governments in respect of the administration of youth justice:

> The Committee is also concerned at the general climate of intolerance and negative public attitudes towards children especially adolescents, which appears to exist in the State party [the UK], including in the media, and may often be the cause of further infringements of their rights. (CRC 2008: para 24)

This appears to provide substantive confirmation of a culture of intolerance directed towards young people, which may help to explain specific shortcomings such as the aforementioned failure to initiate any form of public inquiry into child deaths in custody. Harmful outcomes are a predictable collateral effect of a generalised ethos of fear and hostility towards the younger generation.

Doing injustice: an endemic problem

This selective overview of problematic aspects of youth justice illustrates a number of key linkages between different aspects of the 'system', the prevailing ethos of control, and the harmful consequences experienced by young people on the receiving end. It appears to be the case that the outcomes observed are not just the consequences of specific policy decisions, organisational practices, or particular forms of troublesome behaviour. Indeed, as we have just observed so distinctive is the form of 'youth justice' practised in the UK that authoritative international observers have seen fit to comment on it in broad and general terms. Comparative investigations also have generated very similar conclusions. Whereas some countries such as 'Japan, Norway and Sweden' have managed to maintain a tolerant approach combined with a minimal use of 'youth imprisonment' (Muncie and Goldson 2006: 208), this has clearly not been the case in the UK. While there are clearly geographical and historical variations within the UK (Haines and Drakeford 1998; Glover and Hibbert 2009) these do not substantially qualify the view that the overarching culture of control remains fundamentally influential. The UK is not alone in pursuing a predominantly punitive approach to young offenders (Muncie and Goldson 2006: 212), and it seems that this indicates another worrying feature of contemporary practice, namely that:

> In many countries it seems abundantly clear that it is possible to claim an adherence to principles of universal rights while simultaneously pursuing policies which exacerbate structural inequalities and punitive institutional regimes. (Muncie and Goldson 2006: 212)

The persistence of such attitudes and practices in the face of widespread and powerful social and economic change and political transitions suggests that we must conclude 'that locking up young people is driven by something other than crime' (p. 213). In some countries, such as the UK, 'prison seems to "work"' as a political and symbolic device, irrespective of the (by now well documented) damage it does to those incarcerated and its failure to achieve the 'principal aim' of reducing levels of offending.

We must not think of the youth justice system as being driven purely by 'symbolic' purposes, however, given that it has a direct and as we have seen damaging impact on many thousands of young people who are disproportionately drawn from certain sectors of the population according to their class, ethnicity, and status ('excluded'). Many young people are harmed directly by the justice system and this is surely unacceptable.

This leads us, in turn, to consider the possibilities for change, both in terms of practices and policies and in the prevailing ethos and attitudes towards young people. Barnardo's, for instance, sets out a plausible programme of reform at the conclusion of its review of the use of custody for 12- to 14-year-olds (Glover and Hibbert 2009: 25), but we must also ask bigger questions about the challenge of making such reforms 'stick' and whether or not they may be counterproductive, to the extent that they appear to reinforce the legitimacy accorded to the overarching framework of the youth justice system.

To return to our starting point in this chapter, a renewed attempt to clarify the circumstances in which children are deemed to be 'vulnerable' seems to replicate the divisive processes encapsulated previously in the notion of 'bifurcation' (Bottoms 1977). Two distinct questions need to be asked here. Firstly, will piecemeal reforms have much impact? And, secondly, will these do more harm than good by contributing to the legitimacy of a punitive worldview?

This leads to an important observation: just as the youth justice system itself has both direct and symbolic effects, so too will initiatives which seek to change or reform it in some way. This needs to be borne in mind as we move on to consider 'what is to be done?' (Lenin 1988 [1902]).

Chapter 8

The road to justice: liberal reform

Making the case for change

In this final part of the book, the focus will shift to the question of how and on what basis we should seek to change the way we deal with young people whose behaviour poses problems for us. The preceding chapters have sought to illustrate the fundamental tensions between the ways in which young people's lives are shaped and the ways in which they are perceived and treated. This has culminated in the forms of injustice discussed in the previous chapter. Concerns about the consequences for young people, and society, have been widely expressed for many years, and the evidence to justify these concerns is persuasive. It is interesting, for example, that Muncie (2009) has recounted the concerns of a prominent inquiry into 'juvenile delinquency' of 1816, in words which still resonate today:

> Dreadful is the situation of the young offender: he becomes the victim of circumstances over which he has no control. The laws of his country operate not to restrain, but to punish him. The tendency of the police is to accelerate his career in crime. If when apprehended, he has not attained the full measure of guilt, the nature of his confinement is almost sure to complete it; and discharged, as he frequently is, penniless, without friends, character or employment, he is driven, for a subsistence, to the renewal of depredations. (Committee into Juvenile Delinquency 1816, quoted in Muncie 2009: 53)

In this one brief passage, there are captured many of the central recurrent problems which have continued to beset the practice of youth justice. Offending is identified as a consequence of particular social circumstances; criminal processes act to criminalise and punish rather than addressing the specific offence; the justice system exacerbates the situation, confirming and reinforcing criminality; and, the experience of social exclusion is intensified by the process, offering little choice but to continue to offend in order to survive. This is not to suggest that this is a complete picture, but rather to highlight the nature of the challenge and the sort of issues which have consistently been the focus for attempts at reform. These have clearly fed approaches based on 'welfarism', for instance, as well as those which emphasise prevention and rehabilitation or social inclusion as key objectives. Equally, we can see clear connections between fears about the damaging effects of incarceration and repeated attempts to assert the value of 'alternatives to custody' and 'community justice' which are still evident in the contemporary era.

It has been suggested by some that recent developments have, indeed, captured this spirit in ways that are distinctive and which may, finally, lead to successful outcomes:

> the 'third way' neo-communitarian crime-control strategy of New Labour with its theoretical roots in left realism is a legitimate long-term strategy for both understanding crime and criminal behaviour in all its many manifestations and for the development of flexible strategies for dealing with a complex and ambiguous social problem. (Hopkins Burke 2008: 239)

Hopkins Burke goes on to suggest that such strategies are grounded in a form of 'contemporary new-liberalism' that seeks to reconcile the 'rights and responsibilities' of all those involved with or affected by crime. On the other hand, he also acknowledges 'legitimate concerns' that 'the rigour' of recent reforms may have pushed things 'too far' (p. 239). We are reminded here of earlier warnings about the 'unintended consequences' of well-intentioned reforms (Thorpe et al. 1980). In order to pursue this question, it will now be helpful to consider in more detail the achievements and consequences of the kind of reforms 'from within' associated with this line of ameliorative argument and policy development, in order to determine whether or not they can lead to positive change or simply more of the same.

The reform(ist) agenda

Reform strategies in youth justice tend to share a number of characteristics and these have been manifested again quite recently in an aspirational document from the Institute for Public Policy Research (Farrington-Douglas and Durante 2009). Youth crime is reported to be an 'unsolved problem' (p. 4), and a set of conventional assumptions (see Chapter 3) is utilised to support this assertion. Youth crime is construed as a minority pursuit, for example, with only a few individuals being responsible for the most sustained and harmful forms of delinquent behaviour (see Graham and Bowling 1995). Public fear of crime is believed to be continually on the rise and this is complemented by a one-sided media perspective which creates a climate in favour of 'tough' and dramatic measures to 'tackle' wrongdoing. Not only is youth offending disproportionately carried out by certain young people, it is also concentrated in particular communities – specifically 'disadvantaged areas' (Farrington-Douglas and Durante 2009: 4). Youth crime is thus to be taken as a 'real' and problematic phenomenon (Lea and Young 1984), but one which is misunderstood, misconstrued, and thus inappropriately addressed. Better understanding should therefore lead to better outcomes for all.

At present, however, it is clear that the 'current policy is not working' (Farrington-Douglas and Durante 2009: 4). In particular, 'coercive' and target-driven intervention strategies have proved to be counter-productive, drawing more minor and early offenders into the formal justice system (a scenario which is peculiarly reminiscent of the position at the start of the 1980s; see Morris and Giller 1987). Increasing 'numbers are processed through police stations and courts' and more young people are ending up 'in custody' (p. 4). Once again, and just as in 1816, the consequences are of no benefit:

> This process is known to have some perverse effects. Arresting young people does not tend to stop them reoffending – in fact the reverse may be the case – and putting children in prison can be very damaging. (Farrington-Douglas and Durante 2009: 4)

Equally perversely, the intensification of the formal response to young people's misdemeanours is not matched by a reduction in public concern but rather an increase in levels of fear, which seems to be justified in light of the punitive actions taken. The consequence is, of course, an increasing clamour for yet more certain and extreme measures for dealing with the problem.

If we were to take a historical view, though, we might not feel that this kind of cyclical process is anything new. Pearson's well known (1983) text on the recurrent (albeit shifting) patterns of public concern and moral panic – focused on demonised sections of the population – has captured this dynamic particularly well. Popular opinion seems to be constantly primed to react to one or another contemporary outrage and this is a project in which the media always seem ready to act as willing accomplices. The parallel of this recurrent pattern within the justice system is a process of action-reaction driven by what Cohen (1985: 19) has described as 'the "we blew it" version of history'. This professional and intellectual perspective on the process of development and reform in the justice system is described by Cohen as highly 'ambivalent', being both committed to the idea of progressive reform and yet conscious that the 'record is not just one of good intentions going wrong now and then, but of continual and disastrous failure' (p. 19). While this model of history and change does not question the underlying ideas and objectives of reform efforts, it does recognise that serious and repeated failures are often evident and that new unanticipated problems may arise as a consequence of 'progress'. This construction of change and adaptation clearly echoes that of Beck (1992), who similarly suggests that the scientists and technocrats of the current era have become increasingly aware of the limitations of their own achievements and their potentially counterproductive effects.

The example Cohen draws upon to exemplify this point is that of the asylums (Rothman 1980), which were originally established as an 'alternative' to more punitive penal settings and over the course of time 'degenerated into mere custodial institutions' (Cohen 1985: 20). What this prompted, though, was a new era of reform which sought once again to humanise the interventions on offer. Thus, in the early years of the twentieth century:

> a new wave of reform energy devoted itself to the search for alternatives, administrative flexibility, discretion, a greater choice of dispositions. The ideal of individual treatment, the case-by-case method and the entry of psychiatric doctrines produced a whole series of innovations – attempts to humanize the prison, probation and parole, indeterminate sentencing, the juvenile court ... (Cohen 1985: 20)

But what happened subsequently did not meet expectations. There was little observable change in the usage of institutional regimes and the new programmes developed became 'supplements, not alternatives', so that the system itself became more pervasive – and interventions more 'arbitrary' – despite the absence of any convincing evidence of their efficacy. As Cohen puts it, yet again 'failure and persistence went hand in hand'; the belief was sustained that it would be possible to get things right in the end. Despite the repeated evidence of failure associated with the 'reform enterprise', its fundamental aims and objectives do not come into question. Reformers continue to believe that it is possible to learn from the errors of our ways, and to adapt accordingly. A conscious and reflexive model of progress retains the capacity for creative and positive developments: 'A new type of liberalism unencumbered by the naïve optimism of its historical predecessors still allows room for manoeuvre. Things can still be improved' (Cohen 1985: 21).

Returning to the IPPR report mentioned earlier, we find that exactly this construction is placed on the 'wrong turns' taken by New Labour over its period in office. Despite the evidence of increased use of custody, and harmful outcomes for young people (Chapter 7), we are reassured that:

> behind Labour's drives for toughness a more effective, more progressive strand to its youth offending policy can clearly be seen and may be gaining ground. The 1998 reforms aimed to put prevention at the heart of youth justice. The Government has also recognised that some of its tough targets were not working, and changed them. Giving the Department for Children, Schools and Families responsibility for youth justice jointly with the Ministry of Justice helped to place the welfare of young people more firmly on the youth justice agenda. The Children's Plan contained a range of measures to help young people avoid crime, including a new focus on positive, structured activities. The Youth Crime Action Plan toned down the rhetoric, and introduced a range of helpful measures to improve the system. (Farrington-Douglas and Durante 2009: 4)

These apparently hopeful signs suggested to the authors of this report that 'a new moment' for progressive change might have been reached.

What is interesting about the implicit strategy incorporated in this account is that it essentially reasserts a series of aspirations which have long featured in the liberal reform agenda, dating back to the beginning of the twentieth century at least, as we saw earlier. Four key elements of a progressive strategy are identified, seemingly: prevention, welfare, constructive activities (social inclusion), and system modification.

These strands of reform are also evident in an earlier IPPR report which recommended a better application of measures that would 'work' (presumably in the sense of preventing offending) 'and ... a more welfare-oriented approach' (Margo and Stevens 2008: 69). This report, too, argues that the existing framework and aspirations of public policy are consistent with an effective and progressive approach to youth offending, claiming that current practice is wasteful and misdirected but not beyond redemption (p. 58). Importantly, the authors argue, we should not 'ignore' behaviour which is socially unacceptable or breaches consensual norms; rather, we should address such behaviour 'in context' – echoing an earlier aspiration to 'tackle' both crime and its causes (Blair 1993)! However, we should not assume either that it is public opinion or the media which will set limits to what can be achieved: reforms have to be 'sold' effectively, and if so, may even be able to change 'the public discourse on youth crime in the UK' (Margo and Stevens 2008: 57). The reform agenda is thus capable of seeking out the middle ground and building on an implicit consensus about the objectives and essential characteristics of an effective youth justice system.

Indeed, it seems almost possible to conclude that the problems encountered historically are not fundamental flaws or unresolvable contradictions, but rather inadequacies in the form and content of implementation measures. Perhaps we have simply been hamstrung by our incomplete knowledge of 'what works' (Hopkins Burke 2008: 181) or perhaps by an undue sensitivity to what we believe to be intractable punitive public attitudes. In fact, it would seem that there is a considerable degree of overlap between popular aspirations and progressive approaches to youth justice: 'there is a good deal of support for prevention' (Allen 2005: 33) and in addition this is backed up by 'scepticism about prison', a 'desire for better alternatives', and 'support for treating rather than punishing underlying problems' (p. 34). With the right tools and appropriate resources, it remains possible to achieve these objectives:

> It requires careful and intelligent assessment of the factors relating to the offence and the offender and a balanced judgement about the best measures to impose ... The answer [to shortfalls] is surely to expand ... services ... (Allen 2005: 33)

Despite his generally critical tone, Pitts (2003) also argues that a reformed youth justice system is capable of having a 'constructive' impact. It clearly cannot be a major driver for social and economic change which would affect the 'nature, level and distribution of youth crime' (p. 97), but by utilising the resources of youth justice practitioners alongside 'high-quality educational, health, housing and welfare provision' it may be possible to change the lives of some of the young people who get 'involved in crime', he suggests. It is not the capabilities or objectives of youth justice services that are the problem, but rather it is the way in which they are 'undermined by the politicization of youth crime'. Similarly to Allen, Pitts blames populism for derailing many good intentions in youth justice. In order to achieve positive change then, it is important to marshal the forces of reform so that they come into alignment and are adapted to a common approach. There is a shared view of the scale and complexity of the task and a conscious awareness of the recurrent dangers of strategic and operational wrong turns. But, even the Youth Justice Board could become a vehicle for positive change, if the subject could be 'de-politicised' (Hopkins Burke 2008: 244).

Interestingly and ironically, perhaps, this kind of assumption sits well with political interests who from the standpoint of the present seek to present recent achievements in youth justice as a catalogue of serious failures. This was the rhetoric of New Labour immediately prior to and on becoming the ruling party, heralding a 'root and branch reform of the youth justice system' (Straw 1997). It was argued, for instance, that the shift to a pre-emptive strategy of 'preventing youth offending' represented a new proactive ethos, clearly at odds with previous reactive forms of intervention which were not geared towards anticipating crime at source. Taken to its logical conclusion, this approach would therefore necessitate an entirely novel framework of services and professional attributes. The emphasis would be on predictive assessment skills and the capacity to deliver reintegrative programmes which would both inhibit young people's propensity to offend and offer them realistic and positive alternative options.

The logic and rhetoric of 'reform' are thus deeply embedded in thought and practice within youth justice. This sits well with the notion of 'reflexive modernity' (Beck et al. 1994) which suggests that human history is a matter of 'trial and error', but that equally we are capable of learning from immediate past mistakes and getting things better (if not right) next time. This is perhaps why certain modes of thinking and variations in practice appear to be strangely familiar when we encounter them in a new guise or under a new name. As we shall see, this is epitomised in the way in which the aspiration for effective 'alternatives to custody' continually re-emerges – each time in a different form, but with familiar characteristics as well, such as the insistence on being 'credible' to the courts.

Reform: strategies and practice

Having considered the logic and trajectory of reformism, we will now move on to reflect on its direct manifestations and the nature of the practices associated with this perspective on change. If there is a recurrent pattern evident in repeated attempts to change youth justice for the better, it can perhaps be represented as a kind of 'sidestepping' movement, whereby the fundamental pillars of support for the system itself are not brought into question, but rather dodged and negotiated. Thus, innovations and new developments are effectively located within the prevailing assumptions and ideologies of criminal justice and do not (cannot?) challenge it directly. The sentencing tariff, the individualisation of interventions, notions of personal responsibility, models of blame and retribution, and the adversarial logic of control all appear to be untouched by the kind of tactics and models of practice advocated by proponents of reform. This is perhaps quite well illustrated by reference to some of the change strategies pursued under this guise, including: promoting prevention/early intervention; offering 'alternatives to custody'; and reframing welfare.

Early intervention/preventive measures

As with other elements of the reformist project, early preventive initiatives appear to display a number of recurrent features. Thus, Intermediate Treatment was developed in the UK in the late 1960s as a model of practice directed at children 'at risk' (Cohen 1985: 60). IT projects were typically developed to include a portfolio of activities, groupwork and broadly educational opportunities, aimed at children whose status was uncertain and who might become clients of either the care or justice systems.

Although IT tended to conflate welfare needs and the risk of offending in ways which are less clear cut in the present day, its aims were quite familiar, being to avoid the possibility of 'institutionalisation' and promote 'normal' forms of upbringing and re-integration into the mainstream of community life. For Cohen, though, it is especially significant that the question of delinquent

157

behaviour was not addressed squarely by such programmes; in fact 'There is a deliberate attempt here to evade the question of whether a rule has actually been broken' (Cohen 1985: 60). The policy climate of the time (the 1960s) was one in which the distinction between the 'deprived' and the 'depraved' was minimised, in the context of a model of 'prevention' based on the assumption that addressing welfare needs would necessarily reduce the likelihood of offending, too. This, though, could be seen as both a conceptual and material weakness:

> The ideology of community treatment and the preventive thrust of the diversion strategy allows for an altogether facile evasion of the delinquent/non-delinquent distinction. (Cohen 1985: 60)

As a result, preventive initiatives such as IT were not faced with the challenge of directly competing with conventional ideologies of punishment and just desserts. The practical consequence of this was that many of the children and young people recruited to IT programmes 'were not subject to any court order at all' (p. 61), leading to the widely observed phenomenon of 'net widening' which has been of repeated concern to many of those involved in youth justice over the years.

More recent attempts to develop preventive programmes have also sought to carve out a space for non-punitive interventions with young people 'at risk', seeking to provide positive opportunities in place of the machinery of surveillance and control. Once again, the language of 'care' and 'control' is blurred, as in the case of the Youth Inclusion and Support Programme (YISP). The YISP is targeted at children and young people from 8–13, thus pre-dating the age of criminal responsibility in some cases. Referral criteria include problem behaviour, but extend beyond this into other aspects of a child's circumstances ('risk factors'), and interventions target a range of welfare needs alongside behaviour management. Typically, YISPs will come under the aegis of 'multi-agency' management structures and will thus achieve the same kind of slippage effect as that alluded to by Cohen (1985: 61) previously: 'Crime and delinquency nets thus not only become blurred in themselves but get tangled up with other welfare, treatment and control nets'. As in its previous manifestation, it seems that 'prevention' measures are not sufficiently ideologically robust in themselves as to be able to operate free of the shadow of the justice system. They operate on or before its fringes, unable to displace either its logic of control or its practices of behaviour management and scrutiny. And equally – where 'prevention' fails – young people come to be increasingly exposed to more rigorous and repressive measures of intervention, having demonstrably 'failed' to make use of the opportunities of reintegration or 'normalisation' offered by way of early intervention programmes. Indeed, and ironically, such outcomes tend to confirm that not only are they increasingly incorrigible as individuals, but also that the prevention project itself is of only limited value, given its visible lack of success in this respect.

Alternatives to custody

As with early prevention, the concept of 'alternatives to custody' has a well-established history and there have been a number of attempts to develop models of practice which will supplant the use of incarceration under this kind of heading. In fact, one of the most comprehensive initiatives of this kind was inspired by a recognition of the earlier shortcomings of Intermediate Treatment. This became 'Intensive Intermediate Treatment' (IIT) in the 1980s, being repositioned to offer courts an option which would be a more 'demanding' community-based measure than had previously been available (Smith, D. 1999). Rather than seek to challenge the sentencing tariff, practitioners and policy makers sought to locate this form of intervention precisely at the point where courts would be likely to consider sending young people to custody. As such, the kind of interventions to be offered in the form of IIT would need to be realistic and 'credible' (Smith, R. 2007). They should, to an extent, incorporate the punitive logic of the secure regimes they sought to displace:

> to be seen by sentencers as suitable ... community corrections have to incorporate appropriate degrees of control, and offer the promise of effectiveness in stopping the delinquent behaviour. (Hudson 1987: 153)

The programmes introduced in the 1980s, often as part of a specific government-funded initiative (Department of Health and Social Security 1983), typically included components such as 'tracking', behaviour management exercises, and sometimes community service. More explicit and active use would be made of 'breach' procedures for a failure to comply as well (Haines and Drakeford 1998; Smith, R. 2007: 10).

At the time – and somewhat against the expectations of its critics (Muncie 2009: 290), this strategy appeared to pay off, in that it was associated with a considerable reduction in the numbers and proportion of young offenders sentenced to custody:

> In 1983, a total of 13,500 14 to 17 year old males were sentenced to immediate custody for indictable offences compared to 3,300 in 1993. This represented a fall from some 15 per cent of all court dispositions to 11 per cent. (Muncie 2009: 291)

Logically, then, it seemed to make good sense to attempt to revitalise this idea as custody rates increased again towards the turn of the century and as the Youth Justice Board began to seek ways of reducing this renewed reliance on locking up young people. It seemed that substantial and demanding community-based programmes could meet perceived public expectations of a punitive response to youth crime while also keeping offenders out of custody (Moore 2004) and so the Intensive Supervision and Surveillance Programme was launched in 2001 (Home Office 2001). Once again, this initiative seemed to be the product of an exercise in managing ambiguity, whereby the expectations of both an allegedly retributive public and a more progressive practitioner community could be satisfied, without perhaps 'disturbing the surface' of a predominantly punitive consensus. As far as its content went the ISSP included little of substance over and above its predecessor, IIT, except perhaps the inclusion of electronic means of surveillance which had not been available in a reliable form twenty years previously (Muncie 2009: 340).

In fact, the ISSP failed fairly spectacularly on all counts, acting neither as a true alternative to custody nor as an effective means of preventing further offending (Gray *et al.* 2007; Smith, R. 2007). And as with 'failed' preventive measures, this evidence only contributes to and compounds the prevailing assumption that liberalising measures of this kind are ineffective as a means of addressing youth offending. By contrast, custody at least offers the comparative certainty of containment for a set period of time.

Reasserting 'welfare'

Despite its history, and its periodic discreditation (see Schur 1973; Thorpe *et al.* 1980; Hudson 1987, for example), the liberal reform perspective retains a degree of fascination with the idea of reinserting welfare principles into the operation of the youth justice system. Strategic attempts to promote a 'needs-led' agenda can be observed in both the minutiae of the justice process and in the broad framing of the system as a whole.

Thus, in the former category, the incorporation of the 'vulnerability' principle into National Standards for Youth Justice (Youth Justice Board 2005) is one such measure. Where young people appear to be at risk of serious harm (or of perpetrating it) provision is made for specific measures to address these needs, with a view to enabling suitable non-custodial provision to be made available where necessary, in place of secure remands or sentences to custody. The need for such measures might appear compelling given the continuing evidence of substantial harm and the death of young people in secure settings (Goldson and Coles 2005). In practice, this appears to have been an ineffective and misconceived form of safeguard which has manifestly failed to protect a number of young people, such as Joseph Scholes, towards whom it would seem to have been intentionally geared (Goldson and Coles 2005: 63).

In broader systemic terms, it is of some significance that approaches to youth justice appear to be divergent within the UK, with Wales notably maintaining a much stronger 'welfare' orientation in policy and practice than England despite their common legislative framework and procedures. It has been argued, for instance, that there is evidence in Wales that 'a distinctive welfarist culture' (Field 2007: 328) is in place which distinguishes it from the overall pattern of youth justice delivery in England (Cross *et al.* 2003). In Wales, it is suggested, there is a greater readiness to take a 'children first' approach, despite the emergence of 'tangible organisational pressures on YOT workers to ... embrace a conflicting construction of young people as "offenders first" ' (Cross *et al.* 2003: 157).

Similar evidence of a continuing espousal of welfare principles has emerged from other studies in Wales, where it seems that both practitioners and sentencers have sustained a commitment to taking young people's needs seriously in the criminal process despite the changing legal and political emphasis following the reforms initiated in 1998 by New Labour. Field (2007: 328) does, however, acknowledge that the availability of evidence of whether or not 'welfare' remains central may well depend to some extent on the analytical approach taken. 'Practice cultures' may convey a rather different impression from analyses of 'political and media discourses' and, indeed, from systemic overviews; at ground level, England and Wales may not be so different after all (Burnett and Appleton 2004). As we have observed, too, it is not unknown for a commitment to meeting the welfare needs of children to be associated with 'objective outcomes that entail more constraint in the community and high custody rates' (Field 2007: 327); the possibility of 'unintended consequences' remains strong:

> analysis of the practice cultures of the 'new' youth justice suggests that a desire to engage constructively with the welfare problems that may underpin offending has not been displaced by dominant 'tough' punitive attitudes. But that is not to say that the belief in earlier and greater intervention will not produce outcomes that, in the end, place greater constraints on liberty for the same offending. (Field 2007: 327)

These three approaches to the pursuit of liberal reform in youth justice have, over time, been able to demonstrate variable degrees of success, as with the inroads achieved by 'alternatives to custody' during the 1980s and (possibly) with the influence of 'welfarism' in Wales in the present. However, these successes seem to be fragile and often unsustainable in the long run. Of course, the possible explanations for these rather discouraging outcomes do vary; it may be that it is just a matter of the ineffective implementation of fundamentally sound ideas, or, alternatively, that we must also consider the possibility that efforts to reform the system 'from within' are bound to fail, given the contextual factors which are endemic to youth justice, such as the 'logic of control' (Cohen 1985).

The limits of reform?

As we have seen, there is a well-established tradition of reform within youth justice, which is essentially pragmatic and has as its objective the moderation of punitive attitudes and practices rather than their abolition. Operating under the shadow of prevailing ideologies of individualised responsibility, moral failure, retribution, and control, modifications in the system are sought which create exceptions and identify possible spaces for alternative forms of practice which are more child/young person friendly. The logic behind this kind of positioning is, however, essentially defensive and reactive, conceding the central legitimacy of the punitive ethos and its associated modalities of blame, personal accountability, and techniques of control.

The challenge of negotiating a legitimate space in what is essentially hostile terrain has resulted in a number of 'accommodations' which have been associated with unintended consequences of various kinds. The argument here is that these are not, primarily, signs of implementation failure, but are, rather, predictable consequences of the tactical decisions which underlie such attempts at reform. In some instances, such as the early intervention programmes of recent years, it may well be the case that their delivery does not coincide clearly with their intended purposes, but their problems extend well beyond localised concerns about the content and outcomes of specific activities. We need therefore to distinguish between practical shortcomings at the point of delivery, on the one hand, and systemic failings, on the other, which arise from the structural and ideological constraints that frame specific reform initiatives. These deficiencies may be linked, but they are also quite clearly different in nature and in their implications and consequences.

The relationship between material consequences and conceptual problems has been evident for some time. Thorpe *et al.* (1980: 22) first drew attention to the effects of 'vertical integration'. Not only did the scope and impact of the combined 'care' and 'justice' systems expand dramatically over the previous decade, but far from being divided along the lines of 'welfare' and 'justice' these two systems were also integrated theoretically and ideologically. Pre-figuring much of the contemporary landscape of early intervention and risk management, they made the following observation:

> (... with certain qualifications) the new system has been deployed with the younger age groups and has adopted a 'preventive' policy. The concept of children 'at risk' is invoked in the identification of a new population for whom social work intervention is appropriate prior to confrontation with the courts. Once such children begin to appear in court, however, they are fairly rapidly phased into the penal system .... It is tempting to argue ... that if social work has already 'failed' ... it is therefore time to try something new and different. Hence there is a form of collusion: the agreement between magistrate and social worker that it is now necessary to remove the child from home .... Hence, too, the emergence of concepts like 'the need for structure' .... (Thorpe *et al.* 1980: 23)

Thus, it is suggested, the very logic of early prevention enables the system to 'extend its scope' and its range of 'intervention and surveillance'. Preventive measures themselves come to act as a 'feeder mechanism' for the formal justice system and eventually, custody. Others, too, have suggested that this process of mutual reinforcement has identifiable consequences for practice and outcomes within youth justice: 'care offenders ... appear to have an accelerated passage through the justice system when compared to young people who do not have such a background', despite having 'less "delinquent" ' characteristics (Haines and Drakeford 1998: 135).

Extending the argument further, Thorpe *et al.* (1980: 100; original emphasis) have suggested that the basis for the conflation of apparently distinct ideas, practices, objectives, and outcomes was a series of common assumptions shared by the differing – and ostensibly alternative – models of intervention: 'Both "treatment" and "punishment" seek to *transform* the *individual* in *anticipation* of his [sic] future actions'. Crucially, both models adopt an individualised approach to young people, their behaviour, and how to deal with it. Thus wider contextual factors and structural influences are discounted as irrelevant either to the task of explaining offending or responding to it. This omission in turn probably contributes to the unrealistic expectations held about most interventions and their 'transformational' effects. The 'attempt to "change an offender's character, habits or behaviour patterns", is common' to both punitive and rehabilitative intervention strategies (p. 100). A failure to respond, though, in the form of re-offending is held to be due to the young person's underlying shortcomings, despite the persistent lack of evidence to show that any form 'of intervention is any more effective than another' (p. 101). If there are inadequacies in the services provided, these are likely to be viewed as technical ('we blew it') and capable of resolution without disturbing the underlying rationale for intervention. However, the fear raised by some is that this will simply lead to an intensification and extension of the mechanisms of control, in the guise of prevention and early intervention (Austin and Krisberg 2002).

'Preventive' measures, then, do not disturb the underlying logic of the justice system, but neither do those reforms which seek to insert alternative options into the portfolio of disposals at the threshold to custody. Indeed, we are acutely aware of the promotional language utilised by such initiatives, which incorporates the promise of being similarly 'tough' as custody, of containing young people, of monitoring their activities, and of imposing demanding corrective programmes on them. It has been observed previously that the re-alignment of Intermediate Treatment during the 1980s was associated with a conscious effort to 're-articulate IT away from a more welfare-oriented youth service provision into an alternative to custody' (Haines and Drakeford 1998: 47).

This was observed also to be replicated in the re-orientation of social services departments' policies and strategies for working with young offenders. Most ceased to prioritise 'prevention' and began to incorporate a new model which 'strongly reflected anti-custody thinking' (Haines and Drakeford 1998: 53). Earlier concerns to deliver broad-based, needs-led prevention programmes were effectively airbrushed out of the picture, in some cases to the extent that 'preventive work ... may not be called prevention' (p. 52). Most social services departments at the time (the mid to late 1980s) were found to be operating this kind of model within youth justice – if not exclusively – and thus appeared to have contributed to the emergence of a 'new orthodoxy' (p. 53). Intermediate Treatment was now to be targeted at 'those at serious risk of custody/residential care' (p. 52) and programmes would be 'offence-focused, not needs-focused'. In order to guard against net-widening, these programmes would only be available for those young offenders liable to face a custodial sentence and would not be confused with welfare provision, to which some participants would have a parallel entitlement. While this agenda was frequently driven by an aspiration to reduce the use of custody and promote 'diversion', it did so primarily by seeking to replicate the mode of thought and intervention style epitomised by custodial settings themselves. This was believed to help both with 'marketing' these schemes to potentially sceptical sentencers in the courts and with clarifying the aims and objectives of IT. In operational terms, then, programmes would be concerned with young people's behaviour and attitudes and work with them would be geared to achieving demonstrable changes in these aspects, with no reference to needs or personal problems (certainly not in their own right). Problematically, though, this was not just a tactical shift, but also effectively downgraded 'welfare' as a consideration – in the context of young people's offending certainly, but possibly more widely too. In other words, changes in practice pragmatically designed to achieve a progressive outcome could not easily be distinguished from changes in thinking that could well (and arguably have) lead to retrograde steps too:

> The ascendancy of new orthodoxy thinking in the 1980s led many to believe that it represented the triumph of *justice* over *welfare*. (Haines and Drakeford 1998: 53; original emphasis)

While it is acknowledged that not all commentators took this view (see Pratt 1989, for instance), Haines and Drakeford insist that the changes of this era were largely driven by a particular interpretation of the 'justice model' (p. 58), grounded in the use of the available machinery of the justice system to 'avoid custody' wherever possible. This, indeed, was what was achieved to a large extent at the time; there was a very sharp 'decline in the use of custody' between 1980 and 1990 (p. 58).

Ironically, though, the short- and medium-term successes of the 1980s may have been at least partly based on a rationale which opened the way for more repressive interventions in the succeeding years. It is not simply at the point of 'alternatives to custody' that the shape of interventions has changed, for instance, and Haines and Drakeford's conclusion in this respect still rings true:

> the nature of direct work with young people on Supervision Orders has tended to be limited to work that deals directly with offending behaviour; and this has primarily been interpreted very narrowly. There has been little explicit recognition that offending behaviour can be related to social, family or material circumstances (as these have a link into the welfare continuum). (Haines and Drakeford 1998: 66)

Somewhat depressingly, they comment further that 'Anyone experienced in working with young people will be familiar with the sterility of these limited methods'! The progressive weakening of 'welfare' as a strand of policy and practice in youth justice has continued and if anything intensified. Contemporary arguments for 'reform', even at the pre-offending stage, are conspicuously couched in terms of the need to confront and change what young people *do*, rather than their social or personal circumstances:

> What each district needs to develop is a spectrum of services and interventions to tackle ASB [Anti-social Behaviour] at different stages:
>
> - work to prevent crime and ASB occurring in the first place by addressing risk factors;
> - intervention at the early stages of ASB to prevent continuation and escalation;

- intervention at the serious and/or persistent stage. (Mayfield and Mills 2008: 82)

Such attempts to modify the prevailing mood of punitive populism are fraught with difficulty in a climate where 'government lacks any social or political capacity of its own' and works solely within a 'framework of social control', it is argued (Waiton 2008: 354). Even attempts to offer supportive services tend to be couched in the language of compulsion and compliance. The 'voluntary' Acceptable Behaviour Contract (ABC) and the Individual Support Order (ISO) have clearly incorporated this kind of terminology. Thus, for example, where a young person is subject to an Anti-social Behaviour Order the court can also make an ISO, which requires him/her to make use of services to help change her/his behaviour, such as provision to address substance misuse, anger management, or counselling. And as a result, the acceptance of 'help' becomes mandatory, in effect.

Even for those who have taken a positive view of some aspects of change in government policy under New Labour, these moves are problematic: 'we currently define and treat too much misbehaviour by young people as a crime to be punished rather than a problem to be solved' (Allen 2007: 25). These outcomes were not accidental, however, and crucially they depended for their legitimation on a willingness to detach 'welfare' considerations from the justice process in the interests of clarity, consistency, and fairness. It is difficult to accept the argument that different 'logics' appear to apply at different points in the system and that progressive developments can sit comfortably alongside more repressive measures without being compromised in some way. Crawford and Newburn (2003), for instance, have argued that 'the referral order and youth offender panel ... hold real promise' for a more inclusive, 'constructive' and 'participative' approach to young people's crimes (p. 237), even during an increasingly interventionist and controlling phase of youth justice policy in general. Yet the very limited scope for referral orders to operate within the justice system – situated firmly within the sentencing tariff and involving programmes which are prescriptive, offence-oriented, and conditional – suggests that they, too, however progressive and 'restorative' their packaging are heavily infused with the penal logic that pervades the wiser youth justice arena. This, indeed, seems to provide further support for the argument that the reformist pursuit of compromise within a hostile climate may be highly problematic and will probably result in counter-productive outcomes.

Beyond compromise, beyond 'reform'

The aim of this chapter has really been to offer a strong warning about 'supping with the devil'. There has been a recurrent mood of optimism among those who have promoted and been involved with attempts to 'reform' youth justice, but experience has shown that such aspirations have rarely come to fruition and there are very often 'unintended consequences' for which young people themselves will pay a heavy price. This is not because of an implementation failure or poor planning, although these may both be in evidence; it is rather because the reform project itself is fundamentally compromised. Even when successes have been achieved these have been impossible to sustain and this is at least partly because of the ideological adjustments necessary. The 'taken for granted' nature of prevailing assumptions and routinised practices within criminal justice act as a kind of default setting to which the system reverts when the going gets tough. Punishment becomes the symbolic benchmark against which alternative forms of intervention are judged and the spectre of 'Safari boy' periodically reappears to stalk our good intentions (*Independent*, 24 September 1994; *Daily Telegraph*, 21 August 2001; *Daily Express*, 24 September 2009).

Seeking to make piecemeal changes from within and make these stick may simply be an unachievable goal given the context. The prevailing discourse of due process, individualised responsibility, behavioural management, and control may just be too pervasive to allow for creative and progressive developments to take place.

Muncie (2009: 383) argues that we should not overlook the 'centrality' of 'cultural contingency and local actors' in mediating and delivering overarching national and global projects, but that their very locality and provisional nature suggest that progressive achievements are fragile exceptions rather than signposts towards a far-reaching radical agenda.

Importantly, though, Munice also cautions against the possibilities of lapsing into a mood of nihilism or 'radical pessimism':

> The 'catastrophic' images raised by some neo-liberal readings of youth governance may help us to identify significant macro social changes, but are less attuned to resistance to change, to contradictions within neo-liberalism ... to the inherent instability of neo-liberal strategies and to the simultaneous emergence of other competing transformational tendencies .... (Muncie 2009: 383)

In setting out the conceptual and structural limits to reform (or more correctly, reformism) the aim is not to generate a mood of despair or a sense that change is impossible. Rather, it is to suggest that we should be more and not less ambitious and should seek change which does aspire to 'transformation', because this is more likely to be better suited to the needs, experiences, and aspirations of young people themselves. We have seen in previous chapters that there is a substantial gulf between their lives and circumstances, on the one hand (see Chapter 1), and the ways in which they are stereotyped and dealt with by the justice system, on the other (see Chapter 7). What we should be seeking is not to modify this system, or simply to limit the damage caused, but rather to promote forms of practice and policy change which will acknowledge, take account of, and respond positively to young people in light of their backgrounds and experience.

It is unfortunate that this project has to be undertaken in an era when there is 'an uneasy relation, if not distinct fracture, between the correctionalist priorities that typify youth justice policy and the more inclusive and benign rationales that' are clearly evident in other aspects of policy directed towards children (Goldson and Muncie 2006: 203). However, as we are reminded, social relations and political forces are in a state of constant flux – 'youth justice systems are dynamic and ever-changing sites of contestation and change' (p. 204). The task in front of us, therefore, is to seek to map out the direction and possibilities for change which are truly 'progressive' and do not accept externally imposed ideological and material constraints.

Chapter 9

The road to justice:
radical alternatives

The art of the possible?

The previous chapter sought to offer a critical appraisal of the achievements and limitations of attempts to promote liberal reforms of youth justice. This is not to suggest that such reforms have made no difference, indeed in some cases they have clearly resulted in beneficial outcomes. However, they also remain susceptible to changes in the prevailing mood and the machinery of criminal justice. The adoption of the language of due process and just desserts, for instance, provides little protection against the compression of the sentencing tariff or the realignment of 'alternatives to custody'. Equally, the dispersal of punitive practices throughout the spectrum of disposals cannot easily be challenged in light of conventional wisdom about individual responsibility and a need for discipline. Thus the limits to reform 'from within' are endemic and certain. For every reduction in the use of custody, or the extension of a bail entitlement, there is likely to be an equal and opposite increase in measures of control. Positive change under such circumstances can only ever be regarded as provisional and is always susceptible to 'knee jerk' reactions from policy makers, the media, law enforcement agencies, or the judiciary.

We should not conclude from this, however, that the ethos of accountability, risk management, and behaviour control is all-pervasive, or that it is impossible to do more than speculate in theoretical terms about modes of practice which are genuinely 'just' and productive for young people and the wider community. The intention at this point is to move on to illustrate some of these possibilities, drawing on evidence from practice as far as possible and demonstrating how these examples are able to offer some insight into the ways in which youth justice could be different, in principle and purpose as well as in its direct manifestation in the operational arena.

In what follows, I shall also seek to distinguish between 'weak' and 'strong' forms of alternative models of practice in recognition that their relationship with conventional models of intervention is sometimes problematic. This will enable us to clarify, for example, just what aspects of 'restorative practice' are capable of offering progressive possibilities, despite the acknowledged limitations of their application in contemporary contexts such as by way of the Referral Order. Similarly, we should be aware of the different ways in which models of 'diversion' operate and whether or not these are consistent with important underlying aims, such as the effective achievement of minimum intervention.

By setting out some ideas about alternative forms of youth justice practice of this kind, I hope to be able to demonstrate that these are more consistent with the substance and context of young people's lived experiences than conventional models. Notions of participation and active engagement are thus to be seen as essential elements of intervention rather than as 'rights' which are forfeited at the point where an offence is committed. The links between these models of practice and the broader context of children's/young people's rights should be made explicit and should not be made conditional on the extent to which they are or are not identified as law abiding citizens (Smith, R. 2010b).

First, though, it will be helpful to consider the important question of the scope of youth justice itself and what it should *not* do, as well as what its central focus should be. Clarity on this point is essential if we are to avoid 'criminalising' large groups of young people.

Prevention and inclusion

Abolitionist arguments (Mathiesen 1974) might advance a case for the eradication of the youth justice system altogether, but at the very least there is a strong case for ending its role in 'early prevention'. This is the point where the pernicious logic(s) of individualised accountability, behaviour management, surveillance and control, and punitive discipline spill over into the pre-criminal arena. In contemporary practice in England and Wales, young people are identified formally (by way of Anti-social Behaviour Orders) or more informally (by being classified among the most 'at risk' of offending in the locality) and are then selected for specialist treatment on the basis of their supposed criminogenic tendencies. Apart from being not very good at the prediction game these measures are unjustifiable for other reasons, as earlier studies have observed:

> to the extent that they still incorporate factors such as employment, substance abuse, educational levels and criminal records of family members ... these techniques continue to use actuarial assessments as though they were clinical assessments, that is, they are using descriptions of the characteristics of populations of offenders to protect the likelihood of reoffending of individual offenders. (Hudson 2003: 49)

This sort of anticipatory measure is problematic for other reasons, too. It is based on socially constructed assumptions about what constitutes criminal or pre-criminal behaviour and where we should look for this. We should clearly be concerned about the consequences of this kind of approach for those populations (particular ethic groups, marginalised populations and young people in general) who come under the microscope, and we should also recognise the consequences of the infusion of so-called 'preventive' activities with the discourses of criminality and 'risk' (Smith, R. 2010b).

These concerns have received some empirical support, too, albeit from Scotland which has historically been purportedly more 'welfarist' than England and Wales. However, recent changes may have modified this to some extent, thereby strengthening the basis for drawing comparable conclusions. The context is one in which the 'holistic and child-centred ethos' of Scottish youth justice 'has been gradually eroded' in favour of a strategy of 'public reassurance and community regeneration' (McAra and McVie 2007: 322). Possibly as a result of this developing trend, it was found that:

> targeted early intervention strategies, far from diminishing the number of offence referrals, are likely to widen the net of potential recipients even further. Greater numbers of children will be identified as at risk and any early hearing involvement will result in constant recycling into the system ... (McAra and McVie 2007: 337)

The 'formal' processes at play here seem to be doing no more than recruiting the 'usual suspects' and classifying them as legitimate objects of concern. The process of 'recycling' appears to continue apace, irrespective of 'whether their offending has diminished in seriousness or frequency' or whether other needs have been 'addressed'. On one level we should probably be concerned because this is visible evidence of the persistence of the phenomenon of net-widening, but in a way more seriously still it offers powerful evidence of the ideological achievements of such practices, cementing in our minds as they do a standardised image of the qualities and characters of those who are, or will become, offenders; and offering a self-referential legitimacy for the kinds of processes put in place to deal with them and contain the 'threat' they represent.

This, in short, is the key justification for pursuing the reconceptualisation of preventive early intervention and its constitutive elements. Whether we see existing practice as an arbitrary separation of 'welfare' and 'justice' (England and Wales) or a colonisation of one by the other (Scotland), the underlying argument is that it is inappropriate and unproductive to view young people 'at risk' or 'in need' through the lens of the criminal justice system. Significantly, this debate was played out once again over the introduction and implementation of the *Every Child Matters*[1] reforms and alternative models of practice appear to operate in the shape of programmes such as SureStart and other community development initiatives. In its aspirations and broad ambition, the *Every Child Matters* policy initiative appeared to offer considerable scope for a new and more inclusive approach to child welfare:

> *Every Child Matters* is, in some ways, a refreshing and radical reform in the ways public services are expected to work with children, young people and families. (Hoyle 2008: 14)

ECM was constituted in a way which set out a series of global objectives for children's well-being in positive terms and proposed a universal service framework to achieve these. Services should be integrated, child-centred, and focused on preventing harmful outcomes by promoting strengths and resilience rather than by identifying problems and addressing deficits. The origins of this policy development are held to lie in the 'model' provided by 'SureStart' (Pugh 2007). This, in turn, was seen as distinctive in that it was a generic programme of intervention aimed at children in their early years, drawing extensively on a wide range of prior research. This body of evidence:

argued for the need to bring services together to respond holistically to the needs of children and families; for the importance of reaching out to vulnerable families and making services accessible; and pointed at the value of working with vulnerable families through mainstream services. (Pugh 2007: 342)

Targeting of these programmes operated at the neighbourhood and community level (Smith, R. 2007: 45), where 'disadvantage' and social exclusion had been identified. Initiatives such as SureStart seemed initially to be aimed at improving the social circumstances of populations experiencing poverty and other forms of material disadvantage and this was a strategy which appeared to be fully in tune with the broader egalitarian intentions of government, at least for a brief period of time following the election of New Labour in 1997. Similar programmes have also been put in place elsewhere, such as in Australia (Freiberg *et al.* 2007: 229). The approach to 'prevention' undertaken under these schemes had many qualities which encouraged a broad spirit of inclusion and reducing inequality, which did not rely on singling out individuals from sections of the community deemed to be 'at risk'. Principles of participation, empowerment, and 'bottom-up' service development clearly informed the initial development of services like SureStart (Alcock 2004) and this was evident in many local projects in their approach to practice (see Potter *et al.* 2005, for example). In this sense, there appeared to be a natural convergence of interest between communities seeking access to improved resources and wishing to address their self-identified needs, and policymakers at statutory agency and government levels who were concerned with conventionally defined social problems such as unemployment, crime and 'disorganised families' (Hey and Bradford 2006: 63).

The idea that people should be involved in deciding their own priorities and having some say in how these are pursued has been influential in shaping the approach to practice taken in a wide range of local projects. There has been 'a stronger focus on what consumers want rather than what providers think they should have', including a recognition that 'children and young people should be more involved in decision-making' (Pugh 2007: 341).

These new initiatives – in the same ways as their historic predecessors such as the Community Development Projects of the 1970s – have begun to prefigure the kind of universal forms of intervention which offer a sense of positive change, owned by those who are the 'targets' of official policy. They work to the extent that they are able to deliver a transfer of resources, power and control and they also work as long as they avoid stigmatising or 'splitting off' individuals or problematised groups from the community. At the same time, however, experience shows that these gains are very often compromised and fragile. For SureStart, therefore, the 'goal posts' kept moving (Pugh 2007: 343) and other related schemes such as The Children's Fund and On Track experienced the same kind of policy slippage, becoming infused under pressure with a specific 'strong emphasis on reducing offending behaviour' (p. 344). It is these changes in focus that have critically undermined the capacity of such projects to contribute to the decriminalisation of young people and wider improvements in their lives. Indeed the language of 'prevention' is problematic in itself, in that it generates a pre-emptive concern with 'problems' and 'risk' rather than focusing more broadly on universal aspirations and broadly 'inclusive' goals: 'To target individual children and young people can be stigmatising and can become a self-fulfilling prophecy' (Pugh 2007: 350). In the context of her broadly positive analysis of recent trends towards greater investment in 'services for children' which 'increasingly' locate children within their communities and promote participation and self-directed change, Pugh still believes that there remains a need to achieve a 'paradigm shift' (p. 351). In other words, these features need to be seen as ends in themselves rather than as means towards other 'preventive' goals such as the reduction of anti-social behaviour and crime by young people. The model of practice which should be the predominant objective should be recognised as successful not if it achieves top-down targets, which as we have seen are highly suspect in any case, but in light of other achievements:

> The 'community empowerment and engagement' model on which Sure Start is based is very different from a very structured intervention targeted at specific children and families. (Pugh 2007: 352)

Community harmony and 'well-being' should be the priority rather than a reduction in official crime figures, given their limited value and unrepresentative nature.

At the threshold of the 'system': pursuing minimum intervention

While it is possible to speculate about approaches to 'youth justice' at the point of entry to the system which do not single out young people for special treatment on the basis of their actual or potential anti-social or criminal behaviour, it is important to locate such strategies within the framework of possibilities constituted by the material contexts of contemporary practice. In other words, we should seek to start from where we are and consider in more detail how radical and progressive forms of practice can (with varying degrees of difficulty) be inserted into the policies, systems, and procedures which constitute the day-to-day reality of youth justice.

These interventions impact initially on young people at the point where they are formally identified as being likely or actual offenders. Increasingly, as we have seen, this distinction has been eroded and the practices to which they become subject are equally difficult to distinguish. In this sense, reasserting the principle of 'minimum intervention' becomes an important element of progressive strategies across a range of sites where young people are problematised in some way. The idea of reducing the level and impact of intervention as far as possible draws its justification from a number of sources, specifically those concerned with preserving the 'rights' of young people and preventing an unwarranted and potentially harmful intrusion in their lives (Smith, R. 2010a). Associated with this perspective, too, is a concern to avoid 'labelling' young people and contaminating them through their contact with a system which is itself directly criminogenic (Schur 1973).

Practice informed by this kind of perspective is therefore also informed by a perceived need to de-escalate the level of intervention and to 'normalise' young people who come to the attention to the forces of law and order. I have previously (Smith, R. 2007) referred to historical examples of 'diversion', and it is clear that there remains a significant commitment to this in aspects of current practice, albeit in a far more unfavourable political and structural climate. At the time of writing, there appears to have been a substantial recent decline in the numbers of young people being formally processed by the justice system (Ministry of Justice 2010a, 2010b) – a *de facto* policy in favour of minimum intervention appears to have been reinstated, although the origins of this are not yet discernible. One prominent and knowledgeable critic, the former head of the Youth Justice Board, has claimed that the decrease in official figures relating to the number of young people who are 'first time entrants to the youth justice system' is no more than an artefact (*Guardian*, 8 January 2009). Changes in police behaviour have led to an increase in the use of various forms of 'summary justice' in his view, especially 'penalty notices for disorder' that are issued for minor acts of anti-social behaviour.

In clarifying the purpose of such devices, the then government argued that they were precisely intended to 'avoid drawing a young person further than necessary into the criminal justice system for low-level offences and anti-social behaviour' (Department for Children, Schools and Families spokeswoman, quoted in the *Guardian*, 8 January 2009). Thus, the use of penalty notices appears to have become a device by which 'something' appears to be done about youth crime and police detection rates are improved and yet young people are also 'diverted' from the criminalising effects of formal incorporation into the justice system. This sort of expedient measure offers the prospect (or perhaps the illusion) of a substantive change in the way young people are dealt with, but its very spirit of pragmatism prevents it from having any sustainable or principled impact on the construction and management of the justice process.

By contrast, there have been attempts to promote a more fundamental strategy of minimum intervention at various points in time and it is these which offer more encouragement for proponents of progressive change. Rutherford's (2002) account of recent history in youth justice suggests that the 1980s were indeed a decade of '*diversion* and *decarceration*' (p. 100; original emphasis), and that these outcomes were achieved because the principle of 'minimal intervention' was embedded 'at all stages of the process' (p. 101), with the credit for this being attributable to the aspirations and efforts of 'practitioners in statutory and voluntary agencies working at the local level' (p. 101). This, in turn, led to an explicit endorsement from government; importantly, though, it was not led or inspired by government but originated at the level of practice.

Other sources have also suggested that there are a number of international jurisdictions in which the principle of avoiding the use of the full force of the law is incorporated at the heart of the process. Thus, for example, Italy is reported to operate a system whereby 'judges seek as far as possible to deal with the offender without the need to arrive at a full trial' (Nelken 2006: 164). The offence may be declared 'irrelevant' where offences are 'trivial'; the judge may administer a 'judicial pardon' in cases where the young person is not expected to reoffend; and even in more serious cases the decision as to whether to proceed to trial can be deferred pending the outcome of a court-approved programme of intervention. Even though a custodial sentence is effectively the only option available should young people be found guilty at a 'full trial', most such sanctions are 'suspended' (p. 165). As a product of this systemic orientation towards 'tolerance', the numbers of young people ending up in custody are low and the rate of custodial sentences is about a fifth of that in England and Wales:

> The low prison numbers are in part the result of the fact that, as compared to England and Wales, many fewer young people face prosecutions and fewer still are convicted. In the 1970s less than 20,000 young people were being reported for crimes. After 1988 this number increased sharply to 45,000, but, remarkably, the number of those being prosecuted (despite this being a system of obligatory prosecution) has remained the same. (Nelken 2006: 167)

Nelken attributes Italy's distinctive – and distinctively tolerant – youth justice system to a specific configuration of social and cultural forces which places more emphasis on the family and less on formal structures and systems of control. Finland is also reputed to be a jurisdiction where a conscious commitment to pursue diversion and embed it at the heart of the youth justice system has taken root (Muncie 2009: 373).

Elsewhere, too, there is evidence of the potential gains to be achieved by the adoption of a strategic approach to the 'diversion' of young people in trouble, as in one UNICEF project in Serbia (Vujacic-Ricer and Hrncic 2007). Significantly, perhaps, this strategy was initiated in the aftermath of a period of conflict and repression within the wider community. It was recognised that to achieve change in youth justice processes a broad coalition would be needed that drew specifically on practitioner expertise and experience. This 'bottom up' approach sought to 'develop a sense of ownership over the project from the beginning' and to ensure that there was a common commitment to the aim of 'bringing about change for children in their communities' (p. 2). Although this initiative is viewed as part of a larger programme designed to institutionalise models of restorative justice, a rights-based approach to minimum intervention is at the core of the strategy, supported by new legislation from 2006 which established a legal basis for diversion.

These diverse models of practice grounded in the principle of limiting the role of the formal justice system seem to share a number of key features. There appears to be a groundswell of support at the level of local practitioners and institutions, for instance; there is a clear sense of a systemic strategy; an acknowledgement of children's distinctive rights is important; and, there is usually a pro-active approach to consensus building and the promotion of a child-centred approach.

As we know from experience in England and Wales, even a comprehensive approach to a diversionary strategy of this kind will not guarantee continuing success, but the important point here is to identify those components which are essential if minimum intervention is to stand any chance of being delivered consistently in practice. It cannot, for example, be restricted to one stage in the criminal justice process, as occurs with Reprimands/Final Warnings, but it must be seen as a principle which infuses all aspects of intervention. As Stout (2006) has observed, in reviewing developments in South Africa, there are considerable risks in allowing diversion to become a feature of a 'bifurcated' youth justice system, only being applicable in practice to those at early stages of the process and in relation to minor offences. This appears to be in stark contrast to the Italian model which allows for diversionary practices in respect of serious matters.

Minimum intervention must also be seen as an end in itself, rather than as a supplementary means of achieving other aims, such as enhanced welfare interventions or models of restorative justice. The absence of principle as much as anything else may have accounted for Rod Morgan's (former chair of the YJB) angry criticisms of the 'smoke and mirror' exercise which reputedly lay behind the increases in diversion rates reported by official sources in 2008 (*Guardian*, 8 January 2009).

Community justice: keeping it local?

Aside from the principles of universal prevention and minimum intervention which have already been introduced, it will also be helpful to consider those alternative models of youth justice which are grounded in 'communities' rather than institutionally patterned. In one (conventional) sense, this can be understood as a variation on the theme of 'alternatives to custody'. But, equally, it can also be interpreted as an argument for forms of intervention that are owned and led by the community rather than simply delivered there. The primary focus of such models is the well-being of communities and young people, rather than simply addressing procedural issues such as 'dealing with' crime and antisocial behaviour. Some attempts to develop community-based models in practice can be identified, although their aims and achievements are variable. Once again, it may well be significant that examples of such initiatives are evident in areas and communities which have previously experienced high levels of conflict and oppressive behaviour, including Serbia, South

Africa, and Northern Ireland. It may be that in these places the focus of attention is necessarily on the task of pursuing social justice across deep divisions and this perhaps changes the way in which the 'crimes' of the young are viewed. Practice examples may appear to be relatively mundane, but the following example from Northern Ireland is in stark contrast to the ASBO-led strategy pursued in large parts of England and Wales:

> A group of young people had begun to hang around on a particular street corner, drinking and playing loud music late at night. Residents were unhappy with the situation, particularly as they were often verbally abused by the group. Parents of some of the youths became aware that paramilitaries had approached the group and they therefore alerted CRJI [Community Restorative Justice Ireland] to avert violence. Two CRJI staff observed the corner over a number of evenings to assess the situation and found that the allegations were accurate. They approached the group and convinced them to attend a meeting to discuss the problems they were causing. CRJI also arranged a separate meeting of local residents to discuss their issues. Finally, both residents and youths met together and agreed a course of action where the youths could still congregate on the corner, but would keep the area clean, keep the noise down and treat the residents with respect. (Mika 2006: 20)

The community orientation of Northern Ireland's youth justice services is embedded in formal statements of policy as well (Youth Justice Agency 2003).

Some models of 'community justice' take a more conventional approach and appear to be designed to replicate accepted forms of adversarial practice in more informal settings, but without calling into question the underlying logic of individualised models of blame and accountability. The North Liverpool Community Justice Centre, for example, appears to prioritise a swift and 'robust' processing of alleged offenders rather than genuine attempts to engage with or involve the community in which it is sited (McKenna 2007). It had 'originally been the intention of the NLCJC to set up a youth reference group including young people from local schools and young offenders' (p. 62), but by the time of the project's evaluation this had not been achieved. Nor had good links been established with local schools. Clearly, this is a very limited and probably unproductive model of 'community justice' and contrasts with other examples which start from the position of seeking to engage and empower communities, such as a scheme in New Zealand identified by Omaji (2003: 146). This project was based on an 'ecological approach ... placing the young offender in the context of both family and community. The model, therefore, locates the focus of intervention with both family and community' and decentres the 'offender'. Offending therefore becomes something for which there is shared ownership and a sense of mutual responsibility. This approach is believed to be more consistent with Maori culture and traditions, too, than Western models of due process and individualised interventions.

On the other hand, there are examples from 'Western' communities of forms of practice which are based on principles of engagement, inclusion and mutuality, as well. In an early issue of the journal *Youth Justice*, Holman (2001) describes one such approach that depends on an organic relationship with local people, drawing on their strengths, recognising the validity of their experience, and being responsive: 'neighbourhood projects start by asking residents what services they want and then set about trying to get resources in order to supply them' (Holman 2001: 50). Thus, practitioners are likely to encounter young people 'in trouble' at a point where they already have a relationship and a degree of mutual understanding, in the same way as the wider community is also familiar with them; these relationships will be 'non-threatening' and provide the basis for constructive dialogue. Holman concludes that: 'Neighbourhood projects almost certainly help some families to hold together, keep some children out of care, and divert some youngsters away from custody' (2001: 50). He contrasts this model of intervention with that espoused by the 'new youth justice' which is detached from communities and everyday experience, has no commitment to 'long-term involvement', does not take an 'integrated' approach to neighbourhoods, and tends to over-react, failing to recognise the 'dangers of swift intervention' (p. 51). One of the features of this account is that it does not paint an idealised and glowing account of the lives and experiences of people in the neighbourhoods concerned, which were poor and disadvantaged in other ways. On the other hand, it emphasises that addressing the issue of 'youth justice' is, and must be, part of a much larger strategy of intervention that is dependent on offering options and opportunities to younger community members without 'labelling' them in any way: 'very needy youngsters did come in but they entered on the basis of being residents not with the label "vandal" or "drug-user" ' (p. 47).

A similar model of intervention is in evidence at the projects run by Kids Company (Gaskell 2008). Their work has derived from a philosophy of providing open access to services and providing safe spaces for young people to be and to seek support in ways that suit them. The basis of the organisation's work is 'a policy of non-exclusion' (Gaskell 2008: 7), given that the young people seeking to make use of the facility are quite likely to have had considerable prior experience of being 'excluded from schools, youth clubs and even Social Services Departments'. The interventions undertaken with young people are 'child-focussed', 'relationship-based', 'non-time limited', 'flexible', and 'empowering'. The underlying assumption appears to be that children and young people whose life experiences have been negative and harmful will need experience of 'positive relationships' before they are able to view themselves and others in a positive light and behave accordingly. The aims of the Kids Company project overall may be quite conventional (p. 79) but the approach is distinctive, not least because it is genuinely inclusive and oriented towards achieving social (rather than criminal) justice. Very different outcome measures are evident:

> Kids Company's street level services are considered by children and young people to be effective at the point of access, with 97% of service users believing that Kids Company helps with … difficulties. Happiness was the most commonly cited outcome, gained by 58% of children and young people accessing Kids Company's services. (Gaskell 2008: 4)

Although, by contrast, addressing the problem of crime is not a primary objective, researchers have found that 'attending Kids Company' does appear to have an effect in terms of a reduction in offending and arrest rates (p. 81). The point is made, though, that these figures should not necessarily be read in the conventional manner as indicating a reduction in criminal activity; rather, they may be linked to a reduced likelihood of being criminalised by justice agencies, on grounds of their visible differences:

> Arrest rates for this client group cannot be assumed to be the same as criminal involvement. Many of the client group are arrested for crimes they did not commit, solely because of their appearance, demeanour, or (seemingly inappropriate) use of public space. (Gaskell 2008: 81)

The acknowledgement that the social construction of criminality must be accounted for in determining what we mean by 'successful outcomes' for young people is very well illustrated by this point and it underlines further the important conceptual distinction between 'formal' and substantive justice.

The primary concern of such interventions is clearly not the issue of young people's behaviour and whether or not they are prone to commit crimes. However, if effective in engaging with young people and reconnecting them with the community, there may be behavioural consequences.

> [Kids Company] gives me something to do in the day. It stops me doing crime, you get me? Instead of going out there to do crime or sell drugs to get money, I'd rather come here and get a bit of an education for life later, you get me? (20-year-old young man, quoted in Gaskell 2008: 109)

Holman (2001: 46) similarly provides evidence that such schemes do have an impact on the direction of young people's lives and whether or not they continue to 'get into trouble'. A relationship between community initiatives such as this and 'youth justice' can therefore be mapped out, despite the observation that they do not set out with the aim of tackling offending behaviour and nor do they rely on conventional definitions of crime and antisocial behaviour to frame their engagement with young people or judge success and failure.

Restorative practice: a progressive model?

Where issues are raised within communities about young people's unacceptable behaviour, there is clearly an expectation that 'something' will be done about it. In light of this, it may be helpful to consider the development of emerging models of restorative justice and their compatibility with underlying concerns about rights and inclusive approaches to work with young people. Some models of restorative justice clearly do not deal with these issues well, and notions such as 'reintegrative shaming' seem too deeply embedded in a culture of blame to offer much of any real value (Marshall 1999: 30). On the other hand, there is an attractive logic to the idea of providing forums within which conflict, exploitation, and oppressive behaviour can be dealt with fairly and straightforwardly by those concerned without recourse to criminalising institutional mechanisms of control.

Attempts to deliver this kind of programme have been evident in Northern Ireland, in particular in recent years (Jacobson and Gibbs 2009). It is suggested that this is a distinctive model of youth justice that contrasts starkly with practices in England and Wales (p. vi). Principles of collaborative problem solving rather than judgement and blame appear to be dominant:

> The system of restorative justice which has been established [in Northern Ireland] involves the use of 'youth conferences' at which the offender, victim (or victim representative), professionals and others are brought together to discuss the offence and its repercussions, and to agree on an action plan for the offender. (Jacobson and Gibbs 2009: v)

The use of 'conferences' as a focal point for re-examining the offence, considering options, and deciding what to do about it has important implications for the way in which youth justice interventions are (or can be) re-defined. This is the case for a number of reasons which have wider consequences. Firstly, it removes the task of resolving the matter from the formalised and politicised setting of the court. In addition, it goes some way to addressing power imbalances. In the Northern Ireland setting it is expected that everyone involved 'shows mutual respect', for instance (p. 6). Questions of blame and responsibility become less central too, as the focus shifts to giving a more nuanced account of what happened and establishing a mutually agreed basis for resolving the matter.

Close parallels are drawn between this model and that of 'family group conferences' which are already quite widely practised in child welfare in the UK and elsewhere, having originated in New Zealand. One such initiative is of note because of some of the ways in which it decentres concerns about offending and locates the young person's 'crime' within a much wider series of questions relating to social context and welfare needs:

> There is a major emphasis on the role of the wider family support network in working with the young person to resolve difficulties seen to be associated with offending behaviour ... In effect RJ [Restorative Justice] becomes one element in a wider focus on the needs of the young person and the activation of social support in meeting those needs. (Mutter *et al.* 2008: 3)

The model developed in this case involved a structured process of distinct 'phases' in which the details of an 'offence' could be presented by youth justice agencies, with the 'victim' or her/his representative giving an account of the impact of the offence and then having a discussion with the young person about how the offence could be 'addressed'. Finally, there would be a period of 'private family time' during which the young person and other family members alone would decide on a plan of action to which others concerned could then respond. This model can be distinguished from others in the way that it operates 'at any stage of a young person's offending career' (p. 3), thus challenging the tariff-based assumptions which seem to inform other forms of restorative practice, such as those associated with pre-court diversion and Referral Orders. In this sense, it might be argued that this scheme prefigures forms of intervention which do not depend on conventional assumptions of guilt, responsibility, and graduated levels of punishment. And yet the question for this particular initiative – just as for restorative justice in general – is to what extent it is able, in practice, to free itself from these deeply embedded expectations. Thus it is clear that referrals in this example 'came as an element of the disposal recommended to the court upon sentencing' (p. 3) and could not, therefore, operate outside existing systems or be entirely free of prior assumptions: 'FGC [Family Group Conference] was not seen as an alternative justice process, rather an alternative approach alongside and complementing the formal youth justice processes' (p. 3).

The tension between competing models of practice in family group conferences has been explored elsewhere too (Jackson 1999), with the suggestion that a thoroughgoing *'family empowerment'* model is not compatible with the *'restorative model'* which is prominent in youth justice. The context is all-important if it operates to constrain discussion and shapes interaction in such a way that the only real question to be addressed is how and to what extent a young person 'makes amends' (Mutter *et al.* 2008: 3; Jacobson and Gibbs 2009: 6) for her/his actions, and this question itself is only addressed within, rather than as an alternative to, established mechanisms which are designed to apportion guilt and impose sanctions accordingly. Jackson (1999: 143), for one, believes that these concerns should not lead us to dismiss the potential contribution of conferences out of hand, suggesting that they can be of value if they are constructed in such a way as to pay 'sufficient attention to the underlying philosophical bases especially family empowerment and a recognition of the social exclusion experienced by many families and young people who get into trouble'. And, she goes on to remind us of the need 'to think carefully about the implications of introducing a radically different way of working into an essentially punitive youth justice system' (p. 144).

This is the central challenge for restorative practices in youth justice, in effect. If it is not simply to be co-opted into established (and essentially repressive) mechanisms for dealing with young people as 'criminals', then how must it be constituted and how can it operate in a transformative manner? Some assessments of restorative practice have certainly raised questions about its limitations, often grounded in their observations of practice (Daly 2002; Nakagawa 2003). Indeed, it is contrasted with 'transformative justice' in that the latter is believe to resist 'co-optation', not least because it is concerned to 'move forward' as opposed to merely attempting to 'restore what was there before' (Nakagawa 2003: 2). Indeed, given that what was already in place included the sort of inequality and discrimination we have already observed, this is an important point. Simply 'restoring' the status quo is likely to do no more than re-establish the unjust social relations and inequalities which form the backdrop and act as drivers for 'youth offending' in the first place. By contrast: 'Transformative justice ... puts an understanding of the structural racism and classism of our existing criminal justice system at the center of the theory' and of practice in those 'few circumstances' where it has been applied (Nakagawa 2003: 2).

It has been suggested, for instance, that restorative youth justice should be firmly grounded in a 'rights-based' approach derived from the principles set out by the UN (Moore and Mitchell 2009: 35). This incorporates provisions such as the 'free and voluntary' basis of participation by both offender and victim alike and it requires that 'power imbalances' should be taken into account in 'restorative processes'. Further to this, interventions should be oriented towards the 'reintegration of the victim and offender into the community'. There are reckoned to be concrete examples of practice which demonstrably incorporate these principles 'within youth justice settings', notably in Canada. It is also suggested that it may be possible to develop practice tools to support a more systematic implementation of rights-based restorative practice. This would include explicit adherence to certain key elements:

Non-discrimination, equality and mutuality;
Best interests, well-being and restoration;
Survival, development and safety;
Participation, voice and volunteerism ... (Moore and Mitchell 2009: 39)

It is clear from this, especially the latter principle of voluntary involvement, that this is a distinctive view of restorative justice which is not always represented in practice (Crawford and Newburn 2003: 134) and in the view of some is relatively unimportant (Masters 2005). On the other hand, it has been suggested that this in particular is an essential component of a genuinely restorative approach because it is the only guarantee of engaging young people themselves, changing experiences and perceptions of the justice system, and indeed impacting on the 'wider social situation' (Haines and O'Mahony 2006: 122). As I have observed previously (Smith, R. 2007: 214), the notion of 'consent' has historically been inscribed in various aspects of the justice system, being a requirement prior to the making of certain court orders in the past. The importance of this principle in restorative justice practices is that it represents a more proportionate reflection of the relationship between 'offender' and 'community' than one which simply compounds pre-existing structural relationships and reinforces young people's sense of powerlessness and systemic unfairness (McAra and McVie 2007). Perhaps this suggests a more subtle reading of the idea of 'restoration' than simply reinstating the *status quo*, but this seems important if we are not simply to use an apparently innovative form of practice as a way of buttressing well-established systemic failings. Real change is possible on this basis.

Signposts and maps: current practice and future possibilities

[T]ransformative justice ... begins with the assumption that we must move forward rather than attempt to restore what was there before. (Nakagawa 2003: 2)

The preceding discussion has sought to identify sites and processes of contemporary practice in and around youth justice which in themselves contain the seeds of progressive change. These are not necessarily or inherently transformational and in some forms can be counterproductive (such as the use of compulsion in restorative interventions), but their reference to underlying principles grounded in notions of 'welfare rights' (Scraton and Haydon 2002) is significant and offers hope. Some would perhaps argue that this is still not enough, especially where 'abolition' is believed to be the only strategy which retains a spirit of radical integrity (Mathiesen 1974). However, the aim here has been to show that it remains possible for those engaged in the here-and-now of everyday practice with young people implicated in the justice system to act in ways which both respect and promote the interests of those affected and at the same time point the way towards forms of justice which account for and redress imbalances in the social fabric itself. The danger inherent in offering no possibility of change to practitioners is that the form of nihilism captured in the phrase 'nothing works' (Muncie 2009: 287) becomes translated into the belief that there is nothing that can 'work', irrespective of what we wish to achieve. Transformation, nonetheless, is an essentially *practical* project that does not result from either simply wishing away the injustices which we do not accept, or lapsing into a spirit of 'radical pessimism' (Muncie 1999).

The importance of seeking to demonstrate what can be achieved, even in adverse circumstances, is grounded in the fact that it shows what is possible even when the odds are against us. This is not an argument for collusion, however, and it should be emphasised that the kind of core principles and practices set out here are not negotiable. Thus, for example, the Referral Order is of necessity an unacceptable site for the implementation of restorative justice because it relies on elements of coercion, unlike other progressive forms of intervention, such as pre-court diversion in the 1980s or some elements of community justice in Northern Ireland. Holding on to these principles in the face of hostile demands is no easy task and we must also accept that ground can be lost as well as gained. Progress is not certain or unidirectional as Cohen (1985) has made abundantly clear. Despite this, we have been reminded from time to time that there is a degree of autonomy (Poulantzas 1978) at the level of individual practitioners and in specific sites of intervention, which may be exercised effectively:

> The degree to which empowerment and restorative values and principles are incorporated in ... practice is influenced by a range of factors largely within the control of statutory systems. It is important to note that workers have a significant degree of autonomy with respect to how they interact with families, who they involve and how they make decisions. (Connolly 2009: 317)

Clearly, there is a risk here of being too idealistic and underestimating the structural constraints and operational challenges we are likely to encounter, but it does offer at least a glimmer of hope for the radical potential for change even in the mundane and yet creative domain of day-to-day practice. Crucially, as Drakeford (2001) has reminded us, it is essential that a rights-based approach continues to be represented at the point of intervention in order to challenge the negative and oppressive impacts of the youth justice system as constituted in the contemporary era.

Chapter 10

Reframing justice for young people

The problem of misalignment

'I can't believe it, they're making a wing for 10 year olds. What's it going to be next? Are they going to start branding people and stuff like that, putting marks on them? Are they going to make a wing for babies, babies going out and killing people?' (Young man in custody, quoted in Lyon *et al*. 2000: 56).

There appears to be a recurrent, perhaps endemic, tension between young people and society. This is manifested in public and political rhetoric, on the one hand, and reflected in the experiences of young people, on the other. Our expectations of them are fraught and ambivalent and this in turn produces uncertainty and frustration as they seek to negotiate the systems and 'pathways' (Haw 2006) mapped out for them. The kind of choices they make are circumscribed in various ways and as a result they may be inclined to pursue options which are not acceptable and which on occasion appear unsettling and even threatening. In light of this, perhaps, confrontation and conflict might seem inevitable. The dynamics of conflict, though, are themselves the product of fluid and unequal social relationships. Power, resources, structure and ideology are all features of these relationships and therefore play a crucial part in shaping the interaction between young people and the community/ies of which they are a part.

Almost inevitably, the young are likely to be disadvantaged in these terms, even before we consider the additional factors which compound inequalities and underpin oppression, such as ethnic difference, poverty and other forms of institutionalised inequity. Unfairness becomes almost the natural order of things. At the same time, in their role as the 'next generation' young people and their behaviour become the subject of intense scrutiny and close control. Attempts to organise and express themselves in distinctive ways are likely to become the subject of concern, as a matter of course, and it is here that the ambiguous messages they receive become especially problematic. Individualism, for example, lies at the heart of the education system and the young are expected to compete for advantage in this context as they are also encouraged to participate in organised sport. Other forms of individualism, though, are less acceptable, if they involve, say, theft or playing loud music. Where the opportunities to 'succeed' are differentially distributed – and – indeed notions of what constitutes 'success' itself may also vary – once again the modes of individual self-expression are likely to reflect these social realities.

In the face of these dynamics, we might reasonably expect to find that the ways in which we deal with young people's behaviour when it gives cause for concern are designed to take account of variable experiences, disadvantage, and embedded injustices. However, this is not the case and perhaps it is not so surprising that unequal social relations are reproduced within our system of justice rather than being redressed through this mechanism. The mistreatment of young people by the justice system – and especially certain categories of young people such as those from certain ethnic minority groups – is by now well documented; as yet, however, there has been little evidence that these 'systemic' wrongs have been recognised at the level of policy and system change. It is possible, nonetheless, to set out both principles and (limited) evidence of prefigurative practices which demonstrate how things could be different and to what sort of youth justice system we should aspire. It is important to continue to make the case that these are practical and achievable goals rather than utopian dreams and this is what I hope to demonstrate in conclusion here.

The lessons of experience: 'lost in transition'?

To begin with we should reflect on the experiences of young people and how these are reflected in various discourses of youth. Once again, it will become evident that there are consistent and substantial discontinuities between the substance of their changing lives and the ways in which these are accounted for, especially by the formal mechanisms of social organisation and control such as the education system (see Chapter 5). This sense of dissonance has been captured well by recent attempts to identify alternative conceptualisations of childhood and youth. Lee (2001), for example, has drawn attention to the tension between 'being' and 'becoming' in childhood and youth, whereby children are held to be simultaneously dependent and independent according to the context and nature of their behaviour. This creates a sense of ambiguity and renders unclear the extent to which they should be held responsible for their actions and treated accordingly. As we have observed, this has led to a series of anomalies in the legal frameworks of childhood as well as problematising explanations of their (deviant) behaviour. While this appears to have been a persistent historical challenge in the constitution of the machinery of social control, it is suggested that this also has a particular contemporary flavour:

> the task of placing people into the categories 'being' and 'becoming', so central to the function of the developmental state, has become more difficult in the age of uncertainty. The masses of poor children, concentrated in towns and cities by modernization and then impoverished by a combination of economic recession and policy responses to it testify to the contemporary difficulties of maintaining a clear being/becoming division. (Lee 2001: 71)

But uncertainty and indeed unacceptable behaviour are not simply the products of impoverishment and it is insufficient to attempt to account for changing patterns and expectations of childhood in this way. Lee (2001: 71) also refers to the 'childhood ambiguities of affluent societies'.

A rather more nuanced theoretical framework is offered by James and James (2004) whose two-dimensional model attempts to address the tension between 'universal' and particular influences on children and young people. They suggest that our models of childhood are derived in different ways from our attempts to resolve two polarities – that between 'structure and agency' and between 'commonality and diversity' (p. 58). The intersection of these tensions gives rise to four possible conceptualisations: the 'tribal child'; the 'minority child'; the 'socially constructed child'; and the 'social structural child'. While children may be seen as 'social actors' on one side, 'childhood' may be viewed as a product of broader social dynamics on the obverse of this. Thus, while it is apparent that notions of childhood and youth are evident in 'every social system' in accordance with the 'social structural' model, it is also important to consider the specific 'features' and 'local contexts' in light of which particular categories of children are 'socially constructed' (p. 60). This analytical framework does not stop here, however, because it also recognises the value of seeing children as 'social actors' who make sense of, and respond to, these structural and ideological influences. They have an active role in making sense of, and taking action in light of, their experiences and the social systems within which they are implicated (Merton 1957; Smith, R. 2000).

While these explanatory frameworks may appear in one sense as alternatives they should rather be taken as interlinked, representing 'four different facets' of the lives of children and young people. In other words, relying over heavily or exclusively on one or other of these models will only provide a partial and distorted view of the subject:

> Taken together they constitute and reflect the totality of the childhoods lived by children throughout the world and, from the perspective of the individual child, it is these same four positions that, in varying proportions, at any given time and in any particular social situation, combine to shape their daily lived experiences. (James and James 2004: 61)

This suggests that explanations of young people's lives and behaviour will need to be constructed as complex and quite fluid accounts, viewing them simultaneously as products and producers of the worlds they inhabit. Perhaps inevitably though, the tendency is towards the development of rather one-sided and static formulations. Young people are believed to be, variously, products of their circumstances, untamed spirits, victims of the 'system', or resisters of social cooptation and conformity. These 'working models' form the basis for the construction of certain prototypical explanatory frameworks which in turn are held to account for behaviours, consequences, change (or the lack of it), and outcomes.

James and James (2004: 61) point out that these are 'sociologically speaking' to be acknowledged as Weberian 'ideal types' and must be viewed as such. In other words, they offer the basis for establishing analytical distinctions and providing a mechanism for varying the perspective we bring to bear on different aspects of children's lives and their 'childhoods'. In concrete terms, as they point out, this can be illustrated by the differing responses to the murder of James Bulger in the UK and a similar event in Norway at roughly the same time. The young killers of James Bulger were readily characterised as 'tribal' children, representing a highly specific and extreme form of wilful, 'evil' behaviour. On the other hand, the response to the killing of one child by others in Norway did not prompt a similar process of 'splitting off'; these children were responded to as 'minority group' children, if anything, for whom the event was a distressing accident linked to their specific social status, perhaps as morally unformed or lacking an 'adult' appreciation of the consequences of their actions. The apparent dissonance between these two positions clearly generates a degree of concern as to how we can generate a theoretically coherent overarching framework for understanding children and young people, while also providing a sufficient basis for making practical choices about how to approach and address the specific problems of childhood and youth. This necessitates developing an interactive model which will provide a means of linking alternative perspectives in a coherent manner:

> At a theoretical level, then, we envisage the relationship between change and continuity in childhood as a reflexive, flexible and evolutionary process in which 'childhood', as a social space inhabited and experienced by individual children, is continuously located within and shaped by successive generations of adults and children. (James and James 2004: 63)

As they acknowledge, this is an abstraction which might provide a valuable analytical frame but does not of itself explain how and why children's lives are experienced and childhood is structured in just the way they are. They go on to suggest that 'the law' as an organising force has an important role in shaping the concrete day-to-day realities of children across all of the 'ideal type' models identified. This is because the law is peculiarly 'concerned with codifying the particular structural characteristics of any given society or culture' (p. 67) and so plays a consistently important part in both organising and representing social relations, even in informal contexts such as friendship networks or 'gangs'. Each of these will have its own system of rules and behavioural expectations that will be more or less explicitly specified. This also helps to explain the emergence of differences, especially where the rules and norms emerging from children's and young people's own interactions and deliberations are in conflict with those of the wider society whose formal expectations may be very different (p. 69).

Importantly, we can observe here a complex pattern of interactions that does not necessarily have a distinct and constant reference point from which to take observations and make judgements. Even the logic and workings of the 'law' are partial and depend on the particular viewpoint and location of those concerned. Even though attempts have been made to supervene these tensions and contradictions through the development of 'universal' instruments like the UN Convention on the Rights of the Child, as James and James observe (p. 81) this is unlikely to represent more than 'the beginning in the process of changing the cultural politics of childhood' (p. 106). In practice, the complex logic and child-centred nature of this kind of instrument has already encountered substantial resistance from entrenched interests, wedded to a limited conceptualisation of children and young people.

The scale of the task: barriers to justice

As the previous section suggests there are encouraging possibilities on offer, both to reframe the ways we think about children and young people and to develop mechanisms and operational frameworks that will enable us to change practice in a progressive direction. But we cannot simply wish away the major obstacles to these developments that are deeply embedded in contemporary attitudes and practices. There continues to be what seems to be a deeply felt need to categorise and control young people in ways which do not engage with their perspectives, their experiences, and their capacities as social actors. This is reflected in a number of conventional practices that deal only with aspects of young people's behaviour and their lives in order to assign them to particular definitional statuses and to legitimise coercive interventions purportedly in the interests of the wider community. In terms of the conceptual distinctions just elaborated, this involves a process of 'social construction', on the one hand which assigns young people to the category of 'tribal child' on the other. Implicated in this process are apparently neutral mechanisms for identifying 'problems' that – in the manner of their operation – in fact apply and institutionalise powerful discriminatory effects. This process is captured most effectively in the notion of 'othering', which utilises ideas and representations of 'difference' to classify and problematise certain groups and communities. Garland (2001: 136) suggests that this is a deliberate process, selecting and turning the spotlight on 'useful' features of those targeted in order to constitute them as 'suitable' enemies. Attention is turned towards recognised and scientifically respectable markers of difference, such as character traits, genetic predispositions and other, more specifically 'situated' distinguishing features that will provide an authentic means of identifying those who pose a potential or actual risk:

> The public knows, without having to be told, that these 'superpredators' and high-rate offenders are young minority males, caught up in the underclass worlds of crime, drugs, broken families, and welfare dependency. The only practical and rational response to such types, as soon as they offend if not before, is to have them 'taken out of circulation' for the protection of the public. (Garland 2001: 136)

In the case of young people, this is constituted as a multi-layered process spanning a range of general (being young) to specific (being 'excluded') characteristics that tends to compound the effects of single indicators to produce a multiplier effect (Kemshall 2008) and thereby to escalate levels of concern, leading in turn to an intensification of response. In this way, specific instruments such as the ASSET tool (Youth Justice Board 2005) have a particular part to play – converting these signifiers into legitimised and 'scientific' indicators of 'risk' and a potential future threat to society. Phoenix (2009) refers to a context of 'repressive welfarism' which underpins this sort of calculative strategy. 'Risk' becomes the modality according to which assessments of young people are carried out, drawing on generalised and specific attributes to generate and justify the foci of concern. Interestingly, too, this approach subsumes the tension between 'welfare' and 'punishment' within a common framework of the objectification and individualisation of young people (p. 114). In contemporary political terms, these shifts are accounted for by the emergence and growing dominance of 'actuarial justice and managerialism and the dominance of risk thinking' in policy and practice (p. 115), as epitomised in Phoenix's view by the *Scaled Approach* (Youth Justice Board 2008).

It is clear, though, that policy prescriptions about risk assessment and the use of standardised tools do not coincide with the experiences or in many cases the practices of youth justice workers. Phoenix (2009: 120) observes that 'YOT workers discussed ASSET as being a "meaningless", "paperwork heavy" system of assessment' that does not allow for a realistic or sufficiently rounded view of young people's circumstances or behaviour. Rather than informing assessments and recommendations ASSET forms would be completed purely to satisfy bureaucratic demands, in a context where any meaning had been stripped from the process by the formulaic nature of the documentation itself: 'you think if I don't understand it how the hell can a young person understand what I'm saying' (YOT worker, interviewed in Phoenix 2009: 121). This problem, though, is overlaid onto what is perhaps a deeper, structural issue of concern. As Phoenix goes on to demonstrate, this type of objectifying risk-based assessment not only distorts the day-to-day activities of practitioners and their interactions with young people, it also comes to act as a representation of 'reality' because it provides the basis of formal accounts presented in decision-making forums such as the courts. Using the only means at their disposals, practitioners found themselves reconstituting welfare needs as risk factors and seeking to broaden the working definition of risk to include a 'risk to' as well as a 'threat from' young people reported for offending. Youth justice workers appeared to know very well that young people were starting to be identified as problematic and coming to the attention of the judicial system, largely because of structural influences and disadvantages in their own lives. However, within their available repertoire of responses, the only available course open to them was to seek to frame recommendations and interventions in terms of the 'risk' represented by the young person. Sometimes, practitioners have been observed to claim that this is the only way to access welfare services when other responsible agencies have not shown the capacity to offer suitable provision (p. 128). The effect, though, is fundamental:

> in the current context … practitioners' efforts to introduce assessments of youthful lawbreaking which highlights service gaps may have unintended consequences. The language of risk and the assumptions contained within it prohibit youth justice workers from expressing their own (professional) assessments about the dearth of services for young people into any meaningful recommendation apart from criminal justice interventions. As a result … the language of risk and the tools at the disposal of youth justice workers in England and Wales have meant that many workers have not found ways to displace, transform or

197

re-package young lawbreakers as anything other than suitable subjects of *criminal justice responses* albeit for non-criminal justice ends. (Phoenix 2009: 130; original emphasis)

As she concludes this amounts to a paradox, whereby the very attempt to utilise the system to access welfare services ('welfarism') necessitates a representation of young people and their behaviour in the language of risk and 'criminogenic need' (see Ward and Stewart 2003); this results both in a heightened use of 'punitive' responses and a further legitimation of the discourse and techniques of 'risk assessment' and 'risk management'. Importantly, here, this process leads to a particular form of objectification of young people, utilising a very narrow and limited frame of reference. As I have noted elsewhere (Smith, R. 2005), the elision of 'welfare' and 'justice' perspectives within the sphere of youth justice has been a recurrent, but sometimes unacknowledged feature of attempts to interpose arguments based on 'need' into a field of knowledge constructed under the authority of the 'law'. The problem which this process exemplifies is one of misrepresentation, which inevitably permeates the youth justice system in its entirety. Young people can only be represented as one-dimensional caricatures of themselves; their lived experiences and their status as social actors (see Chapter 1) are not recognised in the terms described by James and James (2004) and they become decontextualised abstractions. Even when they are 'socially constructed' as 'tribal', this fails to connect their 'wilful' individual behaviour to the 'structural' aspects of their lives or their 'minority' status as children and thus essential considerations such as discrimination and oppression are excluded from the picture. In place of these partial, unrepresentative, and ultimately damaging portrayals of young people who we encounter in the justice system, we must seek to re-establish a comprehensive, honest, and fair approach to the challenge of, firstly, understanding them, and secondly, of developing effective forms of practice with them. As Kemshall (2008: 30) puts it, the 'tension between risks and rights needs to be located within a broader context of social opportunity and choice' and supported by a renewed 'emphasis upon the resources young people have to enable them to make the "right choice" about risk'. A process of engagement and inclusion is necessary in order to enable young people to 'exercise responsibility' (Smith, R. 2010a). Simply imposing solutions on them is unlikely to do more than confirm their 'fatalistic' preconceptions about the world and their place within it. Empowerment rather than greater control seems to be the message we should draw from these reflections.

Justice and young people: a realistic goal?

How, then, can change be achieved? The contemporary climate is gloomy, dominated by an (international) consensus on the need to be 'tough' on youth crime and a domestic context of high levels of punitive sanctions and a continued commitment to the idea of criminalising children from the age of 10. Short-term improvements – such as the current reduction in custody rates – may be no more than that and are unlikely to be sustainable unless they are informed by the kind of progressive rationale introduced in the previous chapter and elsewhere (Barton *et al.* 2007). Longer-term and more substantial improvements will be dependent on the mobilisation of a series of constituencies around a set of principles and operational frameworks that are robust and defensible.

Of considerable importance is the overarching framework of the UN Convention on the Rights of the Child, not least because its comprehensive rights programme encompasses a 'joined up' view of young people and their 'developing capacities' (Lansdown 2005) which locates rights in relation to youth justice processes squarely within their wider, generic 'welfare' rights (Scraton and Haydon 2002; Smith, R. 2010a). This is particularly significant, because it offers not just a comprehensive, global practical tool for securing the basic elements of social justice for young people, but also a conceptual framework that can demonstrate the crucial importance of creating and sustaining effective links between generic entitlements and safeguards which apply specifically to those who have been implicated in criminal justice processes. In other words, it underlines the central need to ensure that young people who are caught up in the youth justice system do not then experience a diminution of their 'universal' rights as children to a decent education, say, or to protection from bullying and racist abuse. One form of 'justice' cannot be achieved without the other and it is therefore simply unsustainable to seek to justify oppressive practices – or even to tacitly accept them – simply on the grounds that young people have forfeited their 'rights' by involving themselves in criminal offences.

Further, the practical reconnection of universal and situated rights through the UN Convention offers confirmation of the interdependency of the components of just treatment of children and young people. This interconnectedness is emphasised in specific terms by the elaboration of detailed frameworks of children's rights within 'juvenile justice' which themselves sit within the broader provisions of the convention itself (Goldson and Muncie 2006: 217). Rights to protection should be guaranteed to all children, for example, but these will require special provisions in institutional settings if they are to be realised. Similarly, participation rights which are in principle extended to children generically do not become invalid once they become embroiled in criminal justice processes. And yet as we have seen, even those aspects of youth justice which purport to promote 'participation', such as the Referral Order, do so in ways that will severely restrict young people's capacity to express themselves openly and honestly.

What, then, are the tasks that might enable those engaged in the production of 'youth justice' to move towards a model of intervention that is capable of really 'doing justice' to young people? Firstly, it seems that there is a need to record and report contemporary practice failures. This may be problematic in terms of access to and uses of information, but we have seen productive examples of such activity from sources which may have seemed unlikely – such as the prisons inspectorate which has drawn attention to the consistent mistreatment of young people in custodial settings. In addition, though, it is important to approach the challenge of maintaining generic rights in specific circumstances where these may be under threat. Young people's participation rights are often compromised by the justice process and it is therefore important to seek out opportunities to let their voices be heard and for their accounts to be incorporated effectively in decision-making processes, according to the kind of practice models discussed in the previous chapter.

Closely allied with the principle of participation is advocacy. For those working with young people in the justice system it will be important to adopt an attitude of 'challenge', especially in relation to the denial or loss of the kind of universal entitlements referred to previously. The tendency to focus on conventional forms of classification – such as 'risk' or 'criminogenic need' – can, as we have seen, shift our attention towards narrowly defined concerns that do not enable us to locate young people within wider contexts or to relate their immediate circumstances to the stories of their lives. Not only is it important to challenge ourselves and thus move away from these restricted channels of thought, it is also important to go on to place generic needs and rights at the centre of our accounts of young people whatever their 'crimes'. These are not optional extras, but fundamental elements of a form of 'pro-social modelling' (Cherry 2005) that might actually 'work'. This may offer us a more radical but equally a more meaningful basis for reconsidering and reconstructing the strategy of changing behaviour by 'demonstrating the behaviour that is desirable' (Rex and Gelsthorpe 2004: 204) to young people receiving youth justice sanctions. What this means for those who are systematically excluded, stereotyped, unheard, and mistreated might be worth due consideration.

A realisation of young people's rights in this respect is underpinned by the principle of (re)integration – namely, the capacity to access universal rights in a material sense as well as in the abstract. This is shown to be crucial by those who observe that the 'dominant version of human rights that is presented at an international level gives a biased emphasis to civil and political rights' (Stanley 2007: 171). These approaches are not sufficient if they do not seek to understand 'long-term economic, social, cultural and development violations' (Stanley 2007: 171). Thus the models of 'community justice' discussed previously that engage young people and promote participation offer a partial solution to the problems of exclusion and 'labelling', but they must be supplemented by strategies that will address the wider problems of social inequality and problematisation reflected in:

> principles of *universality, comprehensiveness* and *re-engaging* the *'social'*. This requires dispensing with forms of conditionality that bolster the 'deserving-undeserving schism' ... and instead provide holistic services that meet the needs and safeguard and promote the well-being of *all* children and young people. (Goldson and Muncie 2006: 222; original emphasis)

It is not possible to achieve thoroughgoing models of social justice if improvements in our working models of youth justice are only applied in particular communities or within contexts marked out and indeed identified for intervention on the grounds of social disadvantage. In this sense, the achievement of fair and universal models of justice for young people is, and will remain, an essentially *political* task and cannot be secured only by improving the systems or mechanisms for determining how best to respond to the crimes of the young. This, of course, presents a fundamental challenge for those in the front line who are expected to take on and give substance to a change agenda which goes well beyond the tasks assigned to them, the working context, and their professional roles and identities. On a day-to-day basis, this means having 'to stick with the uncomfortable business of explaining complexity in places where the simplicity of blame and shame are preferred' and maintaining the 'determination to advance the best interests of children at times and places where a hostile reaction can be assured', in order to locate interventions explicitly in a context of 'the differences in power which exist in society at large' (Drakeford 2001: 44).

Yet retaining a commitment to change and a sense of what is possible, and where the opportunities are to initiate progressive developments, may still be realistic, reasonable, and achievable. In this sense, it is important to think in terms of 'prefigurative' action which incorporates a sense of what is possible and how the principles of rights and social justice can be validated and current practice – the 'unfinished' nature of this project is recognised, but its value in terms of identifying what can be achieved should not be under-estimated.

Visions and reality: a footnote

Retaining a belief about the potential for radical change and the achievement of social justice for young people has been difficult in recent years in particular. I sometimes talk about my experiences in quite different times, during the 1980s, that now seem almost too long ago and too far away to offer any insights relevant to the present day. Would it be possible even to conceive of 'custody-free zones' (Haines and Drakeford 1998) in the present day? And more pessimistically, what did we really achieve if youth justice did become a bit more liberal, when young people were simultaneously faced with mass unemployment and the (completely illogical) loss of their benefit entitlements at the same time?

Nonetheless, there are certain lessons from that era which are transferable, I believe, and which should offer us some continuity of 'critical hope' (Leonard 1997). I believed then, and still do now, that the principled dedication and activism of a generation of radical practitioners did 'make a difference'. This came about not just through being in the right place at the right time, but also because certain key principles were embedded in and articulated in practice, such as minimum intervention, diversion, participation, universal rights and community justice. These are all terms which have a contemporary resonance and as indicated previously are all practised currently in various ways in different settings. It may be hopelessly over-optimistic, but nonetheless it seems a good place to end – with the suggestion that a concerted and principled 'movement' towards 'doing justice to young people' remains a practical and achievable goal.

References

Adamson, S. (2003) *Youth Crime: Offender Based Approaches to Reduction.* Sheffield Hallam University: Sheffield.

Agnew, R. (1999) 'A general strain theory of community differences in crime rates', *Journal of Research in Crime and Delinquency*, 36 (2): 123–55.

Alcock, P. (2004) 'Participation or pathology: contradictions in area-based policy', *Social Policy and Society*, 3: 87–96.

Aldridge, J., Parker, H. and Measham, F. (1998) 'Rethinking young people's drug use', *Health Education*, 5: 164–72.

Allen, R. (2005) 'Rethinking retribution: a critique of simple justice, *Criminal Justice Matters*, 60 (1): 32–9.

Allen, R. (2007) 'From punishment to problem solving: a new approach to children in trouble' in Davies, Z. and McMahon, W. (eds) *Debating Youth Justice: From Punishment to Problem Solving?* King's College, London, 7–53.

Alsaker, F. (1995) 'Is puberty a critical period for socialization?', *Journal of Adolescence*, 18: 427–44.

Althusser, L. (1971) *Lenin and Philosophy and Other Essays.* London: Verso.

Archer, L. and Yamashita, H. (2003) 'Knowing their limits? Identities, inequalities and inner city school leavers' post-16 aspirations', *Journal of Education Policy*, 18 (1): 53–69.

Armstrong, D., Hine, J., Hacking, S., Armaos, R., Jones, R., Klessinger, N. and France, A. (2005) *Children, Risk and Crime: The On Track Youth Lifestyles Surveys.* Home Office: London.

Arnett, J. (1999) 'Adolescent storm and stress, reconsidered', *American Psychologist*, 54: 317–26.

Arnull, E., Archer, D., Eagle, S., Gammampila, A., Johnston, V., Miller, K. and Pitcher, J. (2005) *Persistent Young Offenders – A Retrospective Study.* YJB: London.

Audit Commission (1996) *Misspent Youth*. Audit Commission: London.

Austin, J. and Krisberg, B. (2002) 'Wider, stronger and different nets: the dialectics of criminal justice reform' in Muncie, J., Hughes, G. and McLaughlin, E. (eds) *Youth Justice: Critical Readings*. Sage: London, 258–74.

Baker, K., Jones, S., Merrington, S. and Roberts, C. (2005) *Further Development of ASSET*. Youth Justice Board: London.

Barboza, G., Sclamberg, L., Oemkhe, J., Korzeniewski, S., Post, L. and Heraux, C. (2009) 'Individual characteristics and the multiple contexts of adolescent bullying: an ecological perspective', *Journal of Youth and Adolescence*, 38 (1): 101–21.

Barclay, G. and Mhlanga, B. (2000) *Ethnic Differences in Decisions on Young Defendants Dealt With by the Crown Prosecution Service*. Home Office: London.

Barclay, G., Munley, A., and Munton, T. (2005) *Race and the Criminal Justice System: An Overview to the Complete Statistics 2003-2004*. Home Office: London.

Barlow, J. (1998) 'Parent-training programmes and behaviour problems: findings from a systematic review', in Buchanan, A. and Hudson, B. (eds) *Parenting, Schooling and Children's Behaviour*. Ashgate: Aldershot, 89–109.

Barrett, M. and McIntosh, M. (1982) *The Anti-Social Family*. Verso: London.

Barry, M. (ed.) (2005) *Youth Policy and Social Inclusion*. Routledge: Abingdon.

Barry, M. (2006) *Youth Offending in Transition*. Routledge: Abingdon.

Barton, A., Corteen, K., Scott, D. and Whyte, D. (eds) (2007) *Expanding the Criminological Imagination*. Willan: Cullompton.

Beck, U. (1992) *Risk Society*. Sage: London.

Beck, U., Giddens, A. and Lash, S. (1994) *Reflexive Modernization, Politics, Tradition and Aesthetics in the Modern Social Order*. Cambridge: Polity Press.

Berridge, D., Brodie, I., Pitts, J., Porteous, D. and Tarling, R. (2001) *The Independent Effects of Permanent Exclusion from School on the Offending Careers of Young People*. Home Office: London.

Blagg, H., Derricourt, N., Finch, J. and Thorpe D. (1986) *The Final Report on the Juvenile Liaison Bureau Corby*. University of Lancaster: Lancaster.

Blair, T. (1993) 'Why crime is a Socialist issue', *New Statesman*, 29 Jan, 27–28.

Bottoms, A. (1977) 'Reflections on the Renaissance of Dangerousness', *Howard Journal*, 16: 70–96.

Bourdieu, P. (1998) *Practical Reason*. Polity Press: Cambridge.

Bowling, B. and Phillips, C. (2002) *Racism, Crime and Justice*. Longman: Harlow.

Bradford, S. and Morgan, R. (2005) 'Transformed youth justice?', *Public Policy & Management*, 25 (5): 283–90.

Briggs, S. (2002) *Working with Adolescents*. Palgrave Macmillan: Basingstoke.

Bronfenbrenner, U. (1979) *The Ecology of Human Development*. Harvard University Press: Cambridge, MA.

Brown, P. (1987) *Schooling Ordinary Kids*. Tavistock: London.

Brown, S. (2005) *Understanding Youth and Crime (2nd edition)*. Open University Press: Buckingham.

Brownlee, I. (1998) 'New Labour: new penology? Punitive rhetoric and the limits of managerialism in criminal justice policy', *Journal of Law and Society*, 25 (3): 313–35.

Buchanan, A. and Hudson, B. (eds) (1998) *Parenting, Schooling and Children's Behaviour*. Ashgate: Aldershot.

Bullock, K. and Jones, B. (2004) *Acceptable Behaviour Contracts: Addressing Antisocial Behaviour in the London Borough of Islington*. Home Office: London.

Burnett, R. and Appleton, C. (2004) 'Joined-up services to tackle youth crime', *British Journal of Criminology*, 44: 34–54.

Centre for Social Justice (2010) *Green Paper on the Family*. Centre for Social Justice: London.

Cherry, S. (2005) *Transforming Behaviour: Pro-social Modelling in Practice*. Willan: Cullompton.

Christie, N. (2000) *Crime Control as Industry (3rd edition)*. Routledge: London.

Chui, W., Tupman, B. and Farlow, W. (2003) 'Listening to young adult offenders: views on the effect of a police-probation initiative on reducing crime', *Howard Journal of Criminal Justice*, 42: 263–81.

Cicourel, A. (1968) *The Social Organisation of Juvenile Justice*. Wiley: New York.

Cloward, R. and Ohlin, L. (1960) *Delinquency and Opportunity: A Theory of Delinquent Gangs*. Free Press: New York.

Cohen, A. (1955) *Delinquent Boys: The Culture of the Gang*. Free Press: New York.

Cohen, S. (1985) *Visions of Social Control*. Polity Press: Cambridge.

Coleman, J. and Hendry, L. (1999) *The Nature of Adolescence (3rd edition)*. London: Routledge.

Coles, B. (2003) 'Young people' in Alcock, P., Erskine, A. and May, M. (eds) *The Student's Companion to Social Policy*. Blackwell: Oxford, pp. 296–302.

Colley, H. and Hodkinson, P. (2001) 'The problem with 'Bridging the Gap': the reversal of structure and agency in addressing social exclusion', *Critical Social Policy*, 21 (3): 335–59.

Committee on the Rights of the Child (1995) *Concluding Observations of the Committee on the Rights of the Child: United Kingdom of Great Britain and Northern Ireland (Eighth Session)*. United Nations: Geneva.

Committee on the Rights of the Child (2002) *Concluding Observations of the Committee on the Rights of the Child: United Kingdom of Great Britain and Northern Ireland (Thirty-first Session)*. United Nations: Geneva.

Committee on the Rights of the Child (2008) *Concluding Observations of the Committee on the Rights of the Child: United Kingdom of Great Britain and Northern Ireland (Forty-ninth Session)*. United Nations: Geneva.

Communities that Care (2005) *Risk and Protective Factors*. Youth Justice Board: London.

Connolly, M. (2009) 'Family group conferences in child welfare: the fit with restorative justice', *Contemporary Justice Review*, 12 (3): 309–19.

Craine, S. (1997) 'The "Black Magic Roundabout": cyclical transitions, social exclusion and alternative careers' in McDonald, R. (ed.) *Youth, the 'Underclass' and Social Exclusion*. Routledge: London, 130–52.

Crawford, A. and Newburn, T. (2003) *Youth Offending and Restorative Justice*. Willan: Cullompton.

Cross, N., Evans, J. and Minkes, J. (2003) 'Still children first? Developments in youth justice in Wales', *Youth Justice*, 2 (3): 151–62.

Daly, K. (2002) 'Restorative justice: the real story', *Punishment & Society*, 4 (1): 55–79.

Department of Health and Social Security (1983) 'Further Development of Intermediate Treatment', *Local Authority Circular 3/83*. DHSS: London.

Department for Education and Skills (2003) *Every Child Matters*. DfES: London.

Department for Education and Skills (2004) *Every Child Matters: Next Steps*. DfES: London.

Department for Education and Skills (2005) *Youth Matters*. DfES: London.

Dishion, T., Andrews, D. and Crosby, L. (1995) 'Antisocial boys and their friends in early adolescence: relationship characteristics, quality and interactional process', *Child Development*, 66: 139–51.

Donzelot, J. (1979) *The Policing of Families*. Johns Hopkins Press: Baltimore, MD.

Downes, D. and Rock, P. (1982) *Understanding Deviance*. Oxford University Press: Oxford.

Downes, D. and Rock, P. (2003) *Understanding Deviance (4th edition)*. Oxford University Press: Oxford.

Drakeford, M. (2001) 'Children's rights and welfare: towards a new synthesis', *Youth Justice*, 1 (1): 40–44.

Eckersley, R. (1997) 'Portraits of youth: understanding young people's relationship with the future', *Futures*, 29 (3): 243–9.

Esbensen, F. and Huizinga, D. (1993) 'Gangs, drugs and delinquency in a survey of urban youth', *Criminology*, 4: 565–89.

Fadipe, M. and Gittens-Bernard, L. (2005) 'Postscript on youth justice' in Barry, M. (ed.) *Youth Policy and Social Inclusion*. Routledge: Abingdon, 227–31.

Farrington-Douglas, J. and Durante, L. (2009) *Towards a Popular, Preventative Youth Justice System*. Institute for Public Policy Research: London.

Featherstone, R. and Deflem, M (2003) 'Anomie and strain: context and consequences of Merton's two theories', *Sociological Inquiry*, 73: 471–89.

Feilzer, M. and Hood, R. (2004) *Differences or Discrimination?* Youth Justice Board: London.

Femia, J. (1981) *Gramsci's Political Thought: Hegemony, Consciousness and the Revolutionary Process*. Oxford University Press: Oxford.

Fenwick, M. and Hayward, K. (2000) 'Youth crime, excitement and consumer culture: the reconstruction of aetiology in contemporary theoretical criminology', in Pickford, J. (ed.) *Youth Justice: Theory and Practice*. Cavendish: London, 31–50.

Fergusson, R. (2007) 'Making sense of the melting pot: multiple discourses in youth justice policy', *Youth Justice*, 7 (3): 179–94.

Ferrell, J. (1994) 'Confronting the agenda of authority: critical criminology, anarchism and urban graffiti' in Barak, G. (ed.) *Varieties of Criminology*. Praeger: Westport, CT, 161–79.

Ferrell, J. (1999) 'Cultural criminology', *Annual Review of Sociology*, 25: 395–418.

Field, S. (2007) 'Practice cultures and the "new" youth justice in (England and) Wales', *British Journal of Criminology*, 47 (2): 311–30.

Fionda, J. (2005) *Devils and Angels: Youth Policy and Crime*. London: Hart.

Fitzgerald, R. (2003) *An Examination of Sex Differences in Delinquency*. Canadian Centre for Justice Statistics: Ottawa, Ontario.

Foucault, M. (1979) *Discipline and Punish*. Penguin: Harmondsworth.

Foucault, M. (1980) *Power/Knowledge*. Pantheon Books: New York.

France, A. (1989) *The Red Lily*. Brentano's: New York.

France, A. (2008) *Understanding Youth in Late Modernity*. Maidenhead: Open University Press.

Freeman, M. (2002) 'Children's rights ten years after ratification' in Franklin, B. (ed.) *The New Handbook of Children's Rights*. Routledge: Abingdon, 97–118.

Freiberg, K., Homel, R. and Lamb, C. (2007) 'The pervasive impact of poverty on children: tackling family adversity and promoting child development through the Pathways to Prevention project', in France, A. and Homel, R. (eds) *Pathways and Crime Prevention: Theory, Policy and Practice*. Willan: Cullompton, 226–46.

Furlong, A. and Cartmel, F. (1997) *Young People and Social Change*. Buckingham: Open University Press.

Galambos, N., Almeida, D., and Petersen, A (1990) 'Masculinity, femininity, and sex role attitudes in early adolescence: exploring gender intensification', *Child Development*, 61: 1905–14.

Garland, D. (2001) *The Culture of Control*. Oxford University Press: Oxford.

Garrett, P. (2004) 'The electronic eye: Emergent surveillant practices in social work with children and families', *European Journal of Social Work*, 7 (1): 57–71.

Gaskell, C. (2008) *Kids Company Help with the Whole Problem*. Kids Company: London.

Ge, X., Jin, R., Natsuaki, M., Gibbons, F., Brody, G., Cutrona, C. and Simons, R. (2006) 'Pubertal maturation and early substance use risks among African American children', *Psychology of Addictive Behaviors*, 20 (4): 404–14.

Giddens, A. (1991) *Modernity and Self-Identity*. Polity Press: Cambridge.

Glover, J. and Hibbert, P. (2009) *Locking Up or Giving Up?* Barnardo's: London.

Goldson, B. (1999) 'Youth (in)justice: contemporary developments in policy and practice' in Goldson, B. (ed.) *Youth Justice: Contemporary Policy and Practice*. Ashgate: Aldershot, 1–27.

Goldson, B. (2002) *Vulnerable Inside*. The Children's Society: London.

Goldson, B. (2006) 'Penal custody: intolerance, irrationality and indifference' in Goldson, B. and Muncie, J. (eds) *Youth Crime and Justice*. Sage: London, 139–56.

Goldson, B. and Chigwada-Bailey, R. (1999) '(What) justice for black children and young people?' in Goldson, B. (ed.) *Youth Justice: Contemporary Policy and Practice*. Ashgate: Aldershot, 51–74.

Goldson, B. and Coles, D. (2005) *In the Care of the State?* Inquest: London.

Goldson, B. and Muncie, J. (2006) 'Critical anatomy: towards a principled youth justice' in Goldson, B. and Muncie, J. (eds) *Youth Crime and Justice*. Sage: London, 203–32.

Graber, J. and Brooks-Gunn, J. (1996) 'Transitions and turning points: navigating the passage from childhood through adolescence', *Developmental Psychology*, 32: 768–76.

Graham, J. and Bowling, B. (1995) *Young People and Crime*. London: Home Office.

Gramsci, A. (1971) *Selections from Prison Notebooks*. Lawrence and Wishart: London.

Gray, E., Taylor, E., Roberts, C., Merrington, S., Fernandez, R. and Moore, R. (2007) *Intensive Supervision and Surveillance Programme: The Final Report*. Youth Justice Board: London.

Griffin, C. (1993) *Representations of Youth*. Polity Press: Cambridge.

Griffin, C. (2004) 'Representations of the Young' in Roche, J., Tucker, S., Thomson, R. and Flynn, R. (eds) *Youth in Society* (2nd edition). London: Sage, 10–18.

Haines, K. and Case, S. (2008) 'The rhetoric and reality of the 'Risk Factor Prevention Paradigm' approach to preventing and reducing youth offending', *Youth Justice*, 8 (1): 5–20.

Haines, K. and Drakeford, M. (1998) *Young People and Youth Justice*. Macmillan: London.

Haines, K. and O'Mahony, D. (2006) 'Restorative approaches, young people and youth justice' in Goldson, B. and Muncie, J. (eds) *Youth Crime and Justice*. Sage: London, 110–24.

Hall, S., Critcher, C., Jefferson, T., Clarke, J. and Roberts, B. (1978) *Policing the Crisis: Mugging, the State and Law and Order*. Macmillan: Basingstoke.

Hallsworth, S. and Young, T. (2008) 'Gang talk and gang talkers: a critique', *Crime, Media, Culture*, 4 (2): 175–95.

Hancock, L. (2006) 'Urban regeneration, young people, crime and criminalisation' in Goldson, B. and Muncie, J. (eds) *Youth Crime and Justice*. Sage: London, 172–86.

Hantrais, L. (2000) *Social Policy in the European Union*. Macmillan: Basingstoke.

Hartnagel, T. (2004) 'The rhetoric of youth justice in Canada', *Criminal Justice*, 4 (4): 355–74.

Hartup, W. (1998) 'The company they keep: friendships and their developmental significance' in Campbell, A. and Muncer. S. (eds) *The Social Child*. Psychology Press: Hove, 143–64.

Haw, K. (2006) 'Risk factors and pathways into and out of crime, misleading, misinterpreted or mythic?: from generative metaphor to professional myth', *Australian and New Zealand Journal of Criminology*, 39 (3): 339–53.

Hayden, C., Williamson, T. and Webber, R., (2007) 'School pupil behaviour and young offenders – using postcode classification to target behaviour support and crime prevention programmes', *British Journal of Criminology*, 47: 293–310.

Hayes, H. (2006) 'Apologies and accounts in youth justice conferencing: reinterpreting research outcomes', *Contemporary Justice Review*, 9 (4): 369–85.

Hayward, K.J. (2002) 'The vilification and pleasures of youthful transgression' in Muncie, J., Hughes, G. and McLaughlin, E. (eds) *Youth Justice: Critical Readings*. London: Sage, 80–93.

Hendrick, H. (2003) *Child Welfare: Historical Dimensions, Contemporary Debate*. Policy Press: Bristol.

Hendrick, H. (2006) 'Histories of youth crime and justice' in Goldson, B. and Muncie, J. (eds) *Youth Crime and Justice*. Sage: London, 3–16.

Hey, V. and Bradford, S. (2006) 'Re-engineering motherhood? Surestart in the community', *Contemporary Issues in Early Childhood*, 7 (1): 53–67.

Heywood, C. (2001) *A History of Childhood*. Cambridge: Polity.

Hine, J. (2004) *Children and Citizenship*. Home Office: London.

Holman, B. (2001) 'Neighbourhood projects and preventing delinquency', *Youth Justice*, 1 (1): 45–52.

Home Office (1985) 'The cautioning of offenders', *Home Office Circular 14/85*. Home Office: London.

Home Office (1997) *No More Excuses*, Cm 3809. Home Office: London.

Home Office (2001) *Criminal Justice: The Way Ahead*, Cm 5074. Home Office: London.

Hope, T. (1998) 'Community crime prevention' in Goldblatt, P. and Lewis, C. (eds) *Reducing Offending: An Assessment of Research Evidence on Ways of Dealing with Offending Behaviour*. Home Office: London, 51–62.

Hopkins Burke, R. (2008) *Young People, Crime and Justice*. Willan: Cullompton.

Howard League (2008) 'Growing up, shut up' *Factsheet*. Howard League: London.

Howell, J. and Egley, A. (2005) 'Moving risk factors into developmental theories of gang membership', *Youth Violence and Juvenile Justice*, 3 (4): 334–54.

Hoyle, D. (2008) 'Problematizing Every Child Matters', *the Encyclopaedia of Informal Education*, available at www.infed.org/socialwork/every_child_matters_a_critique.htm, accessed 21 June 2010.

Hudson, B. (1987) *Justice Through Punishment*. Macmillan: Basingstoke.

Hudson, B. (2003) *Justice in the Risk Society*. Sage: London.

Jackson, S. (1999) 'Family group conferences and youth justice: the new panacea?', in Goldson, B. (ed.) *Youth Justice: Contemporary Policy and Practice*. Ashgate: Aldershot, 127–47.

Jacobson, J. and Gibbs, P. (2009) *Making Amends: Restorative Youth Justice in Northern Ireland*. Prison Reform Trust: London.

James, A. and James, A. (2004) *Constructing Childhood*. Basingstoke: Palgrave.

Jakhu, A. (2004) *Children's Support Panel Evaluation Report*. London Borough of Brent: London.

Jenks, C. (1996) *Childhood*. Routledge: Abingdon.

Johnston, L., MacDonald, R., Mason, P., Ridley, L. and Webster, C. (2000) *Snakes and Ladders*. Policy Press: Bristol.

Jones, A. and Singer, L. (2008) *Statistics on Race and the Criminal Justice System – 2006/7*. Ministry of Justice: London.

Jones, D. (2001) 'Questioning New Labour's youth justice strategy: a review article', *Youth Justice*, 1 (3): 14–26.

Jones, T. and Newburn, T. (2006) *Policy Transfer and Criminal Justice*. Open University Press: Buckingham.

Judd, L. (1967) 'The normal psychological development of the American adolescent: a review', *California Medicine*, 107 (6): 465–70.

Kehily, M. (2007) 'Education' in Robb, M. (ed.) *Youth in Context: Frameworks, Settings and Encounters*. Sage: London.

Kehily, M. and Pattman, R. (2006) 'Middle class struggle? Identity work and leisure among sixth formers in the UK', *British Journal of Sociology of Education*, 27 (1): 37–52.

Keith, B. (2006) *Report of the Zahid Mubarek Inquiry (Vol. 1)*. The Stationery Office: London.

Kemshall, H. (2008) 'Rights, risk and justice: understanding and responding to youth risk', *Youth Justice*, 8 (1): 21–37.

Kitsuse, J. (1962) 'Societal reaction to deviant behaviour: problems of theory and method', *Social Problems*, 9: 247–56.

Kuhn, T. (1970) *The Structure of Scientific Revolutions*. University of Chicago Press: Chicago.

Lansdown, G. (2005) *The Evolving Capacities of the Child*. Geneva: UNICEF Innocenti Research Centre.

Larson, R. and Ham, M. (1993) 'Stress and 'Storm and Stress' in early adolescence: the relationship of negative events with dysphoric affect', *Developmental Psychology*, 29: 130–40.

Lea, J. and Young, J. (1984) *What is to be Done about Law and Order?* Penguin: Harmondsworth.

Lee, N. (2001) *Childhood and Society*. Maidenhead: Open University Press.

Lemert, E. (1967) *Human Deviance: Social Problems and Social Control*. Prentice Hall: Englewood Cliffs, NJ.

Lenin, V. (1988 [1902]) *What Is To Be Done?*, Penguin: Harmondsworth.

Leonard, P. (1997) *Postmodern Welfare: Reconstructing an Emancipatory Project*. Sage: London.

Lipsky, M. (1980) *Street Level Bureaucracy*. Russell Sage Foundation: New York.

Lord Chancellor and Secretary of State for Justice (2008) *Government Response to the Justice Select Committee's Report: Towards Effective Sentencing*. The Stationery Office: London.

Loury, G. (2000) 'Social exclusion and ethnic groups: the challenge to economics' in Pleskovic, B. and Stiglitz, J. (eds) *Annual World Bank Conference on Development Economics 1999*. World Bank: Washington, DC.

Lyon, J., Denison, C. and Wilson, A. (2000) *'Tell Them So They Listen': Messages from Young People in Custody*. Home Office: London.

McAra, L. and McVie, S. (2007) 'Youth justice? The impact of system contact on patterns of desistance from offending', *European Journal of Criminology*, 4 (3): 315–45.

McKenna, K. (2007) *Evaluation of the North Liverpool Community Justice Centre*. Ministry of Justice: London.

McLaughlin, E. and Muncie, J. (2000) 'The criminal justice system: New Labour's new partnerships' in Clarke, J., Gewirtz, S. and McLaughlin, E. (eds) *New Managerialism New Welfare?* Sage. London: 169–85.

MacDonald, R. and Marsh, J. (2005) *Disconnected Youth?* Palgrave Macmillan: Basingstoke.

Macpherson, W. (1999) *The Stephen Lawrence Inquiry*, Cm 4262-1. The Stationery Office: London.

Margo, J. and Stevens, A. (2008) *Make Me a Criminal: Preventing Youth Crime*. Institute for Public Policy Research: London.

Marshall, T. (1985) *Alternatives to Criminal Courts*. Gower: Aldershot.

Marshall. T. (1988) 'Out of court: more or less justice?' in Matthews, R. (ed.) *Informal Justice*. Sage: London, 25–50.

Marshall, T. (1999) *Restorative Justice: An Overview*. Home Office: London.

Masters, G. (2005) 'Restorative justice and youth justice' in Bateman, T. and Pitts, J. (eds) *The RHP Companion to Youth Justice*. Russell House: Lyme Regis, 179–85.

Mastrigt van, S. and Farrington, D. (2009) 'Co-offending, age, gender and crime type: implications for criminal justice policy', *British Journal of Criminology*, 49: 552–73.

Mathiesen, T. (1974) *The Politics of Abolition*. Martin Robertson: Oxford.

Matza, D. (1964) *Delinquency and Drift*. Wiley: New York.

Matza, D. (1969) *Becoming Deviant*. Prentice-Hall: Englewood Cliffs, NJ.

May, T., Gyateng, T. and Hough, M. (2010) *Differential Treatment in the Justice System*. Equality and Human Rights Commission: London.

Mayfield, G. and Mills, A. (2008) 'Towards a balanced and practical approach to anti-social behaviour management' in Squires, P. (ed.) *ASBO Nation*. Policy Press: Bristol, 73–86.

Merton, R. (1957) *Social Theory and Social Structure*. Free Press: Glencoe, IL.

Mika, H. (2006) *Community-based Restorative Justice in Northern Ireland*. Queens University: Belfast.

Ministry of Justice (2010a) *Population in Custody Monthly Tables March 2010 England and Wales*. Ministry of Justice: London.

Ministry of Justice (2010b) *Population in Custody Monthly Tables April 2010 England and Wales*. Ministry of Justice: London.

Moffitt, T. (1993) 'Adolescence-limited and life-course-persistent antisocial behaviour: a developmental taxonomy', *Psychological Review*, 100 (4): 674–701.

Moore, R., Gray, E., Roberts, C., Taylor, E. and Merrington, S. (2006) *Managing Serious and Persistent Offenders in the Community*. Willan: Cullompton.

Morgan, Harris Burrows (2001) *Youth Inclusion Programme: Evaluation Overview*, unpublished.

Morgan Harris Burrows (2003) *Evaluation of the Youth Inclusion Programme*. Youth Justice Board: London.

Moore, R. (2004) 'Intensive supervision and surveillance programmes for young offenders: the evidence base so far' in Burnett, R. and Roberts, C. (eds) *What Works in Probation and Youth Justice*. Willan: Cullompton, 159–79.

Moore, S. and Mitchell, R. (2009) 'Rights-based restorative justice: evaluating compliance with international standards', *Youth Justice*, 9 (1): 27–43.

Morris, A. and Giller, H. (1987) *Understanding Juvenile Justice*. Croom Helm: London.

Morris, A., Giller, H., Geach, H. and Szwed, E. (1980) *Justice for Children*. Macmillan: London.

Muncie, J. (1999) 'Institutionalised intolerance: youth justice and the 1998 Crime and Disorder Act', *Critical Social Policy*, 19 (2): 147–175.

Muncie, J. (2002) 'A new deal for youth? Early intervention and correctionalism', in Hughes, G. McLaughlin, E. and Muncie, J. (eds) *Crime Prevention and Community Safety: New Directions*. Sage: London, 142–62.

Muncie, J. (2008) 'The "Punitive Turn" in juvenile justice: cultures of control and rights compliance in Western Europe and the USA', *Youth Justice*, 8 (2): 107–21.

Muncie, J. (2009) *Youth & Crime (3rd edition)*. Sage: London.

Muncie, J. and Goldson, B. (2006) 'States of transition: convergence and diversity in international youth justice' in Muncie, J. and Goldson, B. (eds) *Comparative Youth Justice*. Sage: London, 196–218.

Murray, C. (1996) 'The emerging British underclass' in Lister, R. (ed.) *Charles Murray and the Underclass: The Developing Debate*. IEA Health and Welfare Unit: London, 23–54.

Mutter, R., Shemmings, D., Dugmore, P. and Hyare, M. (2008) 'Family group conferences in youth justice', *Health and Social Care in the Community*, doi 10.1111/j 1385-2524.

Nagin, D., Farrington, D. and Moffitt, T. (1995) 'Life-course trajectories of different types of offenders', *Criminology*, 33: 111–39.

Nakagawa, S. (2003) 'Beyond punishment: restorative vs. transformative justice', *Justice Matters*, 5 (3): 13–14.

Nelken, D. (2006) 'Italy: a lesson in tolerance?' in Muncie, J. and Goldson, B. (eds) *Comparative Youth Justice*. Sage: London, 159–76.

Newburn, T. (2007) *Criminology*. Willan: Cullompton.

Omaji, P. (2003) *Responding to Youth Crime*. Hawkins Press: Leichhardt, NSW.

Patterson, G. (1998) 'Continuities – a search for causal mechanisms: comment on the special section', *Developmental Psychology*, 34: 1263–8.

Pearson, G. (1983) *Hooligan: A History of Respectable Fears*. Macmillan: Basingstoke.

Percy-Smith, J. (2000) 'Introduction: the contours of social exclusion' in Percy-Smith, J. (ed.) *Policy Responses to Social Exclusion*. Open University Press: Buckingham, 1–21.

Phoenix, J. (2009) 'Beyond risk assessment: the return of repressive welfarism?', in Barry, M. and McNeill, F. (eds) *Youth Offending and Youth Justice*. Jessica Kingsley: London, 113–31.

Piquero, A. (2000) 'Frequency, specialization and violence in offending careers', *Journal of Research in Crime and Delinquency*, 37: 392–418.

Pitts, J. (2002) 'Amnesia and discontinuity', Speech to National Association of Youth Justice Conference, Milton Keynes, 14th June.

Pitts, J. (2003) 'Youth justice in England and Wales' in Matthews, R. and Young, J. (eds) *The New Politics of Crime and Punishment*. Willan: Cullompton, 71–99.

Pitts, J. (2008) *Reluctant Gangsters*. Willan: Cullompton.

Portes, A. (1998) Social capital: its origins and applications in modern sociology. *Annual Review of Sociology*, 24: 1–24.

Potter, C., Schneider, J., Lee, S. and Carpenter, J. (2005) *Sure Start Ferryhill/Clayton: Third Year Evaluation Report*. University of Durham: Durham.

Poulantzas, N. (1978) *State, Power, Socialism*. Verso: London.

Powell, M. (1999) 'Introduction' in Powell, M. (ed.) *New Labour, New Welfare State?* Policy Press: Bristol, 1–28.

Pratt, J. (1989) 'Corporatism: the third model of juvenile justice', *British Journal of Criminology*, 29: 236–54.

Presdee, M. (1994) 'Young people, culture and the construction of crime: doing wrong versus doing crime' in Barak, G. (ed.) *Varieties of Criminology*. Praeger: Westport, CT, 179–88.

Pugh, G. (2007) 'Policies in the UK to promote well being of children and young people, in France A. and Homel R. (eds) *Pathways and Crime Prevention: Theory, Policy and Practice*. Willan: Cullompton, 337–53.

Quinney, R. (1970) *The Social Reality of Crime*. Little, Brown: Boston, MA.

Quinney, R. (1974) *Critique of the Legal Order*. Little, Brown: Boston, MA.

Raffe, D. (2003) 'Pathways linking education and work: a review of concepts, research and policy debates', *Journal of Youth Studies*, 6 (1): 3–19.

Rex, S. and Gelsthorpe, L. (2004) 'Using community service to encourage inclusive citizenship' in Burnett, R. and Roberts, C. (eds) *What Works in Probation and Youth Justice: Developing Evidence-Based Practice*. Willan: Cullompton, 198–216.

Roberts, K. (2007) 'Youth transitions and generations: a response to Wyn and Woodman', *Journal of Youth Studies*, 10: 263–9.

Rock, P. (2007) 'Sociological theories of crime' in Maguire, M., Morgan, R. and Reiner, R. (eds) *The Oxford Handbook of Criminology (4th edition)*. Oxford University Press: Oxford, 3–42.

Rose, N. (1999) *Governing the Soul (2nd edition)*. Free Association Books: London.

Rothman, D. (1980) *Conscience and Convenience: The Asylum and its Alternatives in Progressive America*. Little, Brown: Boston, MA.

Rutherford, A. (2002) 'Youth justice and social inclusion', *Youth Justice*, 2 (2): 100–7.

Rutter, M., Giller, H. and Hagell, A. (1998a) *Antisocial Behaviour by Young People*. Cambridge University Press: Cambridge.

Rutter M., Giller H. and Hagell A. (1998b) *Antisocial Behaviour by Young People: The Main Messages from a Major New Review of the Research*. Social Information Systems: Knutsford.

Rutter, M., Graham, P., Chadwick, O. and Yule, W. (1976) 'Adolescent turmoil: fact or fiction?', *Child Psychology and Psychiatry*, 17: 35–56.

Ryan, M. (2008) 'Youth and the critical agenda: negotiating contradictory discourses', *The Australian Educational Researcher*, 35 (2): 71–88.

Sampson, R. and Laub, J. (1993) *Crime in the Making: Pathways and Turning Points Through Life*. Harvard University Press: Cambridge, MA.

Sampson, R. and Laub, J. (2005) 'A life-course view of the development of crime', *Annals AAPSS*, 602: 12–45.

Sampson, R., Morenoff, J. and Raudenbush, S. (2005) 'Social anatomy of racial and ethnic disparities in violence', *American Journal of Public Health*, 95: 224–32.

Scraton, P. and Haydon, D. (2002) 'Challenging the criminalisation of children and young people: securing a rights-based agenda' in Muncie, J., Hughes, G. and McLaughlin, E. (eds) *Youth Justice: Critical Readings*. Sage: London, 311–28.

Schur, E. (1973) *Radical Non-Intervention*. Prentice-Hall: Englewood Cliffs, NJ.

Sebastian, C., Burnett, S. and Blakemore, S-J. (2008) 'Development of the self concept during adolescence', *Trends in Cognitive Science*, 12 (11): 441–6.

Smith, C. and Farrington, D. (2004) 'Continuities in antisocial behaviour and parenting across three generations', *Journal of Child Psychology and Psychiatry*, 45: 230–47.

Smith, D. (1995) *Criminology for Social Work*. Macmillan: Basingstoke.

Smith, D. (1999) 'Social work with young people in trouble: memory and prospect' in Goldson, B. (ed.) *Youth Justice: Contemporary Policy and Practice*. Ashgate: Aldershot, 148–69.

Smith, D. (2004) *The Links Between Victimization and Offending*. Centre for Law and Society: University of Edinburgh, Edinburgh.

Smith, D. and McVie, S. (2003) 'Theory and method in the Edinburgh Study of Youth Transitions and Crime', *British Journal of Criminology*, 43 (1): 169–95.

Smith, D., McVie, S., Woodward, R., Shute, J., Flint, J. and McAra, L. (2001) *The Edinburgh Study of Youth Transitions and Crime: Key Findings at Ages 12 and 13*. University of Edinburgh: Edinburgh.

Smith, P., Cowie, H. and Blades, M. (2003) *Understanding Children's Development (4th edition)*. Oxford: Blackwell.

Smith, R. (1989) *Diversion in Practice*. MPhil thesis, University of Leicester.

Smith, R. (1998) *No Lessons Learnt*. London: The Children's Society.

Smith, R. (2000) 'Order and disorder: the contradictions of childhood', *Children & Society*, 14 (1): 3–10.

Smith, R. (2001) 'Foucault's Law: The Crime and Disorder Act 1998', *Youth Justice*, 1 (2): 17–29.

Smith, R. (2003) *Youth Justice: Ideas, Policy, Practice*. Willan: Cullompton.

Smith, R. (2005) 'Welfare versus justice: again!', *Youth Justice*, 5 (1): 3–16.

Smith, R. (2006) 'Actuarialism and early intervention in contemporary youth justice' in Goldson, B. and Muncie, J. (eds) *Youth Crime and Justice*. Sage: London, 92–109.

Smith, R. (2007) *Youth Justice: Ideas, Policy, Practice (2nd edition)*. Willan: Cullompton.

Smith, R. (2009) 'Childhood, agency and youth justice', *Children & Society*, 23 (4): 252–64.

Smith, R. (2010a) 'Children's rights and youth justice: 20 years of no progress', *Child Care in Practice*, 16 (1): 3–17.

Smith, R. (2010b) 'Social work, risk, power', *Sociological Research Online*, 15 (1): available at http://www.socresonline.org.uk/15/1/4.html, doi:10.5153/sro.2101

Social Exclusion Unit (1998) *Bringing Britain Together: A National Strategy for Neighbourhood Renewal*. The Stationery Office: London.

Social Exclusion Unit (2001) *Preventing Social Exclusion*. The Stationery Office: London.

Social Exclusion Unit (2002) *Reducing Re-Offending by Ex-Prisoners*. The Stationery Office: London.

Squires, P. and Stephen, D. (2005) *Rougher Justice*. Willan: Cullompton.

Stanley, E. (2007) 'Towards a criminology for human rights' in Barton, A., Corteen, K., Scott, D. and Whyte, D. (eds) *Expanding the Criminological Imagination*. Willan: Cullompton, 168–97.

Stephenson, M. (2007) *Young People and Offending: Education, Youth Justice and Social Inclusion*. Willan: Cullompton.

Stevens, M. and Crook, J. (1986) 'What the devil is Intermediate Treatment?', *Social Work Today*, 18 (2): 10–11.

Stout, B. (2006) 'Is diversion the appropriate emphasis for South African child justice?', *Youth Justice*, 6 (2): 129–42.

Straw, J. (1997) 'Foreword' in Home Office *No More Excuses*. The Stationery Office: London.

Taylor, C. (2006) *Young People in Care and Criminal Behaviour*. Jessica Kingsley: London.

Taylor, J., McGue, M. and Iacono, W. (2000) 'Sex differences, assortative mating and cultural transmission effects on adolescent delinquency: a twin family study', *Journal of Child Psychology and Psychiatry*, 41: 443–40.

Thomson, R., Bell, R., Holland, J., Henderson, S., McGrellis, S. and Sharpe, S. (2002) 'Critical moments: choice, chance and opportunity in young people's narratives of transition', *Sociology*, 36 (2): 335–54.

Thornberry, T., Krohn, M., Lizotte, A., Smith, C. and Tobin, K. (2003) *Gangs and Delinquency in Developmental Perspective*. Cambridge University Press: Cambridge.

Thorpe, D., Smith, D., Green, C. and Paley, J. (1980) *Out of Care*. George Allen and Unwin: London.

Timimi, S. (2005) *Naughty Boys*. Palgrave Macmillan: Basingstoke.

Vaughan, K. (2003) 'Changing Lanes: Young People Making Sense of Pathways', paper to NZCER Annual Conference, 8 August, accessed online 14 June 2010, http://www.nzcer.org.nz/pdfs/12223.pdf

Vaughan, K. and Roberts, J. (2007) 'Developing a "productive" account of young people's transition perspectives', *Journal of Education and Work*, 20 (3): 91–106.

Vujacic-Ricer and Hrncic, J. (2007) *Thematic Review of UNICEF's Contribution to Juvenile Justice System Reform in Montenegro, Romania, Serbia and Tajikistan*. Geneva: UNICEF.

Wacquant, L. (2003) *Urban Outcasts*. Polity Press: Cambridge.

Waiton, S. (2008) 'Asocial not anti-social: the "Respect Agenda" and the "therapeutic me"' in Squires, P. (ed.) *ASBO Nation*. Policy Press: Bristol, 337–58.

Walker, J., Thompson, C., Laing, K., Raybould, S., Coombes, M., Procter, S. and Wren, C. (2007) *Youth Inclusion and Support Panels: Preventing Crime and Antisocial Behaviour*. Institute of Health and Society: Newcastle University, Newcastle.

Walklate, S. (2004) *Gender, Crime and Criminal Justice (2nd edition)*. Willan: Cullompton.

Ward, T. and Stewart, C. (2003) 'Criminogenic needs and human needs: a theoretical critique', *Psychology, Crime and Law*, 9 (3): 125–43.

Webber, C. (2007) 'Revaluating relative deprivation theory', *Theoretical Criminology*, 11 (1): 95–118.

Webster, C. (2006) ' "Race", youth crime and justice' in Goldson, B. and Muncie, J. (eds) *Youth Crime and Justice*. Sage: London, 30–46.

Webster, C., Simpson, D., MacDonald, R., Abbas, A., Cieslik, M., Shildrick, T. and Simpson, M. (2004) *Poor Transitions: Social Exclusion and Young Adults*. Policy Press: Bristol.

Weiner, A. (1977) 'Cognitive and social-emotional development in adolescence', *Journal of Pediatric Psychology*, 3 (2): 87–92.

White, R. and Cuneen, C. (2006) 'Social class, youth crime and justice' in Goldson, B. and Muncie, J. (eds) *Youth Crime and Justice*. Sage: London, 17–29.

Willis, P. (1977) *Learning to Labour*. Saxon House: Farnborough.

Wilson, D. and Rees, G. (eds) (2006) *Just Justice*. The Children's Society: London.

Wilson, H. (1962) *Delinquency and Child Neglect*. Allen and Unwin: London.

Wilson, H. (1974) 'Parenting in poverty', *British Journal of Social Work*, 4 (3): 241–54.

Wilson, H. (1975) 'Juvenile delinquency, parental criminality and social handicap', *British Journal of Criminology*, 15 (3): 241–50.

Wilson, H. (1980) 'Parental supervision: a neglected aspect of delinquency', *British Journal of Criminology*, 20 (3): 203–35.

Wilson, J. (1975) *Thinking About Crime*. Vintage Press: New York.

Wyn J. and Woodman D., (2006) 'Generation, youth and social change in Australia', *Journal of Youth Studies*, 9: 495–514.

Yar, M. and Penna, S. (2004) 'Critical Reflections on Jock Young's The Exclusive Society', *British Journal of Criminology*, 44: 533–49.

Yates, J. (2006) *An Ethnography of Youth and Crime in a Working Class Community*. PhD thesis, De Montfort University, Leicester.

Young, J. (1999) *The Exclusive Society*. Sage: London.

Young, J. (2004) 'Crime and the dialectics of inclusion/exclusion', *British Journal of Criminology*, 44: 550–61.

Young, J. and Matthews, R. (2003) 'New Labour, crime control and social exclusion' in Matthews, R. and Young, J. (eds) *The New Politics of Crime and Punishment*. Willan: Cullompton, 1–32.

Youth Justice Agency (2003) *Corporate Plan 2003-05: Business Plan 2003-04*. Youth Justice Agency: Belfast.

Youth Justice Board (2005) *Annual Report and Accounts 2004/05*. Youth Justice Board: London.

Youth Justice Board (2008) *Youth Justice: A Scaled Approach*. Youth Justice Board: London.

Youth Justice Board (2010a) *Youth Rehabilitation Order with Intensive Supervision and Surveillance (ISS): Operational Guidance*. YJB: London.

Youth Justice Board (2010b) 'Assessment: Asset – Young Offender profile', http://www.yjb.gov.uk/en-gb/practitioners/Assessment/Asset.htm, accessed 18th June 2010.

Youth Justice Board (2010c) *National Standards for Youth Justice (revised edition)*. Youth Justice Board: London.

Index

Judd, L. 12
Junior Youth Inclusion projects 133
justice-based position, compared to
welfarist position 121–2
Justice for Children 114
juvenile delinquency, 19th century
view of 150

Kehily, M. 16
Keith, B. 141
Kemshall, H. 196, 198
Kids Company 182–3
Kitsuse, J. 75
Krisberg, B. 113, 164
Kuhn, T. 113

labelling 50–1, 106, 135, 136, 176,
201
Lansdown, G. 199
Laub, J. 28, 29, 52–3, 57, 60, 61–3, 64
Lawrence, Stephen 139, 141
Lea, J. 152
Lee, N. 192
legislative measures, welfare of
children 121
Lemert, E. 55, 135
Lenin, V. 149
Leonard, P. 202
'life course' criminologies 63–4
Loury, G. 93
Lyon, J. 190

MacDonald, R. 16, 17–18, 20–1, 23,
24
MacPherson, W. 138, 139, 141
Major, John 123
Maori culture 181
Margo, J. 155
Marsh, J. 16, 17–18, 20–1, 23, 24
Marshall, T. 114, 183
Masters, G. 187
Mastrigt van, S. 57
materiality of power 83–8
Mathiesen, T. 129, 171, 187
Matthews, R. 93, 100, 109

Matza, D. 31, 42–4, 45, 48–9, 69, 70,
135
May, T. 139, 140, 141
Mayfield, G. 167
McAra, L. 172, 187
McIntosh, M. 81
McKenna, K. 180
McLaughlin, E. 134
McVie, S. 26, 172, 187
media 47, 116, 152, 153, 155
Merton, R. 31, 35–44, 45–6, 48–9, 69,
193
Mettray penal colony 84
Mhlanga, B. 141
micro-management 117
Mika, H. 180
Mills, A. 167
minimum intervention 175–9
minority child 192, 194, 198
Mitchell, R. 186
Moffit, T. 63
Moore, R. 51, 84, 85, 86–8, 160
Moore, S. 186
Morgan, Rod 179
Morris, A. 113, 114, 152
MOSAIC 132
Mubarek, Zahid 141
multi-agency management structures
158
Multi-Systemic Therapy 86
Muncie, J. 45, 47–8, 51, 59, 75, 88–9,
111, 112, 117, 124, 125–6, 134, 145,
146, 148, 150, 160, 168, 169, 178,
188, 200, 201
Murray, C. 102
Mutter, R. 184, 185

Nagin, D. 63
Nakagawa, S. 186, 187
naming and shaming 125
National Standards for Youth Justice
161
NEETs 95–6
neighbourhood projects 181
Nelken, D. 177–8

Stephenson, M. 104, 107
stereotypes 19, 28, 105
Stevens, A. 155
Stevens, M. 114
Stewart, C. 198
'storm and stress' 12, 13
Stout, B. 179
Straw, J. 156
'street kids' 27
structural influences 48, 134, 164,
  197
'Summer Splash' 133
Supervision Orders 166
SureStart 97, 173, 174, 175
systemic discrimination 138–42

talking tough 124
'targeted' interventions 103, 131–6
Taylor, C. 20, 77
Taylor, J. 57
teenage pregnancy 95–6
Teenage Pregnancy Initiative 97
Thatcher, Margaret 116
The Children's Fund 175
'The Exclusive Society' 99
'The Law' 74–5
'third way' 94, 151
Thomson, R. 14
Thornberry, T. 65, 66, 67, 69
Thorpe, D. 113, 114, 151, 160, 163,
  164
Timimi, S. 58
'together at home' 80
transformative justice 186, 187–8
transitions 10, 18–20 *see also* change;
  turning points
travellers 126
'tribal children' 192, 194, 195, 198
truancy 95
turning points 20, 57, 61–2 *see also*
  change; transitions

UN Committee on the Rights of the
  Child 126, 146–7
UN Convention on the Rights of

the Child 126, 143–4, 145, 195,
  199–200
unintended consequences 113, 151,
  162, 163, 168
United States 125

Vaughan, K. 31–2, 33
vulnerability principle 161

Wacquant, L. 22, 23
Waiton, S. 167
Wales 127–8, 161–2
Walker, J. 135–6, 137
Walklate, S. 22
Ward, T. 198
Webber, C. 41, 42, 44
Webster, C. 36, 37, 104
Weiner, A. 12, 13, 14
welfarism 113, 123–4, 151
  rejection of 119
  in Wales 127–8, 161–2
White, R. 109, 112, 145
Willis, P. 15, 16, 23
Wilson, D. 137
Wilson, H. 52, 56, 60
Wilson, J. 52
Woodman, D. 20
Wyn, J. 20

Yamashita, H. 32–3, 34
Yar, M. 45
young criminals, becoming 108–10
Young, J. 23, 45, 49, 93, 99, 100, 109,
  152
Young, T. 64
youth, production of 10–29
  difference and diversity 21–4
  expectations and influences of
    15–18
  explanatory frameworks 25–8
  definition of normal development
    11–14
  stages of adolescence 18–21
  working models of normal
    development 10–11